CELTIC BIBLE COMMENTARY
VOLUME I

THE WINGED MAN

The Good News According to Matthew

CELTIC BIBLE COMMENTARY
VOLUME I

THE WINGED MAN

The Good News According to Matthew

KENNETH McINTOSH, EDITOR

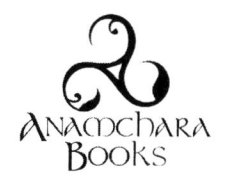

ANAMCHARA BOOKS

THE WINGED MAN:
The Good News According to Matthew

CELTIC BIBLE COMMENTARY VOLUME 1

Copyright © 2017 by Anamchara Books, a division of Harding House Publishing Service, Inc. All rights reserved. No part of this publication may be reproduced or transmitted in any form or by any means, electronic or mechanical, including photocopying, recording, taping, or any information storage and retrieval system, without permission from the publisher.

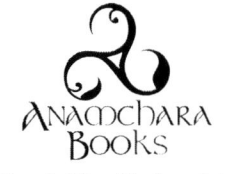

Anamchara Books
Vestal, New York 13850
www.anamcharabooks.com

ISBN: 978-1-62524-472-7
ebook ISBN: 978-1-62524-458-1

Editor: Kenneth McIntosh.
Cover design by Micaela Grace Sanna.

Scripture labeled NIV is from the Holy Bible, New International Version®, NIV® Copyright © 1973, 1978, 1984, 2011 by Biblica, Inc.® Used by permission. All rights reserved worldwide.

APPRECIATION

I've enjoyed serving as general editor for this project and extend gratitude to each of the contributors: David Cole, Teresa Monica Cross, Jack Gillespie, Paul John Martin, and my wife Marsha McIntosh. Steve Robinson did a mighty job helping us with the Bible translation. Micaela Sanna made magic with the beautiful visual illustrations. Discussions held at group retreats with the Community of Aidan and Hilda, both in Oxfordshire, England, and Albuquerque, New Mexico, helped develop and expand ideas found in this book. Simon Reed offered invaluable feedback, both in person and via e-mail. Numerous reviewers, including Camden Flath at Anamchara Books, read and critiqued the commentaries. Most of all, Anamchara Book's executive editor Ellyn Sanna contributed articles, edited and enhanced the writings, and sparked the concept of a Celtic Bible commentary. Several years ago, as we bumped along in a little sedan, driving between hedgerows in Devon, England, Ellyn said to me, "What would you think of doing a Celtic-themed Bible?" The rest, as they say, is history.

TABLE OF CONTENTS

The Peacock's Feathers:
    Principles of Celtic Bible Interpretation   9

The Noblest of Gifts: The Bible in Celtic Lands   51

Blessing   67

Introduction   69

Chapter One   80

Chapter Two   88

Chapter Three   95

Chapter Four   101

Chapter Five   108

Chapter Six   116

Chapter Seven   122

Chapter Eight   129

Chapter Nine   136

Chapter Ten   145

Chapter Eleven   153

Chapter Twelve   160

Chapter Thirteen   169

Chapter Fourteen   178

Chapter Fifteen   187

Chapter Sixteen   195

Chapter Seventeen	202
Chapter Eighteen	208
Chapter Nineteen	218
Chapter Twenty	227
Chapter Twenty-One	236
Chapter Twenty-Two	245
Chapter Twenty-Three	254
Chapter Twenty-Four	263
Chapter Twenty-Five	272
Chapter Twenty-Six	282
Chapter Twenty-Seven	293
Chapter Twenty-Eight	303
A Few Notes	310
Glossary of Celtic Names & Terminology	315
Suggested Readings	320
Contributors	326

THE PEACOCK'S FEATHERS
Principles of Celtic Bible Interpretation

For there are many ways,
indeed an infinite number,
of interpreting the Scriptures,
just as in one and the same feather of a peacock
and even in the same small portion of the feather,
we see a marvelously beautiful variety
of innumerable colors.
—John Scottus Eriugena, *Periphyseon*, 866 CE[1]

When a peacock's tail feathers are raised for courting, they transect the bird's body and form an extraordinary fan shape. The "eyes" seem to jump out from gauze-like feathers; they oscillate and sparkle with iridescent hues. The tapestry of shapes and colors changes constantly, depending on the peacock's motions, the angle of sunlight on the filaments of its tail, and the relative locations of the bird and viewer. This display of plumage is truly one of nature's great marvels—and when Eriugena compared the Bible to a peacock's feathers, he was saying

10 THE GOSPEL OF MATTHEW

something about the Bible that many modern Christians might find quite radical.

John Scottus Eriugena, whose name translates as "John the Irishman from Ireland," has been described as a poet, mystic, philosopher, and theologian, one of the most accomplished thinkers of the Early Middle Ages.[2] Like many of his Gaelic brethren, Eriugena believed that the mystery and beauty of the Bible required the readers to look at each portion of Scripture from multiple perspectives. As readers view Scripture first from one angle and then from another, the written words of God reveal new, surprising, and life-giving truths. Like the splendor of the peacock's train, the beauty of Scripture is dynamic, ever-changing, catching light and meaning from its context that deepens and illuminates new hues and patterns.

This perspective does not in any way diminish the importance of Scripture. Celtic Christians of the Early Middle Ages had a deep and reverent respect for the Bible. Patrick declared in his *Letter to the Soldiers*, "These are . . . words which never lie: those of God and his Apostles and prophets."[3] The Anglo-Saxon historian Bede, who differed from his Celtic brethren in some significant ways, nonetheless lauded the fact that they "diligently followed whatever pure and devout customs that they learned in the prophets, the Gospels and the writings of the Apostles."[4] According to Celtic Scholars Herren and Brown, "British Christianity . . . was governed by a total reliance on the authority of the Scriptures, the corollary of which was a marked distrust of any theology that was not Scripture based."[5]

A legendary incident in the life of Columba attests to his intense passion for Scripture, although the story is not flattering of the saint. Columba coveted a copy of the Psalms belonging to a neighboring monastery, but the owners would not let him remove that special book from their library. Columba therefore set about stealthily copying the text. When his covert scribal work was discovered, he insisted that he be allowed to keep his copy of the book. When this claim was denied, the holy man resorted to warlike behavior that has been sadly endemic to Celts throughout history. He rallied his O'Neil clansmen to take up arms against the offending monastery, and when the dust settled, the blood of a thousand Irishmen stained sanctified ground. As a punishment, the synod of Ireland banished Columba from his beloved native land—a judgment that led him to evangelize the Picts (in modern-day Scotland). This tale, although it portrays Columba in a less than admirable light, does illustrate the value that the Celtic saints placed on the Bible.[6]

Yet the ways that the ancient Gaels interpreted Scripture differs markedly from the way that Christians today approach the same texts. This is an important lesson to bear in mind, as those who love the Bible *differently* are sometimes accused of not valuing the Bible at all. And perhaps the ancient multifold approach to Bible reading could be useful in our time, to fill up what may be lacking in our modern approach. Learning how our ancestors in the faith approached the words of God may offer us a chance to read more deeply.

TREASURES FROM AFAR

*Once every three years the fleet of Tarshish came,
bringing gold, silver, ivory, apes, and peacocks.*
—1 Kings 10:22

In Bible days, the peacock's mystique owed much to its exotic origins; it came from the faraway and fabled East. Europeans in the Middle Ages still felt much the same about peacocks, as well as other imported wonders.

Living in the British Isles, the Celts were never far from the sea, and there was always the possibility that something strange and wonderful would arrive on a nearby shore: fabric, spices, foreign persons, or, best of all and as valuable to the Celts as gold, previously unknown knowledge. The Celtic scholar-saints coveted such foreign wisdom.

Those of us who live in the twenty-first century often value—and romanticize—Celtic Christianity for the ways it differs from other forms of faith. Celtic saints are portrayed as dreamy-eyed mystics, living in a magical world beyond the fringes of the Roman Empire. In reality, Celtic Christians did differ from their neighbors in some ways, but their commonalities with the rest of the Christian world outweighed their differences. As modern Christians, we often forget that medieval Christianity as a whole looked at the world, Scripture, and even God in ways that may seem strange to some of us today.

Celtic scholars were familiar with the medieval world's great Bible interpreters. Although they had their own theologians, the great African theologian Augustine of Hippo also influenced their thinking.[7] Enthralled by the tales of the Desert Fathers and Mothers, the Gaels devoured the saints' lives written by Anthony, Paul of Thebes, and others. The Celts were also conversant with the writers and thinkers of the Egyptian Church, including Origen. Enamored with monastic life, the Celts eagerly read the writings of John Cassian, who brought the Desert monastic way from Palestine to nearby France.[8] They also delighted in Jerome's work, which he conducted in Bethlehem (with the help of two female scholars), translating the Hebrew and Greek texts into Latin.

Syrians may also have influenced the Celtic Church. Columbanus relates how, when he was in Europe, a Syrian woman gave him food in an emergency, telling him, "I am a stranger like yourself, and come from the distant sun of the East." Albert Cook of Yale, regarded as one of the greatest philologists of the late nineteenth and early twentieth centuries, said, "In Gaul, Syrian and Eastern monasticism was flourishing when Christianity passed over to Ireland. In Irish monasticism we should therefore expect to find traces of Syrian and Oriental practices."[9] Syrian influence is particularly intriguing, insofar as the early Syriac churches were strongly influenced by their Jewish neighbors, and students of Celtic Christianity have noted how practices of the Celtic churches reflect those of Judaism.

⌘ TREASURES FROM THE CELTIC WORLD ⌘

While learning from civilizations around the world, the Celts also valued the contributions of their own local authors. Pelagius is sometimes considered the earliest representative of a distinctly Celtic Christian faith. This fifth-century Welshman often butted heads theologically with Augustine of Hippo. Pelagius emphasized free will and the pursuit of moral perfection in Christian life, while Augustine placed greater weight on Divine election and salvation by God's grace alone. Augustine prevailed outside of the Celtic realms, but Pelagius' influence continued in Gaelic lands. A survey of citations by Irish scribes found Augustine quoted eleven times, Origen twenty-one times, Jerome one hundred and sixteen—and Pelagius quoted 1,316 times.[10] Apparently, when Imperial authorities declared Pelagius a heretic, the Celts refused to read the memo!

The Celtic Christians of the Early Middle Ages worked hard to mine all the riches of Scripture, employing multiple dimensions of interpretation. But before we look at their techniques, we might ask how these ancient methods of Bible study have been preserved. Where can we find their understandings? Modern scholars know Gaelic Bible interpretations of the Early Middle ages via three types of written works: glosses, commentaries, and homilies.

Glosses are written comments added by readers to the margins of existent texts, much as modern readers might write notes in the borders and highlight favorite passages in a book. Glosses are common in ancient Celtic copies of the Psalms and Gospels, and also in less sacred books. Sometimes, a single text might have multiple glosses, added by successive readers. More than 12,000 of these marginal writings have survived, most of them written in the Irish language. (Not all the notations are spiritual or theological in nature; for example, one anonymous ninth-century scribe scrawled in the Ogham alphabet, "Ale is killing us," a confession that may have indicated he was suffering from a nasty hangover.[11])

The Celts also wrote books of formal commentary on the Bible that were meant to be read in tandem with the Scriptures themselves. The tradition of Celtic Bible commentary began early in the fourth century, when the first Celtic theologian, Morgan of Wales, wrote his commentaries on the Pauline Epistles. Another commentary, *On the Miracles of Holy Scripture*, written by an Irishman in the year 655, touches on numerous biblical texts spanning from Genesis to the Acts of the Apostles.[12] Others, such as Cummian's commentary on Mark and Eriugena's commentary on John, are specific to a certain book of the Bible.

In addition to glosses and commentaries, modern scholars have ancient Celtic sermon notes. Love for the Bible coupled with the Celts' bardic talents produced exceptional sermons, and we are fortunate that many were written down. These homilies are particularly useful in understanding how biblical themes were used to address everyday concerns.

Added together, their glosses, commentaries, and sermon notes enable us to see the ways that Gaelic Christians interpreted the Bible. We can divide Celtic Bible interpretation into three broad categories, or methods of interpretation—reading in three dimensions, as it were, with each dimension revealing different shades of meaning, all part of the same iridescent fan of light and truth. Medieval theologians favored this threefold approach because it corresponded to the triune nature of humanity: body, mind, and soul.

It seems to me that each of the three dimensions can be likened to an aspect of the peacock's plumage. The first way of reading the Bible is the "grounded" or literal approach, corresponding to the physical structure of a peacock feather. The second way of reading the Bible is on the level of symbolism, equivalent to the manner in which the human eye perceives patterns in peacock plumage. The third way of Bible reading is that of imagination, likened to the way these birds have inspired artists to create new and dazzling visions. Each of the three dimensions is valuable: this approach is "both-and" rather than "either-or." Quoting Ecclesiastes "a threefold cord is not quickly broken" (4:12).[13]

PRACTICING THE CELTIC WAY

In the following sections we'll look at each of these three dimensions of interpretation. Each section will begin with ancient examples, followed by a consideration of the abiding relevance of the principle under discussion, and concluded with an example of how we might examine a Scripture passage from that perspective.

We should remember, as we read and practice these methods of interpretation, that the Celts did not ponder the Bible as isolated individuals (the rare exceptions being occasional hermits) but in community. Three forms of communal information-sharing are apparent. First, since monasteries were the backbone of Celtic spirituality, almost all Bible interpretation was conducted in a context of shared spiritual life. Second, it is clear that there was exchange of information—books, letters, and envoys—throughout the world where the faith had spread. The seaways could be used like the Internet is used today, linking thinkers spatially distant from one another. Finally, there was an exchange of ideas over time. Since all books were hand-copied, they were highly prized and carefully handled, so many lasted for centuries. As Bible texts were passed down over long years, different readers in succession wrote glosses in the margins, sometimes in response to the glosses written by their predecessors. These comments beside the texts therefore became a sort of conversation across time, a precious compilation of different readers' wisdom.

In the New Testament Epistles, the word "you" is usually plural (a fact we miss, since only the American South's "y'all" offers an English-language version of the second-person plural pronoun that exists in many other languages). The ancient Celts provide a healthy model of reading the Bible with "you-all," a community of individuals in vital and intimate relationship with one another, across both time and space.

⋈ THE FIRST DIMENSION: GROUNDED IN PHYSICAL REALITY ⋈

> *Reason herself…if we could*
> *but listen to her more carefully,*
> *insists that we should understand*
> *the relation which exists between*
> *the sacred texts and reality.*
> —Eriugena, *Periphyseon*

Gazing at a peacock shaking its fanned tail feathers, viewers are mesmerized by the way light catches and reveals shifting and shimmering iridescent colors. But few who fix their eyes on this astonishing spectrum realize the cause of the peacock's changing hues: microscopic crystal-like structures within the vanes of each feather reflect different properties of light, depending on how they are spaced. If it weren't for this complex physical arrangement, the peacock would not be so stunning.

In a similar way, the peacock-like diversity of meaning in Scripture depends upon correspondence with physical reality. The first dimension of Celtic Bible interpretation, the physical grounding of each passage,[14] begins with consideration of the ways its message is set within space and time.

This approach to understanding the Bible seems common sense to most modern readers—in fact, for many today it is the only way they know to read Scripture. "Focus on the *ad litteram* sense," writes biblical scholar Michael Graves in *The Inspiration and Interpretation of Scripture*, "is what most distinctively characterizes modern biblical studies, both in the academy and in the church."[15]

Yet this has not always been the case. For long periods of church history, symbolic interpretations were regarded as more important than the literal meanings. Origen, one of the most dedicated and influential scholars of the Bible in early church history, said, "The Scriptures were composed through the spirit of God and they have not only that meaning which is obvious, but also another which is hidden from the majority of readers. For the contents of Scripture are the outward forms of certain mysteries and the images of divine things."[16] Eucherius, founder of the monastic center at Lerins, France, who had a significant impact on Irish Christianity, also emphasized the multiple levels of meaning in the Bible. He encouraged readers to "see through the surface [historical] level of Scripture to its 'higher' spiritual meaning."[17]

While the great scholars of the wider world encouraged the Gaels to seek out the higher symbolic meanings of the Bible, one of their own teachers emphasized the literal sense. The Welshman Pelagius was a brilliant Bible scholar whose commentaries contain very little symbolic interpretation; in fact, his expositions of Scripture read much like modern Evangelical commentaries. Pelagius emphasized human capacity to choose for or against God, potential that was implanted in each individual as a bearer of God's image (Genesis 1:26). God bestowed knowledge leading to salvation, said Pelagius, and the Bible was the foremost revelation of the Divine will. For this reason,

Pelagius focused on legal and didactic texts (as opposed to stories) in the Bible, and he explained these commandments in their most literal sense. "Pelagians trusted a virtuous ascetic to read and interpret the Scriptures for him- or herself," write Michael W. Herren and Shirley Ann Brown, "believing it was better to trust the reader's own interpretation than to absorb a commentary author's 'false allegorisation of the law.'"[18] Although Christians outside the British Isles deemed Pelagius a heretic, his writings held sway over the Celtic saints for four hundred years, and therefore his literal interpretations of the Bible counterbalanced the more symbolic readings that were also an aspect of the Celts' understanding of the Bible.

Celtic Christianity is pervaded by a sense that the sacred is grounded in the natural world. This meant that for the Celts, there were two books of God available for human interpretation—the Book of God written in ink on vellum, and the vastly larger Book of God that comprised all of Creation.[19] Since God expressed God's self through the medium of the material world, the Celts had to be open to the grounded interpretation of the Scriptures, as well as the symbolic.

In the seventh century, a scholar known as the "Irish Augustine" wrote a commentary titled *On the Miracles of Scripture*, which reveals a peculiarly Hibernian grounded perspective.[20] This commentary sets out to provide "natural" explanations for all of the miracles in the Bible.[21] The Irish Augustine reads the whole Bible from the firmly grounded perspective that "all of God's acts . . . must have been accomplished in accordance with nature and not in contravention of its laws."[22] If this treatise on miracles had been written in the modern era, readers would consider it a "scientific" approach to the Bible's wonders.

One striking example of the Irish Augustine's approach is the section "On the Incarnation of Our Lord Jesus Christ, and his birth from the Virgin Mary." Contemplating what many Christians would consider the superlative miracle in all history, the Irish Augustine claims that the Virgin Birth was a natural event. "Although it is indeed contrary to all of human experience for conception to be accomplished without a man's seed, it was not outside of nature" because "we can point to . . . animals generated without the intercourse of parents . . . birds and . . . many fish."[23] In our time, biologists confirm these examples of parthenogenesis in nature. The Irish Augustine was both a keen observer of the natural world, and an ingenious interpreter of Scripture, qualities reflecting the Celtic allegiance to God's revelation in both "books" of God—the Bible and the natural environment.

The Continuing Relevance of the Celts' Grounded Interpretation

Reading the Bible as grounded in time and space is a practice with perennial value because God has addressed humanity through the medium of the physical world; the Bible has specific historical and geographical contexts. Since Scriptures are rooted in history, the Bible should—to a significant degree—be read in light of its physical origins.[24]

Although at first glance the Celtic grounded approach resembles the method of Bible study employed by most Christians today, it differs from contemporary literalism in two regards. First, this grounded reading was balanced by symbolic and imaginative insights. Second, the Celts' reading—unlike that often employed in American Evangelical circles—regarded the letter of the Biblical text as *a* voice, but *not the only voice*, of God's utterance.

For the past five centuries, Protestant Bible scholarship has been strongly influenced by the Reformer's motto "*Sola Scriptura.*"[25] In its more restrictive sense, this means that the Bible is regarded as the supreme authority in all matters of Christian doctrine and practice. In some literalist churches, that doctrine is expanded to assert the Bible's overruling authority in all fields of human knowledge, including science, economics, health, and politics.

This totalizing of the Bible works for many people today, but other believers find it difficult to swallow. Bible scholar Peter Enns confesses, "The Bible can become a challenge to one's faith in God rather than the source of faith, a problem to be overcome rather than the answer to our problems."[26] This troubling-of-faith is apparent in the lives of college students reared in literalist homes and then exposed to scientific knowledge. Many American Evangelicals deny evolution (due to its contradiction with a literalist reading of Genesis 1) and deny climate change (based on a literalist reading of Genesis 8:22).[27] That can lead to painful struggles between what students have been told is Bible truth and the realities of the physical world—but this unfortunate collision is not inevitable. "The problem," as Peter Enns says, "is coming to the Bible with expectations it's not set up to bear."[28]

Celtic Christians in the Early Middle Ages understood Scripture and the world in a way that would have avoided this conflict. Since God's revelation is transmitted to humans both in the Bible *and* in the physical universe, the Bible need not be regarded as the sole repository of all human knowledge. There are truths revealed in Scripture and then there are innumerable further truths coming to light as God speaks through the natural environment.

The Celtic grounded reading of the Bible has the potential to transform an authoritarian form of interpretation into one that's more open to exchange of ideas. For some modern Christians, when the Bible appears to contradict observations of the natural world, the Bible trumps reality. But in the Celtic understanding, God speaks in stereo—both through the Scriptures and through gains in human knowledge. Perceived differences between God's "two books" can be welcomed as occasions for dialogue between the two forms of revelation, with the possibility that gains in scientific knowledge will necessitate revised interpretations of the Scriptures. Such revisions are not "giving in to science" or compromising the Bible—they are blessed opportunities to view the peacock's beauty in a new way.

An Example of Grounded Bible Reading: Mark 10:46–52

We will use the same passage that follows as an example of how to use each of the three different approaches to biblical interpretation. You may wish to refer back again to this passage before you read about its meanings from a symbolic and then an imaginative approach.

> *They came to Jericho. As he went out from Jericho, with his disciples and a great multitude, the son of Timaeus, Bartimaeus, a blind beggar, was sitting by the road. When he heard that it was Jesus the Nazarene, he began to cry out, and say, "Jesus, you son of David, have mercy on me!" Many rebuked him, that he should be quiet, but he cried out much more, "You son of David, have mercy on me!"*
>
> *Jesus stood still, and said, "Call him."*
>
> *They called the blind man, saying to him, "Take courage! Get up. He is calling you!"*
>
> *He, casting away his cloak, sprang up, and came to Jesus.*
>
> *Jesus asked him, "What do you want me to do for you?"*
>
> *The blind man said to him, "Teacher, that I may see again."*
>
> *Jesus said to him, "Go your way. Your faith has made you well." Immediately he received his sight, and followed Jesus on the way.*

Reading this from a grounded perspective, we might begin by asking what we can know about the physical condition of blindness, particularly in the ancient Middle East. Biblehub.com, a popular Bible study website, provides this information: "This distressing malady is very prevalent in the East. Many physical causes in those countries unite to injure the organs of vision. The sun is hot, and in the atmosphere floats a very fine dust, which enters and frets the eye." More specifically, "Blindness from birth is the result of a form of this disease known as *ophthalmia neonatorum* which sets in a few days after birth. Sometimes ophthalmia accompanies malarial fever."[29]

Following the example of the Irish Augustine in his work *On the Miracles of Scripture*, we might ask, "Can this healing be explained in terms of natural law?" It could in fact be a case of psychosomatic blindness, such as that experienced by "that blind, deaf, and dumb boy" Tommy, in the Who rock opera. If psychological trauma caused Bartimaeus to go blind, then the overwhelming psychological power of Christ's verbal blessing might have cured him.

If the blindness was the sort of physical malady noted in the quotes above, then there was no medical cure existent at the time. Interpreters open to a more supernatural healing might enumerate which parts of the optical lens or neural organs of the eye might have been damaged, and how Jesus was able to miraculously perform by mere touch an operation surpassing what can be done by all the best technology of our age.

In the following sections, we'll see how adding levels of interpretation multiplies the ways this same text can be understood and applied to life.

⋈ THE SECOND DIMENSION: ASCENDING TO THE LEVEL OF SYMBOLISM ⋈

> And this variety of interpretation
> is not contrary to nature.
> —Eriugena, *Periphyseon*

The beauty of the peacock's train lies not just in the variety of shimmering colors, but also in the pattern displayed by the outstretched fan. The first thing you notice are the "eyes," ovals within ovals that jump out from the background color. Next, one discerns the arrangement of these "eyes" within the entire train; viewed together, they form a fractal design in which replication of smaller elements produces a larger pattern. No wonder that Hindus, Buddhists, Jews, Christians, and Muslims have all interpreted the peacock as having mystical significance. The beauty and complexity of its plumage beckons us to contemplate the splendor and mystery of a larger reality.

Contemplating the prevalence and complexity of designs in nature, Augustine of Hippo (354–430) formulated a "sacramental vision of reality." In this view, "in even the least interesting bit of matter, there is a link to God."[30] This sacramental view of reality was inspired by Scripture itself: "For the invisible things of God since the creation of the world are clearly seen, being perceived through the things that are made" (Romans 1:20).

Eucherius of Gaul (380–449) likened the Bible to Nature: both are multidimensional forms of revelation. He wrote a book titled *Formula for a Spiritual Understanding*, influential in the Irish medieval monasteries, in which he invited readers past the purely historical meaning of Scripture into deeper, more spiritual meanings, based upon the Bible itself. Listing elements of the natural world referred to in Scripture, such as the sun, moon, trees, fire, stones, and animals, he then pointed out other scriptural examples where that same object was used in a clearly metaphorical way. Eucherius discerned that throughout the Bible "there was the text you could read on the page in front of you, and there was the more real, more permanent and higher meaning to which it pointed through its symbolic codes."[31]

Such a metaphorical reading of Scripture is indeed pervasive in the Bible. The Apostle Paul was fond of symbolic interpretation. In 1 Corinthians 10:4, he refers to the rock that Moses struck in Sinai and says, "They drank from the spiritual rock that accompanied them, and that rock was Christ." In Galatians chapter 4, Paul mentions Abraham's two sons by two mothers and then later declares, "These things contain an allegory, for these are two covenants" (vs. 24).[32] In these examples, Paul illustrates the kind of interpretation that would become common in the Early Middle Ages, seeing through the historical level of the Hebrew Bible to discern a higher spiritual meaning that speaks of Christ. No wonder then that "virtually all ancient Christians believed that the Old Testament had spiritual meaning beyond the literal sense."[33]

Some early Christians had another pressing reason to adopt this method of interpretation: they were trying to preserve the Hebrew scriptures as being suitable for Christianity. Not all Christians agreed that these older scriptures still had value in the post-Incarnation world.

Marcion (85–160), a Christian living in what is today Turkey, noted that the "Old Testament God" did things that seem unworthy of the God revealed in Christ. Could a God who demanded genocide of unbelievers (1 Samuel 15) be the same as a God who loves the world (John 3:16) and *is* love (John 4:8)? Could the same Divine Spirit command, "Do not leave alive anything that breathes" (Deuteronomy 20:16) and then speak through Jesus' lips saying, "Love your enemies" (Matthew 5:44)? Marcion had a simple answer: do away with the Old Testament.

Origen (184–254), a Christian scholar living in Alexandria, Egypt, agreed with Marcion on one crucial point: "Some Old Testament portrayals of God are unworthy of God."[34] Yet Origen's life was devoted to study of the Hebrew scriptures, which he treasured. As Eric Seibert writes in *Disturbing Divine Behavior*, "Origen retained the Old Testament and sought to interpret it in such a way as to exclude from its depiction of God the qualities Marcion condemned. Marcion denied the validity of allegory. Origen spent his life employing allegory and seeking to justify the method."[35] Origen defended Christian use of the Hebrew scriptures by interpreting the genocide passages symbolically. The Christian should read commands to slay pagans, Origen said, as symbolic calls to eradicate sin and disobedience. He wrote: "If the horrible wars related in the Old Testament were not to be interpreted in a spiritual sense, the apostles would never have transmitted the Jewish books for reading in the church to followers of Christ."[36]

A century later, Augustine also used symbolic interpretation to deal with troubling Old Testament passages. How could a God of love possibly call for smashing the heads of Babylonian infants (Psalm 137:9)? According to Bible scholar Kenton L. Sparks, Augustine interpreted that verse as follows: "The 'infants' of Babylon were not literal children but rather the vices of the Babylonians."[37]

As a Celtic example of figurative reading, the earliest surviving commentary on the Gospel of Mark, written in 610 by the Irish monk Cummian, offers numerous examples of symbolic interpretation. Referring to the mistreatment of Jesus by the Sanhedrin (Mark 14:65), Cummian offers these observations: "This was so that by his guilt he might remove our guilt; that by the blindfold on his face he might take the blindfold from our hearts; that by receiving the spits, he might wash the face of our soul, that by the blows, by which he was struck on the head, he might heal the head of the human race, which is Adam."[38] These insights flow from Cummian's knowledge of other scriptures, and his theological emphasis on the gospel as the outworking of God's mercy. His broader knowledge led him to see God's kindness even in a series of horrible events.

As another example of Celtic symbolic interpretation, Aleran the Wise of County Meath, Ireland, wrote a book in 664 titled *The Mystical Interpretation of the Genealogy of Our Lord Jesus Christ*, in which he went through the genealogy of Christ that introduces Matthew's Gospel and gives a symbolic meaning for each name listed. For example, one ancestor of Christ was Obed, whose name means "servant" in

Hebrew, and Aleran commented, "Christ came not to be served but to serve, even taking on the form of a servant.... The Christian likewise may serve the Lord with that servitude which is not out of fear, but with the spirit of the adoption of sons."[39]

The Continuing Relevance of the Celts' Symbolic Interpretation

Interpreters in the modern era, part of a larger trend that favors didactic language over imaginative wording, have been dismissive of symbolic understanding of the Bible. In modernity, "The one who speaks powerfully is not the poet," writes George Aichele in *Sign, Text and Scripture*, "but the scientist or engineer, who uses words to represent or manipulate the world."[40] Yet some of the greatest thinkers of our age have championed the importance of symbolism.

Huston Smith, a well-known Christian scholar of comparative religions, wrote, "*Exegesis that stops with the literal meaning of a text... cannot do the text full justice.* Classical Christianity took it for granted that literalism could not do the full job, which is why 'Jesus spoke to them in parables.'" Smith concludes, "Religion's technical language is symbolism, the science of relations between the multiple levels of reality."[41]

C. S. Lewis, the twentieth-century grand spokesman of Christianity, asserted that "allegory belongs to 'the very nature of thought and language.' It is a fragment of the perennial language, signaling immaterial feelings by material images that remain constant across the ages and around the world."[42] Lewis dedicated several chapters to the importance of symbolic interpretation in his book *Reflections on the Psalms*. He wrote that since "pagan utterances can carry a second meaning... we shall expect the Scriptures to do this more momentously and more often."[43]

Following in the tradition of Saint Augustine, Lewis addressed Psalm 137 as a text that benefits from symbolic reading. "From this point of view I can use even the horrible passage in 137 about dashing the Babylonian babies against the stones. I know things in the inner world which are like babies; the infantile beginning of small indulgences, small resentments, which may one day become dipsomania or settled hatred . . . against all such petty infants . . . the advice of the Psalms is best."[44]

Marcus Borg, one of the twenty-first century's most insightful Jesus scholars, was a defender of symbolic Bible interpretation. He called metaphor *"the more-than-literal meaning of language"* and affirmed that "there is more than one justification for using a metaphorical approach to the Bible. One reason is that much of its language is obviously metaphorical . . . even when a text contains historical memory, its more-than-literal meaning matters most. For example, the exile in Babylon in the sixth century BCE really happened, but the way the story is told gives it a more-than-historical meaning. It became a metaphorical narrative of exile and return, abiding images of the human condition and its remedy."[45]

In another book, Borg emphasized that "metaphor is about surplus of meaning, not a deficiency of meaning." The Gospel accounts include *"memory metaphorized*—stories that contain the memory of something that happened, but that are told in such a way as to give them a more than historical-factual meaning." An example is Mark's account of Jesus' journey to Jerusalem leading to his sacrificial death. Borg explained, "Jesus really did make a journey from Galilee to Jerusalem that ended in his execution. This is history remembered. But the way Mark tells the story of Jesus' journey gives it a more-than-historical meaning. In Mark it is a story of *what it means to follow Jesus* . . . for Mark (and early Christianity generally), to be a *disciple* is to *follow* Jesus on *the way* to Jerusalem . . . to follow Jesus is to join him on this journey of transformation and confrontation. The story of

Jesus' final journey is a metaphorical narrative about the meaning of discipleship."[46]

Following a similar train of thought, Wheaton College biblical studies professor Michael Graves wrote, "If Scripture is to speak credibly to contemporary Christians, the exposition of Scripture must move beyond recounting the *ad litteram* sense.... Therefore, although it is often not obvious to modern Christians, we have much to learn from the Church Fathers about how to interpret Scripture beyond the literal level."[47]

There is another factor that highlights the contemporary importance of symbolic interpretation. The Bible is critiqued today for the same reason that it was questioned in the second century—the perilous shadow of its violent passages. At a time when the world is reeling from religious terrorism, Christ's followers hesitate to add fuel to an already destructive conflagration.

Philip Jenkins, Distinguished Senior Fellow at the Institute for Studies of Religion at Baylor University, questions whether the Quran endorses violence more than the Bible—and answers in the negative: "If the founding text shapes the whole religion, then Judaism and Christianity deserve the utmost condemnation as religions of savagery." He goes on, however, to note, "Of course, they are no such thing; nor is Islam."[48] As Jenkins points out, Abrahamic religions each have scriptures that can be used to promote violence or peace, and if they are to result in peace, then the teachers of religion must learn to talk about violent passages constructively. Jenkins reminds us that in the accounts of genocide in the Hebrew scriptures, "we have a constructed narrative in which particular authors and editors have taken a story and framed it in ways that made sense to them. It is a story with a point or theme, and one that is aimed at a particular audience."[49]

Investigating the conquest of Canaan, archaeologists find evidence that differs from the Bible tales. According to Jenkins, "Archaeologist William Dever concludes that . . . evidence 'supports almost nothing of the biblical account of a large scale concerted Israelite military invasion of Canaan.'"[50] So why would the Bible writers exaggerate tales of how they exterminated their enemies, down to the noncombatants? The answer may be that the Bible was mostly written after the Babylonian exile, a time at which Jews were wondering: how can we make sure history does not repeat for us? To ensure Israel's future purity, the Bible writers portrayed a golden age of Israel, before they fell into God's disfavor. This golden age was marked by absolute loyalty to God's commandments. The wars in Canaan were portrayed as the utter extermination of everything that did not faithfully worship God, as an illustration of the way that faithful Israel should expunge everything ungodly from their midst. The Bible stories of genocide may have been composed to point to a larger truth—the need to utterly eradicate idolatry—rather than a straightforward recounting of history. Thus, the best current scholarship supports the instincts of the ancient interpreters: in a culture of literary traditions quite different from ours today, biblical tales of violence were intended to be understood for their spiritual meaning rather than taken as literal history.

Professor Michael concurs, saying, "The Philistines are typologized in the Old Testament as the ultimate 'other' in a manner that, even if it reflects historical realities to some extent, also places a theological overlay on top of history. The Church Fathers' belief in a higher sense gave them a framework within which to perceive such theological overlays. For reasons such as these, the interpretations that the Church Fathers identified as the spiritual sense sometimes correlate with ideas genuinely found in the biblical texts."[51]

So there are compelling reasons—both the symbolic nature of many Bible passages and the continuing need to properly interpret violent passages—that commend the "more-than-literal" reading of Scripture. But some church historians allege that the Middle Ages were the Dark Ages in terms of Bible reading. Allegorical analysis of the Bible led to a profusion of ridiculous and unmerited interpretations.

If today's Christians again embrace the symbolic nature of Scripture, will that lead to confusion?

This question wrongly supposes, however, that the literal meaning is always more easily understood than the symbolic meaning. In fact, the "clear and simple" meaning of the Bible is often the product of a group's or an individual's bias. Graves observed, "Many modern teachers of Scripture arbitrarily devise their own (sometimes idiosyncratic) applications of biblical texts and impose them on others as if with divine authority."[52] Similarly, Bible scholar N. T. Wright noted, "We imagine that we are 'reading the text straight,' and that if somebody disagrees with us it must be because they, unlike ourselves, are secretly using 'presuppositions' of this or that sort. This is simply naive, and actually astonishingly arrogant and dangerous. . . . Evangelicals often use the phrase 'authority of scripture' when they *mean* the authority of evangelical or Protestant theology, since the assumption is made that we (Evangelicals or Protestants) are the ones who know and believe what the Bible is saying."[53]

An illustration may serve to show the problem of discerning a "clear" literal meaning. I've often heard Christians say something along these lines: "The Bible does not command slavery—God never desired human bondage." I am thankful they read Scripture that way, but this was not always the "clear" meaning of the Bible. In fact, a vast array of Bible tracts, sermons, and theological arguments before America's Civil War cited chapter and verse to support the viewpoint that the simple, literal, and clear reading of the text demonstrated God's approval—nay, insistence upon!—slavery. How is it that the Bible is very "clear" on something at one point in history, then clearly the opposite a century later?

Perhaps because the "literal" and "clear" interpretation may actually depend on the readers' frame of reference more than on the wording of the text itself. Both literal and symbolic interpretations may be skewed by the readers' bias,[54] and both ways of reading can be safeguarded similarly. First, interpretations should derive directly from the text under consideration, in its context, and in comparison with similar Scriptures (see the example that follows here). Second, Christian exegesis should always be done with reference to Christ, as suggested by Luke 24:27.

Literalists claim that medieval allegorizing harmed the church, but in fact almost all ancient symbolic interpretations were based on these safeguards. Over and over, the commentaries of the Early Middle Ages point the reader to Christ and extol various virtues of the Savior. This hardly did any disservice to the Christian faith; rather, the more-than-literal readings of the Bible served to bolster Jesus' centrality in spiritual life.

There's a third safeguard against readers' bias: any true interpretation should promote obedience to the greatest commands—love of God and neighbor. Augustine put this eloquently in his *Confessions*: "See how stupid it is, among so large a mass of entirely correct interpretations which can be elicited from these words, to rashly assert that a particular one has the best claim to Moses' view, and by destructive disputes to offend against charity itself, which is the principle of everything he said in the texts we are trying to expound."[55] In other words, if we argue over interpretations and harm others in so doing, we've got it wrong even if we get it right!

An Example of Symbolic Bible Reading: Mark 10:46–52

An obvious place to begin contemplation of this text's symbolism is the word "blind." A scan of that term throughout the Scriptures reveals a number of similar healing stories, but also a weighty number of passages where blindness/loss of sight is used symbolically, indicating either spiritual or judicial blindness. (Compare Deut. 16:19, 1 Sam. 12:3, Prov. 28:27, Mt. 5:29, Mt. 6:23, Mt. 18:9, and Luke 6:39.) Blindness, therefore, was a common metaphorical device, both among Jews and early Christians.

Reading the broader setting around this passage affirms the metaphorical sense of blindness in the story, one that's both spiritual and moral in nature. The healing of Bartimaeus is proceeded by conflicts with religious teachers (9:38–41, 42–49; 10:1–12), and then the spiritual blindness of Jesus' own disciples (10:35–45). Matthew, writing shortly after Mark, will condemn the Pharisees who oppose Jesus as "blind guides" (Mt. 23). Bartimaeus' healing is followed by multiple pronouncements of judgment on those who refuse to see God's truth in their midst (Mark 11:12–25, 27–33, and 12:1–12). All this is leading up to the ultimate case of blindness toward justice, which is Jesus' false trial, torture, and execution, in chapters 14 through 15.

In contrast with all the symbolic blindness around him, Bartimaeus, despite opposition from those around him, knows to call out to Jesus. "Many rebuked him and told him to be quiet, but he called out all the more, 'Son of David, have mercy on me!'" (vs. 48). Having noted the themes of spiritual blindness and faith, this verse represents the opposition to discipleship that Jesus' followers in every age must face. In fact, Bartimaeus' confession is so perfect that it has been used (with the substitution of "God" for "David") for centuries as the "Jesus Prayer." The passage ends with another evocative phrase, one that surely held a breadth of meaning in the writer's mind: he "followed Jesus on the way" (the Greek word *odos* meant "path, road, journey"). In the first century, "Christian" was rarely used to refer to Christ's followers; instead, the common designation was "People of the Way" (Acts 9:2). So this passage is a complete narrative of one man's conversion. He was spiritually blind, not unlike many of his fellows; then he called out to Jesus, asking for Divine mercy, despite the castigation of his peers; Jesus transformed him, bringing illumination; and finally, Bartimaeus entered into the community of believers, committing his life to the ongoing journey of discipleship.

Where a physically grounded reading yielded interesting but hardly applicable facts about physical blindness, a metaphorical approach models the way that Christ transforms lives. Like Bartimaeus, we can recognize our places of darkness, can call for Christ to touch us, can be illuminated, and can then embark on a lifelong path among the company of Jesus' followers. With the addition of "second-dimension" reading, we see the larger pattern of the peacock's plumage in this text.

The Third Dimension: Imagining

There are almost innumerable . . . drawings
if you take the trouble to look very closely,
and penetrate with your eyes
to the secrets of the artistry,
you will notice such intricacies,
so delicate and subtle, so close together,
and well-knitted . . . so fresh still in their colorings
that you will not hesitate to declare
that all these things must have been
the result of the work, not of men, but of angels.
—Gerald of Wales, 1185, describing the Book of Kells

For over a thousand years, the Book of Kells has evoked praise and wonder. Its full-page illuminations require a contemplative gaze: first, you see the large design, like the gilded frame of a picture or the form of a carpet. Then, looking closer, you discern portraits: a large letter, an animal, or a human figure. Gazing more closely, a third dimension is apparent: a seemingly infinite maze of knotwork, geometric patterns, dots of bright color, and lines so small they could only be

THE PEACOCK'S FEATHERS   ☘   35

drawn using a magnifying stone. "The decorative scheme of the entire Book of Kells," wrote Georgetown Professor John Pfordresher, "is thus a single, repeating visual metaphor for a theological reality that has ever subtler, even deeper levels of organization and meaning."[56]

In the Gospel of Matthew section, the Book of Kells presents a stunning full-page portrayal of Christ, enclosed within a lavish frame of swirls and geometric patterns. Jesus gazes at the viewer and holds a large, bright red book on his knee. This image of the Bible is central to the entire page; the eye is drawn to it immediately. To the left and the right of Christ's head are a mirrored pair of peacocks. Each sits atop a chalice filled with grapes—the Eucharist. Their tails are cascades of bright colors in intricate design.

What do these peacocks represent? The peacock, which annually sheds then re-grows its glorious train, is a time-honored Christ symbol. These peacocks may also, on the other hand, signify the Bible, the image of which is so prominent on this page. We recall Eriugena's peacock analogy and the fact that Eriugena shared the same Irish monastic background as the scribes who made the Book of Kells.

Pfordresher explained the connection between the imaginative art of the Book of Kells and the Celtic approach to Scripture: "For the Iona community, God's book was mysterious, never to be fully comprehended. Rather than seeking one, single meaning for a word or a sentence, this tradition prized multiplicity, layers of meaning, expecting a complexity and richness beyond the limits of any one reading. . . . The imaginative response to this in the Book of Kells is the analogous complexity of its ornamentation, functioning as a visual metaphor for the value presumed inherent in the text."[57]

Another example of Celtic illuminated Scriptures, the Lindisfarne Gospels, expressed the multiplicity of meanings inherent in the text by another device: mixing alphabets. Michelle Brown wrote, "These pages feature letters of Latin, Greek, Runic, and Ogam inspiration."[58] The very shape of letters could be revelatory; for example

THE GOSPEL OF MATTHEW

the Greek capital Delta (Δ) might be used in place of the Latin letter D in *Deus*, signifying the fact that God is always a Trinity. (The triangle is a symbolic representation of the Trinity.) This multiplicity of signifiers in a text reminded the reader that there were layers of meaning in every passage—layers that pointed to the hidden depths of God's being.

This third dimension of Celtic Bible interpretation differs from the levels of grounded and symbolic readings in that it consciously seeks to go *beyond* meanings found in the text itself. After the hard work of asking, "What does the text say?" the reader proceeds to speculative questions—"What might be left unsaid?" "What happened before and after the story?"—and then on to the really vital question: "What does this say to us, here and now?"

For the Celts, God is ultimately a mystery; there will always be Divine secrets beyond human kenning. At a certain point, physical realities serve only as a portal to the infinite. The only way to pass that entryway is to travel by imagination.

Storytelling has been a benchmark of Celtic cultures from at least the early Iron Age. The Bards were the most honored members of Celtic society; they were greater than kings, since a good singer-storyteller could raise another man up to become king—or cast him down in disrepute. Living in colder regions, Celtic societies depended on their tale-tellers to keep each village and clan inspired through the long, threatening winters. Wordsmiths were honored as much as blacksmiths, and they were just as essential for survival.

Creative forms of expression possess a raw power, activated by our ancestral instincts. "For members of an oral culture," wrote Aichele, "poetic language, like the speech of God in Genesis 1, casts a spell over reality. The poet's words are true because they make things real—they create reality. The powerfully spoken (or 'winged') words of the poet cannot be denied."[59] Perhaps the Celts took to the Bible so readily because its stories are derived from oral tellings, and the

Celts, coming straight to Christianity from an oral culture, understood Scripture accordingly.[60]

The literalist may be disappointed to realize that the Bible is to such a large degree comprised of story. Far from being "God's little instruction book" it is "God's enormous storybook." For the Celts this was not a drawback—quite the opposite. Stories had shaped their lives since the Bronze Age. Stories gave them power and pride; stories enabled them to overcome all manner of deadly foes. Stories were the very blood that ran in Celtic veins, and they were filled with wonder and delight to have so many stories about the King of Mystery and his people.

As soon as Christians arrived in Celtic lands with the gospel, the art of storytelling was applied to the life-giving narratives of the new Christian faith. Writings such as *Altus Prosator* (*The High First-Sower*), *In Tenga Bithnua* (*The Ever-New Tongue*), and *Saltair Na Rann* (*The Psalter of the Quatrains*) fuse bardic storytelling skills with Bible narratives, resulting in uniquely Celtic works of adoration to God. These do not claim to be scriptural commentary; they are works of imagination inspired by the Scriptures and proceeding on a trajectory beyond them.

The High First-Sower, allegedly composed by Columba, is written in Latin with uniquely Celtic phraseology. For instance, the word in the title, *Prosator*, is literally "the first one to sow," a term from Gaelic farming. Poetic in form, *Altus Prosator* has a stanza for each letter of the alphabet, a form perhaps inspired by similar biblical psalms. Its subject is the great work of God, from creation to judgment. Such an epic theme requires all the varied skills of human creative writing, and the *Altus Prosator* does not disappoint; images sourced from the Bible, Christian apocrypha, bardic nature poems, and Greek mythology weave together in a paean of Divine praise. Describing the flood, the narrative invokes "the swelling whirlpools of Cocytus, covered by Scyllas"—references to Greek mythology.[61] Moses' ascent of Mount Sinai is described with dramatic concrete imagery: "Who has ascended Mount Sinai to speak with the Lord, has heard the thunder sounding exceedingly and the noise of the great resounding trumpet, has seen the lightning flashing in a ring and lights and missiles and crashing stones, save Moses, judge of the people of Israel?"[62] From the earthly plane, the narrator lifts the reader to heaven where "in the fervent resounding chanting of hymns by thousands of angels flourishing in their holy dances . . . the Trinity receives threefold praise eternally."[63]

The Ever-New Tongue is an even more creative work, written in Irish. "Far from simply being a commentary on the testimony of the Bible," wrote John Carey, "it purports to be a separate heavenly revelation, unveiling all the mysteries of the universe."[64] Allusions are drawn from the Bible, Gnostic writings, travel literature, gemology, and astronomy, but, said Carey, "its contents have been transformed in the crucible of the author's imagination to become part of his own unique, fantastic vision of reality. *In Tenga Bithnua* is, indeed, one of the most remarkable examples . . . of that inspired fusion of learning and creativity which distinguishes so much of early Irish literature."[65] The central theme—the universal revelation of Divine utterance—is echoed today by the motto of the United Church of Christ, "God is still speaking."

The very first words reflect the majesty of this tale: "The High King of the world, who is mightier than every king, who is loftier than every power, who is fiercer than every dragon, who is gentler than every child, who is brighter than suns, who is holier than every elder, who is more vengeful than men, who is more loving than every mother, the only Son of God the Father, bestowed this account upon the many peoples of the world, concerning the world's form and creation."[66]

The epic is filled with lovely imaginative details such as this comment on the creation of humanity: "And there is in it material from the sun and the stars of heaven also; so that is what makes the brightness and light in people's eyes."[67] This insight not only charms; it is scientifically true, for, as Carl Sagan said, "We are made of starstuff."[68] *The Ever-New Tongue* also reveals that the entirety of the universe was originally contained "in the round many-shaped aggregation of the material of the world . . . in the round many-shaped mass from which the world was extracted,"[69] a phrase evocative of the singularity that physicists posit before the Big Bang.[70] The symphony of creation's beauty ends with an invitation to eternal glory "where the good has not been lacking, and is not lacking, and will never be lacking," and the exhortation, "May we all reach that kingdom, may we deserve it, may we dwell in it world without end, Amen."[71]

The Psalter of the Quatrains is another example of imaginative extrapolation from Scripture. "In the process of putting the Bible story into medieval Irish verse, it transforms it and imbues it with an Irish flavor," Carey wrote. "The *Saltair* gives us an unparalleled opportunity to look at the panorama of the Scriptures through the eyes of the tradition to which this book is devoted; and to experience some of the vivid, colourful, imaginative sensibility which that tradition brought to the church's teachings."[72] It interweaves Hellenistic legend with New Testament imagery: "That is virginal Olympus without movement or stir, according the noble account of the ancient sages; its name is 'the third holy heaven.'"[73] And there are unique Celtic phrases, such as "the King of every splendid substance, our mighty tree."[74] Also in this work, God is "the bright King of mysteries," a fitting title in a poetic work that aims to lift the reader into the realm of the numinous.

These imaginative writings defy categorization in the Christian literary traditions; perhaps they could be characterized as Celtic *Midrash*, the ancient rabbinic commentary on the Hebrew scriptures that is attached to the biblical text. The comparison may seem strange at first: what do the Gaels and the Jews have in common at this time of the Early Middle Ages? But it is not far-fetched. "In the virulently anti-Jewish world of the sixth to eighth centuries," Herren and Brown note, "the British and Irish Churches preserved a deep regard for the most Jewish aspects of Christianity."[75]

Like the Celts, Jewish interpreters expected their scriptures to yield multiple levels of meaning and diverse interpretations. Furthermore, they expected God to *continue* speaking through the Torah. Rabbi Sandy Eisenberg Sasso explains that by "grounding themselves in the biblical narrative," Midrash "retold the ancient story in the light of new realities and changing conditions.... The Rabbis said that when God revealed the Ten Commandments at Sinai, not only the Exodus generation stood at the foot of the mountain, but all generations of Israel yet to come. They believed that revelation did not take place once upon a time but all the time."[76]

The Continuing Relevance of the Celts' Imaginative Reading

"Customarily, when we read the Bible we listen to its ancient words, allowing it to tell us our ancestors' stories. But what would it mean to read the Bible by allowing it to help us tell the stories of *our* lives? What if we read our joys, our fears, and our doubts into the biblical narrative?"[77] Rabbi Eisenberg Sasso's invitation for readers to create their own Midrash can also serve as our call to engage in Celtic Midrash—imaginative reading of Scripture.

This might be considered the *application* stage of Celtic Bible study, but it goes beyond the way some modern interpreters use that word. Too often the Bible is reduced to the role of "God's rulebook," a moral and spiritual instruction manual. In the Celtic view, however, the peacock-beauty of Scripture is more than merely instructional; the Celtic imaginative approach beckons us to draw wonder and inspiration from the Bible, transforming us into Christ-likeness. This is not the old cliché question, "What would Jesus do?" but rather, "What *is* Jesus *doing now* within human beings and the world?"

When we read with imagination, we directly engage with the Bible as narrative (in other words, story)—and story is the most powerful form of communication. As Andover Newton Professor of Bible Gregory Mobley explains, stories are potent because they fill a fundamental human need for mastery over chaos: "Once we have a story, we have direction, shape, motive.... We no longer have chaos, we have meaning and order. And the story we create will represent this meaning and order." From our very beginnings, "Humans are storytellers, meaning-makers, and pattern-tracers. Even before we learn to count, we are constantly putting two and two together, tying episodes together into the daisy-chain cause-and-effect sequences we know as stories."[78] Studies show that our brains acquire new information more effectively through narratives, and reading stories makes us more prone to compassionate behavior. An article in the *Harvard Business Review* concludes, "When you want to motivate, persuade, or be remembered, start with a story of human struggle and eventual triumph. It will capture people's hearts—by first attracting their brains."[79]

Perhaps the power of narrative, coupled with our capacity to imagine, can provide a new understanding of the Bible's relevance. While the Bible continues to work in a strictly literalist sense for many Christians today, many others struggle with the Scriptures. The Bible leads some to faith, but for others it is a stumbling block in faith's way. Embracing the Bible as narrative may provide us with a renewed handle on the Bible's value and authority. As N. T. Wright writes, "Authority is not the power to control people, to crush them, and keep them in little boxes. The church often tries to do that—to tidy people up. Nor is the Bible as the Vehicle of God's authority meant to be information for the legalist."[80]

The Bible's greater "authority" is that of inspiration, largely imparted in the form of stories. Again quoting Wright: "Story authority, as Jesus knew only too well, is the authority that really works. Throw a rule book at people's head, or offer them a list of doctrines, and they can duck or avoid it, or simply disagree and go away. Tell them a story, though, and you invite them to come into a different world; you invite them to share a world-view or better still a 'God-view.' . . . Stories determine how people see themselves and how they see the world.

Stories determine how they experience God, and the world, and themselves, and others. Great revolutionary movements have told stories about the past and present and future. They have invited people to see themselves in that light, and people's lives have been changed. If that happens at a merely human level, how much more when it is God himself, the Creator, breathing through his word."[81]

The Scriptures do indeed possess life-changing power—the power of inspiration. "Inspiration" can be trivialized to holiday cards or cheerful little tabloid stories, but the word can also convey the consuming fire of the Spirit setting mortals ablaze with purpose and passion. An oft-cited verse declares that "every Scripture is inspired by God" or, as more literally translated in the World English Bible, "every Scripture is God-breathed" (2 Timothy 3:16). The text refers to Genesis 2 when God created Adam and "breathed into his nostrils the breath of life." So the Bible's own claim to inspiration is not primarily about having all the facts straight or providing the best set of rules; inspiration is the imparting of life.

The Scriptures are meant to transform us, so that we can say, "It is no longer I who live but Christ living in me" (Galatians 2:2). To this end, God calls us through both the book of Nature and the books of Scripture. As we engage the Bible with our imagination, we allow our souls to be filled with God's breath, transforming us into the Divine nature (2 Peter 1:4).

An Example of Imaginative Reading: Mark 10:46–52

Imaginative reading can be deep and powerful, and especially so when it is your own imagination at work. As Greg Mobley says, "The task of theology is the linking of our individual story to the biggest story we can imagine,"[82] and only you can link God's story to your own.

To that end, I've suggested the following three steps. I know it's tempting to skip over the exercises in a book and "get on to the meat."

But it will benefit you to take time for contemplation as suggested here. Doing so will enable you to firm up in your mind what you've learned so far and—most important—help you to connect your story to God's story.

1. Reread Mark 10:46–52 on page 22.
2. Imagine yourself as Bartimaeus—or, alternatively, as a bystander to this incident. Be as sensual as you can while imagining the scene, keeping in mind that you are blind at the beginning of the story. What does the air feel like against your face? What do you smell? What do you hear? Pay close attention to your emotions as you perceive the messages your senses bring you.
3. Now connect the story of Bartimaeus with memories that are *your* story. When have you felt the kind of feelings that the story invokes in you? What story would you tell along with this one? *Imagine how this story can alter your story* as it unwinds into the future.

For the Celts, the Bible was something amazing and wondrous. Like the world of Nature, it was to be "read" attentively, with the commitment and fascination the lover feels for the beloved. In today's world, where reading is done purely for pleasure or information, we have lost the knack of reading with the Celts' passionate, open receptivity to Mystery, the immense larger and deeper Reality that underlies all life.

But that approach to reading Scripture is not lost to us. With practice, we too can learn to open our hearts and minds to the gift of the Divine Word. When we do, we will find that it enters us as the Breath of God, inspiring us and transforming us in unpredictable ways—and then sweeping through us like a flame that kindles new life and healing in the world around us.

1. John Scottus Eriugena, *Periphyseon on the Division of Nature*, trans. I. P. Sheldon-Williams (Washington, DC: Dumbarton-Oaks, 1987), 390.
2. Dirdre Carabine, *John Scottus Eriugena* (New York: Oxford University Press, 2000), 13.
3. *Patrick's Letter to the Soldiers*, quoted by Oliver Davies in *Celtic Spirituality* (New York: Paulist Press, 1999), 88–89.
4. Bede, quoted by Leslie Hardinge in *The Celtic Church in Britain* (New York: Teach Services, 2005), 30.
5. Michael W. Herren and Shirley Ann Brown, *Christ in Celtic Christianity: Britain and Ireland from the Fifth to the Tenth Century* (Woodbridge, Suffolk, UK: Boydell Press, 2012), 106.
6. Joseph Falaky Nagy, *Conversing with Angels and Ancients: Literary Myths of Medieval Ireland* (Ithaca, NY: Cornell University Press, 1997), 147.
7. Thomas O'Loughlin, *Celtic Theology: Humanity, World and God in Early Irish Writings* (London: Continuum, 2005), 78. O'Loughlin indicates that Adomnán wrote *De Loci Sanctis* as a response to Augustine's call for such a book.
8. Ibid., 53.
9. Albert S. Cook, "The Name Caedmon," in *Publications of the Modern Language Association of America*, VI, 1891: 16.
10. Hardinge, 16.
11. Anglandicus, "Massive Scribal Hangovers: One Ninth Century Confession," December 7, 2014, http://anglandicus.blogspot.com/2014/12/massive-scribal-hangovers-one-ninth.html. [Accessed December 11, 2015.]
12. John Carey, *King of Mysteries: Early Irish Religious Writings* (Dublin: Four Courts Press, 2000), 51–74.
13. The term "three-dimensional" makes sense to our modern minds, but it is anachronistic to the early Christian Celts. (It was first used in 1872, according to the *Merriam-Webster's Collegiate Dictionary*). Hardinge (*The Celtic Church in Britain*, 18), describes a threefold division with ancient Irish and Latin terms distinguishing *stoir* (as in storehouse, referring to the literal sense of the text), *sens* (allegory), and *run* (the "hidden" or mystical meaning). This choice of three divisions can be compared with Origen's interpretive schema that was widely circulated throughout the world in the late Classical Era and the Early Middle Ages. Corresponding to the three elements of human beings (body, soul, and spirit), Origen postulated three layers of meaning in each biblical text (literal, moral, and spiritual). For Origen's three-part division, see Karlfried Froehlich, *Biblical Interpretation in the Early Church* (Philadelphia: Fortress Press, 1984), 17. Origen's three-level interpretive scheme was expanded in the Middle Ages into a "four-senses" approach (literal, moral, allegorical, and anagogical). For the fourfold scheme, see "Hermeneutics" in the online *Encyclopedia Britannica* at https://www.britannica.com/topic/hermeneutics-principles-of-biblical-interpretation. [Accessed Nov. 19, 2015.] I choose not to follow the exact terms of any of the ancient interpretive divisions, believing that the threefold division of literal, symbolic, and imaginative perspectives fits better with modern constructs

of reality—hence my own "three-dimensional" approach. This model does, however, correspond loosely with the three ancient terms listed by Hardinge.

14. I refer to "grounding" rather than "literal" for several reasons. I believe that this level of interpretation as practiced in the Insular Early Middle Ages is only very roughly similar to modern literalism (as I explain later in the chapter). "Grounded" holds the sense that it is the level of interpretation tied most closely to the surface of reality, the meanings pertaining to the visible world as opposed to a deeper, more mystical reading. The word "grounded" also refers to the Earth itself, and the connection with the organic world rooted in the soil of our planet is indicated in this approach. Finally, Bible narratives are "grounded" in the sense that they are "tied down" or "anchored" to their origins in time and space.
15. Michael Graves, *The Inspiration and Interpretation of Scripture: What the Early Church Can Teach Us* (Grand Rapids, MI: Eerdmans, 2014), Kindle edition, location 2890.
16. Ibid., Kindle location 1091.
17. Thomas O'Loughlin, *Journeys on the Edges: The Celtic Tradition* (New York: Maryknoll, 2000), 39.
18. Herren and Brown, 119.
19. Ibid., 35.
20. The name "Irish Augustine" comes from the fact that the work was erroneously believed for a time to be the work of Augustine of Hippo.
21. John Carey, *King of Mysteries: Early Irish Religious Writings* (Dublin: Colour Books, 2000), 51.
22. Ibid.
23. Ibid., 63.
24. Since many of the Bible texts have been substantially rewritten, collated, or redacted, we might do well to also add these redactors to this statement regarding writers.
25. In the Late Middle Ages, the Christian church was wracked by schism and scandal. The Protestant Reformers, seeking to restore the church to its purity, defied the Pope and separated from the leadership of the Roman church, creating the need for a new locus of authority. Scripture fulfilled that role, but doing so required the gradual reformulation of the Bible and its authority, first in the form of *Sola Scriptura* and later the doctrine of infallibility. Even the Catholic Church was influenced by the Protestants' doctrine insofar as the Counter-Reformation reformulated Catholic doctrine as reaction to the Reformers.
26. Peter Enns, *The Bible Tells Me So: Why Defending Scripture Has Made Us Unable to Read It* (New York: HarperCollins, 2014), 6.
27. White evangelical Protestants are particularly likely to believe that humans have existed in their present form since the beginning of time. According to the Pew Research Center, roughly two-thirds (64%) of white evangelical Americans express this view, as do half of all black Protestants (50%). By comparison, only 15 percent of white mainline Protestant Americans share this opinion. ("Public's Views on Human Evolution," December 30, 2013, http://www.pewforum.

org/2013/12/30/publics-views-on-human-evolution/ [accessed November 17, 2016]). Recent data from the Yale Project on Climate Change Communication suggests that while 64 percent of Americans think global warming is real and caused by human beings, only 44 percent of evangelicals do, according to Chris Mooney, "How to Convince Conservative Christians That Climate Change Is Real," *Mother Jones*, May 2, 2014, http://www.motherjones.com/environment/2014/05/inquiring-minds-katharine-hayhoe-faith-climate.

28. Enns, 8.
29. "Blindness," Bible Hub, http://biblehub.com/topical/b/blindness.htm. [Accessed Nov. 26, 2015.]
30. O'Loughlin, *Journeys on the Edges*, 36–37.
31. Ibid., 39–40.
32. Bible scholars are uncertain that Paul of Tarsus actually wrote all of the epistles that bear his name, so I limit examples to those books deemed undeniably Pauline.
33. Graves, Kindle location 1088.
34. Eric A. Seibert, *Disturbing Divine Behavior: Troubling Old Testament Images of God*, (Minneapolis, MN: Fortress Press, 2009), 63.
35. Ibid.
36. Ibid.
37. Kenton L. Sparks, *God's Word in Human Words: An Evangelical Appropriation of Critical Biblical Scholarship* (Grand Rapids, MI: Baker, 2008), 28.
38. Anglandicus, "Cummian's Commentary on Mark," May 17, 2012, http://anglandicus.blogspot.com/2012/05/cummians-commentary-on-mark.html. [Accessed November 19, 2015.]
39. Ibid., "Aleran the Wise: Commentary on the Genealogy of Jesus," May 27, 2012, http://anglandicus.blogspot.com/2012_05_01_archive.html. [Accessed November 19, 2015.]
40. George Aichele, *Sign, Text and Scripture: Semiotics and the Bible* (London: Bloomsbury T&T Clark, 1997), 11.
41. Huston Smith, *The Soul of Christianity: Restoring the Great Tradition* (San Francisco: Harper, 2005), 19, 23. Italics are Smith's.
42. Quoted by Philip Zaleski & Carol Zaleski in *The Fellowship: the Literary Lives of the Inklings*, (New York: Farrar, Straus and Giroux, 2015), 182.
43. C. S. Lewis, *The Inspirational Writings of C.S. Lewis: Surprised by Joy, Reflections on the Psalms, The Four Loves and The Business of Heaven* (New York: International Press, 1991), 187.
44. Ibid., 200.
45. Marcus J. Borg, *The Heart of Christianity: Recovering a Life of Faith* (San Francisco, Harper, 2003), 49.
46. ———, *Jesus: Uncovering the Life, Teachings, and Surprising Relevance of a Spiritual Revolutionary* (San Francisco: HarperOne, 2008), HarperCollins e-books location 927. (Italics in the original.)
47. Graves, Kindle location 2916.
48. Philip Jenkins, *Laying Down the Sword: Why We Can't Ignore the Bible's Violent Verses* (New

York: HarperCollins, 2011), 13.
49. Ibid., 210.
50. Ibid., 57.
51. Graves, Kindle location 1091.
52. Ibid., Kindle location 2914.
53. N. T. Wright, "How Can the Bible Be Authoritative?" http://ntwrightpage.com/Wright_Bible_Authoritative.htm. [Accessed Nov. 27, 2015.] The Laing Lecture, 1989, and the Griffith Thomas Lecture, 1989, originally published in *Vox Evangelica*, 1991, 21: 7–32.
54. Postmodern Bible interpreters increasingly point to the question of whether interpretations come from the perspective of privilege or that of the dispossessed. Racial minorities, women, people of other religions, and LGBTQ persons have historically been on the receiving end of disempowering interpretations.
55. Saint Augustine, *Confessions: A New Translation by Henry Chadwick* (New York, Oxford University Press, 1992), 265.
56. John Pfordresher, *Jesus and the Emergence of Catholic Imagination* (Mahwah, NJ: Paulist, 1998), 221.
57. Ibid., 220.
58. Michelle P. Brown, "Southumbrian Book Culture: The Interface Between Insular and Anglo-Saxon," in Colum Hourihane, *Insular & Anglo-Saxon: Art & Thought in the Early Medieval Period* (Princeton, NJ: Princeton University Press, 2011), 31.
59. Aichele, 10.
60. For an outstanding treatment of the entire Bible in light of storytelling form, see Gregory Mobley, *The Return of the Chaos Monsters—and Other Backstories of the Bible* (Grand Rapids, MI: Eerdmans, 2012).
61. Carey, 40.
62. Ibid., 44.
63. Ibid., 47.
64. Ibid., 75.
65. Ibid.
66. Ibid., 77.
67. Ibid., 79.
68. Carl Sagan, *Cosmos* (New York: Random House, 2011), 115.
69. Carey, 81.
70. On the website Universe Today, Frasier Cain writes, "The scientific consensus is that the Universe is expanding, having gotten its start in a single point 13.7 billion years ago. . . . But what came before the Big Bang? Since all matter and energy was tangled up into a single point of infinite volume and density, it's hard to imagine how you could look to a time before that. Cosmologist Martin Bojowald and others from Penn State University thinks it's possible. . . . According to Bojowald, a mathematical technique called Loop Quantum Gravity, which combines relativity and quantum mechanics, gives a different view of the early Universe. Instead of being infinitely small and dense, it was compacted down into a ball of some volume and density . . . very similar to the space-

time geometry we have in our current Universe. (http://www.universetoday.com/2026/before-the-big-bang-2/#, accessed September 12, 2016.)
71. Carey., 96.
72. Ibid., 97.
73. Ibid., 102.
74. Ibid.
75. Herren and Brown, 109.
76. Sandy Eisenberg Sasso, *Midrash: Reading the Bible with Question Marks* (Brewster, MA: Paraclete Press, 2007), 7, 37.
77. Ibid., 3.
78. Mobley, Kindle location 109.
79. Paul J. Zak, "Why Your Brain Loves Good Storytelling," *Harvard Business Review*, October 28, 2014, https://hbr.org/2014/10/why-your-brain-loves-good-storytelling/. [Accessed November 30, 2015.].
80. Wright.
81. Ibid.
82. Mobley, location 116.

THE GOSPEL OF MATTHEW

THE NOBLEST OF GIFTS
The Bible in Celtic Lands

One of the noblest gifts of the Holy Spirit
is Holy Scripture, by which all ignorance is enlightened,
and all worldly sorrow comforted,
by which all spiritual light is kindled.
—Leabhar Brac, *Medieval Irish Manuscript* [83]

It may be cliché that "God works in mysterious ways," but that certainly is true when it comes to the coming of the Christian faith—and with it the Bible—into the lives of the Celtic peoples.

THE GIFT-BEARERS: HOW THE BIBLE CAME TO CELTIC LANDS

Early in the fifth century, Irish slavers kidnapped an adolescent named Maewyn Succat, stealing him from his home in what is modern-day Wales or Scotland. The raiders threw him in the bottom of their hide-covered boat and took him to their land across the Irish Sea. This seemingly minor incident began a series of events that changed world history.

Maewyn had been raised a nominal Christian, but in bondage, his faith increased. Homesick, lonely, he prayed to God more than a hundred times each day. Miraculously, he escaped from Eire (Ireland) and returned to his family and home. More miraculously, he heard God's call to return to Eire, and he obeyed, bringing the story of Christ with him. Most miraculously of all, by the time of his death, Maewyn—now known as Patrick—had persuaded most of the Irish to follow Jesus. He did so simply by walking and talking, treating each person he met with respect.

Patrick left several written documents, his autobiographical *Confession* and a letter. These are the only existent writings revealing the inner thoughts of a person living in Ireland at that time. Patrick claimed he was poorly educated, but in two short documents he quotes or alludes to Scripture 340 times, citing forty-nine different books of the Bible.[84] It seems Patrick was so immersed in the Bible that its words had fused with his own speech. This meant that as the Irish received Patrick's message, they simultaneously received the wording of the Bible.

When Patrick arrived, Ireland was one of the last fully sovereign Celtic regions. Almost a thousand years earlier, cultures with roughly similar linguistic and cultural patterns had conquered most of Europe. The Greeks described these conquerors as *Keltoi*, hence our modern broad designation of "Celts." But at the time of Patrick, there was no sense of "Celtic" identity. Rome had pushed these tribes to the edges of their empire, where they identified themselves by specific tribal or clan affiliations.

Patrick was neither the first Christian to reach Ireland, nor was he the first missionary in Celtic lands. The Britons, under Roman occupation, had received the new faith centuries earlier—hence Patrick was raised Christian. During Patrick's lifetime, the Welsh theologian Pelagius was already famous, both in the British Isles and in Rome.

Patrick was especially important, however, because Saxons advancing across England had brought their beliefs to the island, which meant that much of Britain had reverted to Pagan beliefs; Patrick laid the foundation for the re-conversion of the Celtic lands. His influence on Ireland was so thorough that from there the message of Christ would rebound throughout the British Isles and then across Europe.

Patrick and his converts saw themselves as part of a universal faith—all of Jesus' followers throughout the world were of "one Savior, one faith, one baptism" (Ephesians 4:5). Yet wherever the new faith engaged with existing cultures, it took on some of the flavor of the local beliefs and customs. Insular churches, far from the established networks of church control, were even more likely to develop their theology and practices in fresh ways, so Celtic churches developed local and regional variations. For example, many Irish churches affirmed women's equality; but there were also island monasteries that forbade women from even stepping ashore. Some Celtic theologians warned of damnation for anyone outside the church, while others believed all humankind would be saved. For the most part, Christian Celts tended to look at the world from a "both-and" perspective rather than an "either-or" mentality, enabling the coexistence of varying spiritual traditions.

THE GIFT RECEIVED: THE BIBLE IN THE EARLY MIDDLE AGES

When we hear the word "Bible," a picture pops up in our minds. We think of one volume, likely bound in leather, containing either sixty-six books (if we're Protestant) or seventy-three (if we're Catholic), written in the language we speak. When we imagine Patrick bringing the Bible to the Pagan Irish, we might envision him carrying a Bible like that. In some ways this would be accurate, but in other respects widely off the mark.

The Physical Book

Judging the Good Book by its cover, early-medieval Bibles would resemble those of today. By the year 200, Christians had begun circulating their scriptures in *codex* form. A codex contains flat pages, sewn together at the spine and encased in front and back covers—in short, the format of a modern printed book.

Why did early Christians write their Bible text in codex style, rather than the format of scrolls, used for a millennium previously? Perhaps it was easier for a persecuted faith to guard its message in more compact form, or maybe bound books were more useful to carry when spreading the message of Christ. No one is certain, but by the fourth century, modern-shaped Bibles were common.

The new format also brought a change in materials. The word "bible" comes from *Byblos*, the Phoenician port that exported papyrus to the Greek world. Papyrus was a thin paper made from crushed river reeds pasted together, and early Jewish and Christian sacred texts were often copied onto this material. By Patrick's time, however, vellum—made from carefully scraped calves' hides—was used for pages.

The Canon

At the time of Ireland's conversion, Christians had only recently agreed upon the list of books that constitute the Bible. This set of biblical texts is known as the *canon*, from the Greek word for "rule" or "measuring stick." For three hundred years after the lifetime of Christ, the Jesus movement debated which books should be regarded as God-inspired scriptures. Some books, such as the four Gospels found in Bibles today, were uncontested. The letters of Paul were also quickly agreed upon. Some early Christians wished to also include in the canon additional books, such as *The Shepherd of Hermas* and the *Epistle of Barnabas.*

Late in the fourth century, a church council and an Egyptian bishop resolved debates over the canon. In 363, the council of Laodicea (in modern-day Turkey) declared that the New Testament consists of twenty-six inspired books, which are still included in today's Bible. The Book of Revelation was excluded, since most Eastern Christians rejected it. However, Bishop Athanasius of Alexandria, Egypt, who held authority over the Eastern churches, added the book of Revelation in 367.

The Council of Laodicea also decreed the extent of the Old Testament canon, which was the same as the forty-six books found in Catholic Bibles today. This list includes what Protestants refer to as "the Old Testament Apocrypha," books that were rejected by the sixteenth-century Reformation.

Celtic monasteries also copied sacred books that were *not* included in either the Old or New Testament canon. The Council of Laodicea had prohibited some of these books; others were used as devotional reading in Eastern and Western churches. Nowadays they are referred to simply as "Apocrypha" (because of the similar wording, Protestants sometimes confuse these with the books that are included in the Old Testament of the Catholic Bible). Irish scholars translated these books, originally written in Greek, Georgian, Syrian, Ethiopic, and Armenian languages, into their own language.[85]

If you asked Patrick, "What are the authorized and inspired books of Sacred Scripture?" he would likely have listed the same seventy-three books found in Catholic Bibles today. However, it is unlikely that he possessed all of those texts in one bound volume; early complete Bibles were rare, costly, and so bulky that they were difficult to transport. More common copies of the Bible would contain the four Gospels, and less often the entire New Testament. Monks used the Psalms for daily prayers, so psalters were also common as bound collections. Other books of the Old Testament would likely be contained in separate volumes.

Patrick's Bible would have been written in Latin, as would most Bibles have been in the Celtic lands during the Middle Ages. At the same time that Patrick preached in Ireland, a scholar named Jerome spent decades living in Bethlehem, adjacent to the alleged birthplace of Jesus, translating the Bible from the original Hebrew and Greek into Latin. Paula and Eustochium, two women proficient in Hebrew, assisted him. The Latin Bible that Jerome produced—called the Vulgate ("Common Version")—was the most-used translation in the history of the Christian faith, the standard text for over a thousand years. Jerome's translation reached the British Isles by the mid-fifth century.

There were other Latin translations, now referred to as "Old Latin" Bibles, before Jerome's version. Numerous scholars had made these, and they varied greatly in quality and translation choices. The majority of Bibles in Ireland and Britain were of this Old Latin variety up until the ninth century; therefore, the Celts read their Scriptures in a considerable variety of translations. The Book of Kells, copied around 800, is a mix of Vulgate and Old Latin translations.

⌘ THE GIFT RETURNED: CELTIC VERSIONS OF THE BIBLE ⌘

Before Patrick, only the Irish intelligentsia (the druids) possessed written language. This was in the form of Ogham lettering, straight lines carved on stone or wood, used for charms or memorials. The vast body of Irish artistic expression existed in oral form.

As soon as Patrick and other Christians introduced the Latin alphabet and the technology of writing with ink on vellum, Hibernian talents leapt onto the possibilities of these new forms. Celtic cultures had long been intoxicated with words; language was a form of magic—the most potent form. The most esteemed members of society were bards. Amergin, the hero who wed the Goddess Eiré and took possession of Ireland from the fairy people, was a bard; so the Irish race was founded upon the arts of word-making. Now, their love of language-play could translate from oral to physical form. The pages of parchment were like naked canvas, pleading for the artist's brush, so they took the curling, flexible shapes of Latin letters and twisted and twirled them across vellum. Insular calligraphers were so enamored of the shapes of letters that they sometimes used non-Latin letters in Latin texts because the foreign letters offered more visual opportunity.

For a millennium before Christianity, the great stories of their gods, demi-gods, and heroes had given identity to the Irish clans; now they had a new set of stories, with exotic lands, mighty champions, and the superlative tales of the God-man. People intoxicated with music also had a hundred-and-fifty poems, ready to set to music and sing for the King of Mysteries. Such marvelous words called forth the beauty of visual art to match their wonders, so the spirals and knotwork and splendid forms previously utilized for carved stones, cauldrons, shields, and jewelry were woven into the playful spell of words on paper. "Looking at all the various forms," wrote Benjamin Tilgham, "one gets the impression that Insular calligraphers were consciously playing with the fact that a letter can be twisted and abstracted into a seemingly infinite variety of forms and yet still ultimately serve to represent the same vocal sound."[86]

The innovative genius of the Irish also produced a very practical breakthrough in the art of writing: the distinction between capital and lower-case letters. "The Cathach of St Columba, dating perhaps from the early 7th century and possibly written by the saint himself," Tilgham noted, "exemplifies one profoundly influential innovation of the Irish monks. To emphasize the beginning of an important passage, the scribes write its first letter much larger than the rest of the text and in a grander style. Slightly embarrassed by the difference in scale, they tend to reduce each succeeding letter by a little until reaching the small scale of the ordinary text. Here, already, is the distinction between capitals and lower case (or in manuscript terms, majuscule and minuscule) which is later a standard feature of the western European script."[87]

Every book had to be laboriously copied by hand; there would be no printing press for another thousand years. Dark ink for lettering came from oak gall, a growth on oak trees caused by insects. In many cases, lettering done with this organic ink has lasted more than a thousand years without fading. Pens made of feathers from geese and other water birds were cut to a chisel point, then dipped in the ink. Some scribes in the late Classical period used pens with copper tips.

A poem, allegedly by Saint Columba, describes the toil involved in hand-copying a manuscript. Note the types of colored inks used by the scribe:

My hand is weary with writing;
My sharp great point is not thick;
My slender-beaked pen juts forth
A beetle-hued draught of bright blue ink.

A steady stream of wisdom springs
From my well-coloured neat fair hand;
On the page it pours its draught of ink
Of the green-skinned holly.

I send my little dripping pen unceasingly
Over an assemblage of books of great beauty,
To enrich the possessions of artists—
Whence my hand is weary with writing.[88]

When we picture a medieval scribe, our mind conjures up the image of a male cleric, but women were also scribes in the Early Middle Ages. The Book of Chad, produced at the same time as the Book of

Kells and the Lindisfarne Gospels, includes glosses revealing that women were involved in the scriptorium where it was produced (in Lichfield, England).[89] Three prayer books produced in Mercia around 800 also appear to have been manufactured by women, as their subject matter focuses on women and their "language lapses subconsciously from the masculine to feminine voice."[90] French female orders in the following century were dedicated to the work of copying and illuminating sacred texts. There are no proven examples of female scribes in Ireland, but it seems likely that they existed, given that the monastery in Kildare was comprised of both men and women, and women were copyists in areas where the Irish had evangelized.

An Old English riddle from the year 709 describes the process of producing vellum and turning it into a book: "An enemy ended my life, deprived me of my physical strength; then he dipped me in water and drew me out again, and put me in the sun where I soon shed all my hair. After that the knife's sharp edge bit into me and all my blemishes were scraped away; fingers folded me and the bird's feather often moved over my brown surface, sprinkling meaningful marks. It swallowed more wood-dye and again traveled over me leaving black tracks. Then a man bound me, he stretched skin over me and adorned me with gold; thus I am enriched by the wondrous work of smiths, wound about with shining metal. Who am I?"[91]

The saying "You can't judge a book by its cover" seems to have been disregarded as much in the Middle Ages as it is now. The eighth-century Stonyhurst Gospel of John, a Hiberno-Saxon illuminated manuscript, is enclosed in a goatskin cover. Pieces of leather were molded over cord to produce the image of the Tree of Life on the front cover—perhaps reminding readers that the contents of John's Gospel were like the tree of paradise, a sacrament offering eternal life. Some Insular manuscripts are missing their covers, but this attests to how richly the original covers were ornamented; Viking raiders sometimes tore pages of books out of their gilded and jeweled covers, discarded the pages, and kept the covers, since the precious metals held value for them that the vellum pages did not.

For the Celtic Christians, however, hand-copied Scriptures were valuable indeed—but that did not prevent them from being well used. Some illuminated Bibles were large and heavy, intended for use as pulpit Bibles, while others were designed to be easily transportable. The seventh-century Saint Cuthbert Gospel, the earliest extant bound book made in Europe, measures only five by four inches. The Gospel of Saint Mulling in Trinity College Dublin and a comparable Irish volume in the British Library contain all four Gospels and are the same compact size. These works are outstanding examples of the scribal art, since it is more difficult to execute elegant script on a small scale, and the latter two examples include illuminated pages similar to larger Bible manuscripts.

Such so-called "pocket Gospels" were designed so that monks could transport them easily on their travels, for purposes of evangelism or pastoral care. They carried these small Bibles secured in leather satchels with shoulder straps. A carved stone from Burra, Shetland, combining Pagan and Christian motifs and possibly dating from the time of the evangelization of the Picts in Northern Scotland, portrays Christian monks, one of them wearing a book-sized satchel affixed by a strap over his neck. Perhaps this was how the Picts first beheld Christianity: meeting cowled monks who carried the written words of the gospel in order to read aloud its life-changing words.[92]

Several saints' legends are illustrative of the Christian Celts' regard for the Scriptures. The first concerns Brigid, the saint who bridges Pagan and Christian traditions, and who is portrayed as the most Christ-like of Irish believers. According to the story, Brigid's charioteer, Aed, tells her that he is sad, for he does not own a copy of the Gospels. Brigid asks Aed to pray with her for a copy of the Sacred Word, and then she reaches into her *sinus* (Latin for "lap" or "bosom") and draws out a copy of the Scriptures.[93] This story highlights the supernatural quality of the texts, their nurturing power, and the cherished nature of the Word. Brigid, the Mary of the Gaels, miraculously conceives the Word (which can be either "Christ" or "Scripture" in Christian symbolism) in the most intimate part of her body.

Two more stories of a saint and the Scriptures concern Columba of Iona. One day Baithéne came to St. Columba and said, "I need one of the brethren to help me go through the text of the psalter I have copied and correct any mistakes." The saint answered, "Why do you bring this trouble on us when there is no need? For in your copy of the psalter there is no mistake—neither one letter too many nor one too few—except that in one place the letter 'i' is missing." When they proofed the entire psalter, it was found to be exactly as the saint predicted.[94] This tale reveals the scrupulous nature of copying the Scriptures. A second story of Columba reveals the great value attached to these manuscripts, and also the fact that a greatly esteemed Abbot like Columba was not above doing the scribal work himself. In fact, copying sacred texts was one of the most important tasks for a leader in the Celtic church. Adomnán, Columba's hagiographer, tells the story:

> Once a book of the week's hymns written out by St. Columba with his own hand fell into the water when the boy who was carrying it in a leather satchel on his shoulders slipped off a bridge over a river in the province of Leinster. The book remained in the water from Christmas to Easter, until it was found on the riverbank by some women out walking. They took it to a priest named Éogenénan, a man of Pictish origin, to whom it had belonged. The book was still in its satchel, which was not merely sodden but had rotted. When Éogenénan opened the satchel, however, he found the book unharmed, as clean and dry as if it had never fallen into the water but had remained in its book case.[95]

A charming and less miraculous insight into scribal life is the famous poem about a scholar and his cat, Pangur Ban. The scribe, like many other writers, knew the quiet sense of companionship a cat can offer while both writer and cat goes about his own business.

I and Pangur Ban my cat,
'Tis a like task we are at:
Hunting mice is his delight,
Hunting words I sit all night.

Better far than praise of men
'Tis to sit with book and pen;
Pangur bears me no ill will,
He too plies his simple skill.

'Tis a merry thing to see
At our tasks how glad are we,
When at home we sit and find
Entertainment to our mind.

Oftentimes a mouse will stray
In the hero Pangur's way;
Oftentimes my keen thought set
Takes a meaning in its net.

'Gainst the wall he sets his eye
Full and fierce and sharp and sly;
'Gainst the wall of knowledge I
All my little wisdom try.

When a mouse darts from its den
O how glad is Pangur then!

THE NOBLEST OF GIFTS

*O what gladness do I prove
When I solve the doubts I love!*

*So in peace our tasks we ply,
Pangur Ban, my cat, and I;
In our arts we find our bliss;
I have mine and he has his.*

*Practice every day has made
Pangur perfect in his trade;
I get wisdom day and night
Turning darkness into light.*[96]

We may imagine the life of early-medieval scribes from a romantic perspective; don't we wish sometimes that we could swap out our stressful job to become a monk sitting in the scriptorium happily scratching away for hours without the stresses of modern life? Yet daily life has never been easy. The end of a seventh-century commentary on Scripture, composed on Iona, says: "Each day brings an almost insupportable amount of ecclesiastical demands from every side and I have had to write the book amidst many laborious preoccupations . . . so do not forget to pray . . . for me."[97]

By the eighth century, Celtic scribes had achieved extraordinary heights of artistry, so that illuminated manuscripts such as the Book of Kells and the Lindisfarne Gospels rank among the greatest works of calligraphy that have ever been produced. The Book of Chad and the Hereford Gospels indicate that Celtic scribes in Western England and Wales rivaled the skills of their brethren on the holy islands of Iona and Lindisfarne.

A look at the materials needed to produce the Book of Kells demonstrates the worth of these calligraphic masterpieces. Rare substances were imported for the colors: purple leaves from Italy, and lapis lazuli for the blue coloring, possibly imported from the Himalaya mountains of India. More precious than the physical elements needed for its composition was the time, effort and extraordinary artistic talent that went into the work. It is estimated that four or five scribes and artists would have taken thirty years to finish the book.[98] Some elements are so tiny that they rival the precision of marks on a dollar bill; they hardly seem possible if done by unaided eyes, and in fact a clue to their composition may reside in the Edinburgh National Museum—a magnifying lens taken from a medieval monastery. With the materials, effort and artistic genius that went into making a masterpiece like the Book of Kells it is no wonder that Gerald of Wales in the twelfth century called it "the work not of men, but of angels."[99]

Even in the increasingly secular twenty-first century, exhibitions of the great Celtic Bible manuscripts draw crowds. Gazing at these works of genius, viewers should remember that for these early-medieval Christians, all their efforts to create visual splendor could only capture flashes of the majesty of God's written Word and glimpses of the High King of Heaven's glory. For them, the worth of the Bible's message far exceeded the value of any physical representation.

It may be difficult for us, living in the twenty-first century, to feel the sense of excitement that the Celts had when reading the Bible. For them, all the stories were new and amazing, in every sense a revelation. We, on the other hand, see the Bible as something very old and—some voices tell us—outdated. The Bible has become fodder in cultural and political battles, so that when some of us hear proclaimed, "the Bible says," they feel a warm sense of comfort—while others might hear "the Bible says" as a veiled sort of threat.

Perhaps we can recapture some of the Celts' enchantment with the Scriptures by gazing at the wondrous art of the Book of Kells and other scribal masterpieces. The Celtic monks worked hard to convey a sense of Divine Mystery in their work and that still shines across the ages. Sometimes, illumination from the ancient past can reveal the road ahead.

83. Martin McNamara, "Love for and Study of the Bible, God's Word, in Early Irish Tradition," in Salvador Ryan and Brendan Leahy, *Treasures of Irish Christianity, Volume II: A People of the Word* (Dublin: Veritas, 2013), 57.
84. Hardinge, 29.
85. Salvador Ryan and Brendan Leahy, *Treasures of Irish Christianity, Volume II: A People of the Word* (Dublin: Veritas, 2013), 61.
86. Benjamin C. Tilgham, "Writing in Tongues: Mixed Scripts and Style in Insular Art," in Colum Hourihane, *Insular & Anglo-Saxon Art & Thought in the Early Medieval Period* (Princeton, NJ: Princeton University Press, 2011), 93.
87. "History of Writing," History World, http://www.historyworld.net/wrldhis/PlainTextHistories.asp?ParagraphID=fle. [Accessed December 2, 2015.]
88. In Maureen O'Rourke Murphy and James MacKillop, editors, *An Irish Literature Reader: Poetry, Prose, Drama* (Syracuse, NY: Syracuse University Press, 2006), 25.
89. Linda Blackford, "University of Kentucky scholar hopes to uncover new clues about origin of 8th-century Gospels," *Lexington Herald-Leader*, July 3, 2014,
90. Brown, 36.
91. George Otto Sims, *Exploring the Book of Kells* (Dublin: O'Brien Press, 2008), 27–28.
92. This is my own reading of the Papil stone, from observing it first hand at the Edinburgh National Museum.
93. Joseph Falaky Nagy, *Conversing with Angels & Ancients: Literary Myths of Medieval Ireland* (Ithaca, NY: Cornell University Press, 1997), 237.
94. Adomnán of Iona, *Life of Saint Columba* (London: Penguin, 1995), 129–130.
95. Ibid., 161.
96. Maureen O'Rourke Murphy and James MacKillop, *Irish Literature: A Reader* (Syracuse, NY: Syracuse University Press, 1987), 22.
97. O'Loughlin, 134.
98. Simms, 65.
99. Giraldis Cambrensis (Gerard of Wales), *The History and Topography of Ireland*, ed. and trans. John O'Meara (New York: Penguin Books, 1982), 84.

66   THE GOSPEL OF MATTHEW

Blessing

My prayer is that reading the Bible the Celtic way will offer you a new journey of adventure and wonder.

May you gaze upon the peacock's feathers:
iridescent, shimmering, dazzling.
May you see the many ways—
indeed an infinite number—
of interpreting the Scriptures.
May your reading be threefold:
grounded,
symbolic
and with imagination.
May you read with the Trinity:
with the High First-Sower,
with the King of Mysteries,
with the Divine Breath filling you.
May your reading restore all that is broken in you,
and may you know
Christ within you,
the Beloved Community around you,
holy Earth beneath you.
AMEN

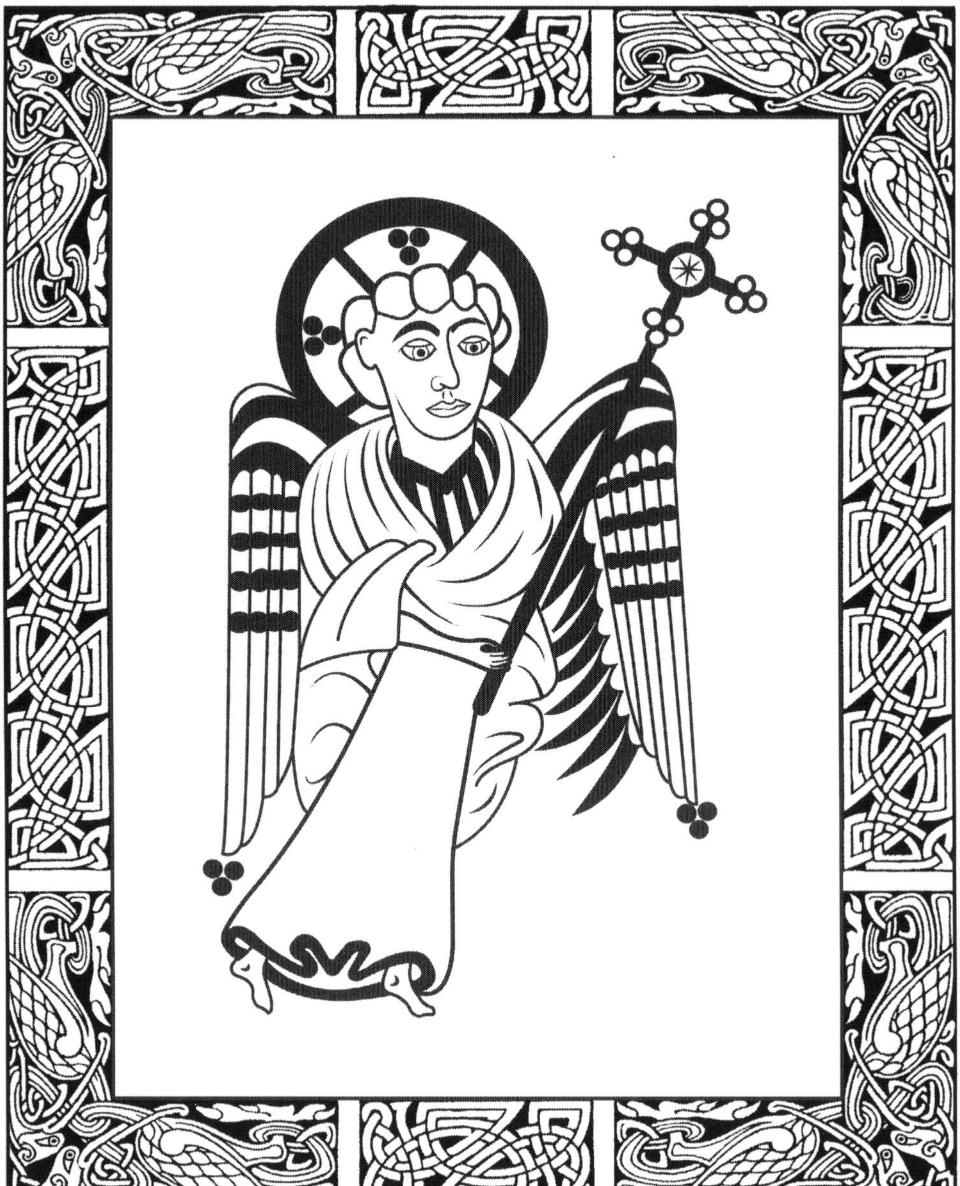

INTRODUCTION
Encountering the Winged Man

The ancient symbol for the Gospel of Matthew—a winged man—has a deep spiritual significance that our modern minds may overlook. While we equate winged human forms with angels, ancient civilizations, including the Celts', perceived wings as a symbol for an embodied connection with a wider and deeper reality.

For the Celts, the winged man was a seer, someone with the ability to fly into the Otherworld and return, bringing with him new vision to share with the more earthbound members of his society. He was both a seeker of wisdom and the proclaimer of truth, a custodian and guardian of divine insight. With this imagery alive in their minds, the Celts would have responded easily and joyfully to the idea that Matthew, author of the first Gospel, was a winged man, bringing wisdom and truth to all the world.

THE FOUR WINGED CREATURES

Ancient Jewish cultural images also included winged creatures—cherubim—though they were far stranger beings than our modern-day images of angels (and *nothing* like the pudgy winged babies that come to mind when we hear the word "cherubs"). The Hebrew scriptures contain ninety-one references to cherubim, but the only explicit description of these mysterious beings is found in the Book of Ezekiel:

> In the fire was what looked like four living creatures. In appearance their form was human, but each of them had four faces and four wings. . . . Under their wings on their four sides they had human hands. All four of them had faces and wings, and the wings of one touched the wings of another. . . . Their faces looked like this: Each of the four had the face of a human being, and on the right side each had the face of a lion, and on the left the face of an ox; each also had the face of an eagle. Such were their faces. They each had two wings spreading out upward, each wing touching that of the creature on either side; and each had two other wings covering its body. (1:5,6,8–11 NIV)

Christianity connected this passage from the Hebrew scripture with the mystic vision described in the Book of Revelation:

> In the center, around the throne, were four living creatures, and they were covered with eyes, in front and in back. The first living creature was like a lion, the second was like an ox, the third had a face like a man, the fourth was like a flying eagle. Each of the four living creatures had six wings and was covered with eyes all around, even under its wings. (4:6–8 NIV)

The theologians of the early Christian church were eager to find connections like these between the Hebrew scripture (the "Old Testament") and the new set of Christian scriptures that was taking shape (the "New Testament"). In the fourth century, Saint Augustine made a connection between the four canonical Gospels and the four living creatures described in both Ezekiel and Revelation. Soon after, early in the fifth century, Saint Jerome assigned to each of the four authors (the "Evangelists") the winged creature that is still traditionally associated with that particular account of the life of Jesus:

- Matthew is symbolized by a winged man, because this Gospel starts with Jesus' genealogy, emphasizing his incarnation as a human being.
- Mark's symbol is a winged lion, a figure of courage and triumph, representing Christ's authority over life and death.
- Luke is represented by a winged calf, a figure of sacrifice, service, and strength; this account begins with the duties of Zacharias in the temple and it focuses on Christ's self-giving on the Cross.
- John is an eagle, a far-seeing creature of the sky that was believed to be able to look straight into the sun. The author of this Gospel differed from the others in that he describes Jesus as the eternal Logos, focusing throughout his account on Jesus' Divine nature.

Inspiration

Encountering the Gospels for the first time, the Celts found a treasure trove of creative inspiration. The designs they painted on their Gospel editions were not merely decoration. Alive with color, pattern, and fanciful images, Celtic script transformed the Latin alphabet, which had been a fairly utilitarian vehicle by which to carry a message, into a rich aesthetic experience. Archeology indicates that the Celts had contact with Egypt's Christians, and art historians see in the Celts' illumined Gospels an artistic union that combined the spiral designs of their metalworking ancestors with the characteristic style of Coptic icons, which were thought to be windows into the spiritual world.

The Celts truly honored, celebrated, and interacted with the Word, in a way few of us have ever dreamed, bringing to the Gospel text their artistic skill, emotional intensity, and an expansive and inclusive imagination, all combined with a sense of creative freedom. They were following no rules, no established tradition. All was fresh and new. The production of their written Gospels was both artistic creation and an act of discovery.

We tend to categorize and recognize distinctions, but the Celts saw things differently. Their perception of the world did not, however, merge everything into a single uniform whole. Instead, in the same way that their designs twisted and twirled and twined, they also interlaced realities, weaving them together so that weft and warp meshed into something far richer and more colorful than the individual strands alone. In reading the Gospels, the Celtic mind found ways to plait together past and present, earth and heaven, along with the world of their ancestors and the new worlds they were encountering.

MATTHEW'S GOOD NEWS

When the Celts read the Gospel of Matthew, it was not dead text codified in ancient times but rather a chance to interlace their own hearts with the living story of Jesus. For us, Matthew's world seems distant and unreal—but for the Celts, it had a fresh immediacy. It pointed to the connections in their own lives between this world and the unseen world. Matthew's story was truly a man with wings, revealing the ways in which humanity can be united with God.

This story was the gospel, a word that today has lost much of its original meaning. It came from an Anglo Saxon word: *godspell*, literally "good-story." (The word that the Celts would have used in their

INTRODUCTION 73

own language, *soisgeul*, had much the same meaning.) The Latin word that the Celts would have read in their Bibles was *evangelium* (a translation of the Greek *euaggelion*), which meant "good news." Matthew was one of the "Evangelists," the people who broadcasted the Good News of Jesus.

In the twenty-first century, we have grown so accustomed to the word "gospel" that we've become numb to its true meaning. To catch a glimpse of that meaning, imagine that you've been given a possible diagnosis of cancer; your heart is weighed down with dread . . . and then—good news!—the diagnosis was a mistake and you have only a minor and curable illness. Or picture your feelings if you had made a terrible mistake at work, one that could cost you your job; you are sick with shame and anxiety . . . but—good news!—you caught the mistake in time to fix it before any harm could take effect. And now think about how you would feel if you learned that a loved one had been in a serious car accident, the terror that would make it nearly impossible for you to breathe . . . but then—good news!—you find out your loved one is safe and sound. This is the same sort of joyful relief that the early church experienced when they heard Jesus' life-promising, hope-giving message. And it was also the Celts' experience when they encountered this amazing, radical story that they had never before heard. The story told by Matthew and the other Evangelists is the good news that reverses humanity's terrible fear of death and darkness. It tells us that when life seems meaningless and unbearable, there is a deeper meaning, a larger hope to cling to. Matthew promised the Celts that their human lives could have wings.

When the early Church put together the New Testament, they placed the Gospels first, not because they were written first (they weren't) but because they told the "Good Story" (the best story ever) that was the foundation for everything in all the books that followed. Matthew's Gospel was placed first of all (though it was not the first written), because the early Church Fathers assigned to it preeminent importance. Matthew's perspective on the Good News emphasizes that Jesus is the Jews' "Chosen One" (*Messiah* in Hebrew, *Christ* in Greek), and it forms a thematic transition between the Hebrew scriptures and the Christian New Testament.

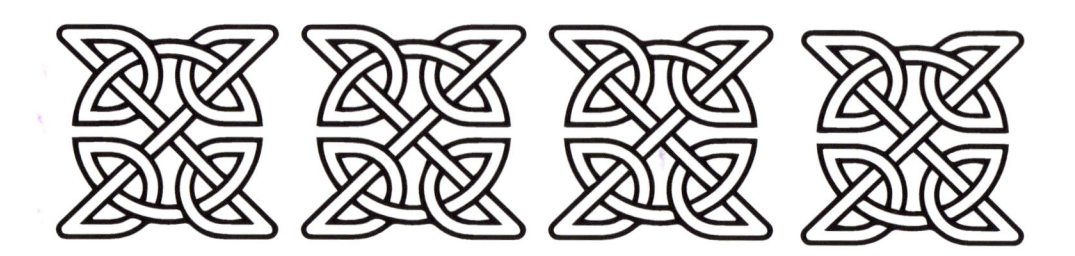

Did someone named Matthew actually write this Gospel? The Celts believed so, because they took the word of Papias, a second-century Turkish bishop. Today, modern Bible scholars dispute Matthew's authorship, but readers through the ages have believed that the tax collector and disciple Matthew (Greek name), also called Levi (Hebrew name), wrote it.

It was written sometime between the years 70 to 100, either in Syria or Galilee. Much of Matthew's text is comprised of quotes from Mark's Gospel and from another document, no longer in existence, called "Q" (from German *quelle* meaning "source"). If an eyewitness—like Matthew the tax collector—had written this Gospel, why would he have borrowed so much of his material? The Celts did not worry about this, however, and instead, they focused on the testimony this Gospel gives to events in the life of Jesus. Like the other canonical Gospels, Matthew's account interprets history, combining sayings and narratives of Jesus.

INTRODUCTION ☘ 75

✠ THE JEWISH GOSPEL ✠

Whoever he was, the author of this Gospel was clearly Jewish. He begins his story with a genealogy to demonstrate the Jewish lineage of "Jesus the Chosen One, the son of David, the son of Abraham." Matthew was writing at least half a century after the death of Jesus, and the context within which he wrote—and his reasons for writing—stemmed from developments that had taken place during those years. He was telling his story to Jewish Christians, a community that was now in conflict. Jewish Christians were being pushed out of the larger communities, located in northern Galilee or Syria, and Matthew was at pains to place his community squarely within its Jewish heritage. The Jesus he portrayed is a Jew, a prophet greater than Moses. Matthew did not think of himself—or Jesus—as someone who had left his ancestral faith and converted to a new religion. Instead, for Matthew, Jesus was the fulfillment of the Hebrew scriptures.

The Jewish flavor of Matthew's Gospel would have been of special interest to Celtic Christians in the Early Middle Ages, since their practices were often similar to Jewish traditions. The Welsh theologian Pelagius (also known as Morgan), commenting on Matthew 5:20, indicated the importance he put on Jewish rules: "For the righteousness of Christ's disciples will be able to stand out above that of the Scribes and Pharisees, as long as they have fulfilled not only the precepts given to the Scribes and Pharisees by Moses and the prophets but also the commandments given by Christ." After Pelagius' time, many of his followers in the Celtic lands continued to urge observance of Hebrew laws. They had several points of conflict with the Roman Church's practices, one of which was their dating of Easter, based on the Jewish dating of Passover, which they held to in defiance of edicts from Rome. Many Celtic Christians observed the Jewish Sabbath Day (rather than Sunday), and some groups celebrated Jewish feast days, followed Old Testament dietary laws, and practiced tithing as described in the Torah. A few scholars have speculated that Jewish laws were easily compatible with druidic law, making them a comfortable fit for the early Celtic Christians. The principles of Bible interpretation practiced by Celtic monks were also similar to Midrash, a form of Jewish commentary.

In contrast with churches elsewhere in Christendom, which developed anti-Semitic prejudices, Celtic Christians found Matthew's Hebrew essence to be an easy fit. They strongly identified with the Jewish context of Jesus' life, and they found the way in which Matthew told the Good News to be instructional, practical, and encouraging. In the centuries that followed, when Christianity still had its own flavor in Celtic lands, the Jewish practice of blessing the small events of daily life was congruent with the Celts' recognition that every-day happenings—rising in the morning, getting dressed, eating meals, working—could be sanctified through small daily rituals.

Matthew's Jesus is also an example of old traditions interlaced with new realities. The Celts may have identified with the way in which Matthew presented Jesus not in the terminology of either-or (either a Jew or a Christian) but as someone who brought new fulfillment to old traditions without negating them, in a way that was similar to how the first Celtic Christians emerged out of Paganism. Matthew's winged man helped the Celts see not only the meshwork between heaven and earth but also the ongoing weave of ancient tradition with current realities.

⊠ THE REALM OF HEAVEN ⊠

The author of Matthew sees Jesus as fulfilling two roles. On the one hand, he is the Divine One who proclaims to us that the Realm of Heaven is nearby—and on the other hand, he is the Human One. In

INTRODUCTION 77

Matthew's account, Jesus is like the winged man who represents both human and Divine qualities.

The Celtic Christians would have joyfully welcomed Matthew's message that the Realm of Heaven was near to them. As Pagans, they had believed in an Otherworld that intersected with this one, and as Christians, they continued to have a sense that at times and in certain places, this world and the Otherworld—the Realm of Heaven—were separated by only the thinnest of membranes. Unlike the Pagan Otherworld, which could be dark and terrifying as well as lovely and filled with light, the Realm of Heaven, as described by Matthew, was a place of justice (6:33), peace (5:9), and gladness (13:44). Matthew's Jesus, both Divine and human, demonstrated that it is possible to live in the heavenly realm now, in this life, in this world—and he used stories and metaphors to help his followers understand the true nature of the Realm of Heaven.

MODERN RELEVANCE

Despite all these common characteristics in their understanding of the Gospels, Celtic Christianity was never a homogenous thing with its own defined orthodoxy. The Christian Celts shared a common love of Scripture, but their interpretations and beliefs varied from individual to individual, from monastery to monastery, and from century to century. The goal of the Celtic Bible Commentary is not to lay claim to any form of historical Celtic practice or belief in an attempt to re-create something that never existed—a comprehensive Celtic theology and practice—but to be inspired and challenged by these contradictory and sometimes clearly mistaken individuals who went before us. We believe the ancient Celts offer us insights that can give hope and meaning to the twenty-first-century world in which we struggle to live a life of faith.

We cannot, of course, read the Gospel of Matthew exactly as the early Celtic Christians would have done. We live in a time that is very different from theirs; our cultural values are far from theirs; and we have been infused since the time we were children with a body of knowledge that would have been alien to them. Furthermore, the modern-English translation of the Greek Scripture that we have created is far from the Latin version with which the Celts were familiar. Even our understanding of "reading" is not the same as theirs. For the Celts, reading the Gospel would have been an all-embracing visual experience, stimulating the eye and the imagination as much as the mind and the heart. We cannot hope to re-create their experience. Instead, our goal is to learn what we can from the ancient Celts—and then see how we can apply it to our own lives in the twenty-first century.

Reading Matthew from a generically Celtic perspective, then, means finding ways to weave its story into our own. It asks us to encounter the Good News as fresh, living, and radical. And it requires that we answer the question: "What does the Good News mean to me, today? What does it mean to the world in which I live? How can I better understand the Realm of Heaven—and encounter its reality in my ordinary life?"

Perhaps the Gospel of Matthew is especially valuable at a time in history when the world seems so full of conflict at all levels—politically, interpersonally, culturally, and even within faith communities. Like us, Matthew was familiar with disagreements among Christ's followers (see, for example, chapter 23). Matthew's Gospel indicates that in such situations, God's ideal for us is to love our enemies (5:43–48); it gives us procedures to work things out when we disagree (18:15–20). Difficult as it may be, caring for our neighbors (even enemy-neighbors) is essential, because ultimately our wholeness depends on how we show love in practical ways (25:31–46). Finally, as we face the complexities of social relationships and other challenges in life, Matthew's Gospel reassures us that we need not fear. We are not alone, for Jesus' presence is always with us (28:20).

We too can have wings.

One

The Book of Matthew begins by outlining the ancestry of Jesus through his father Joseph's blood line, going back to Abraham, and then describing the circumstances of Jesus' birth. After Joseph and Mary are legally wed, but before they have sex, Mary becomes pregnant. In Matthew's portrayal of these events, Joseph does not shame Mary or accuse her of wrongdoing, and instead cares for her. One night, Joseph is visited by an angel, who tells him he should not doubt his decision to marry Mary: her pregnancy was caused by the Holy Spirit, and she will give birth to a son. The angel tells Joseph that Mary's son should be named Jesus and that he will fulfill the prophecy of a child born to a virgin woman who will save all humanity from its failure and wrongdoing. Joseph wakes and does as the angel instructed, caring for Mary and refraining from sex with her until her son is born. Joseph names the newborn child Jesus, just as the angel told him to.

Since this was the beginning of the story of Jesus' life and the first of the Gospels, the Celtic artists who created illumined manuscripts such as the Lindisfarne Gospels and the Book of Kells took pains to make

CHAPTER ONE   ☘   81

this first page as sumptuous as possible in terms of design, calligraphy, and color, filling an entire page with a single word or short phrase. The "Monogram Page" in the Book of Kells, for example, consists entirely of the Chi Rho that was the abbreviation for Christ. Intertwined with the calligraphy of the letters themselves are circles within circles, triskelions, human faces, angels, an otter eating a fish, and a mother cat with her kittens. These images, which for the Celts were part of the entire experience of contemplating this first chapter of Matthew, indicate the all-encompassing enormity of the Incarnation.

⌘ THE VIRGIN BIRTH ⌘

Is a belief in a miraculous virgin birth necessary for us to believe in the Incarnation? That question has plagued Christians for centuries. In some instances, the virgin birth has been pulled out from the entire story as the fulcrum on which the whole Gospel rests. Modern Christianity has struggled with the seeming contradictions between science and a literal understanding of various biblical accounts (and not only in regard to the virgin birth). Medieval Celtic Christians also experienced this struggle, but with sometimes different conclusions. It was quite possible, some concluded, to believe passionately and wholeheartedly in the Incarnation, while still applying a scientific mind to the details of the story recounted in Matthew 1.

"Miracles do not, in fact, break the laws of nature," wrote a twentieth-century Celtic Christian, C. S. Lewis. "There is an activity of God displayed throughout creation," the famous apologist explained, "a wholesale activity," and the miracles recorded in Scripture "perform the very same things as this wholesale activity, but at a different speed and on a smaller scale." Lewis concluded: "The miracles in fact are a retelling in small letters of the very same story that is written across the whole world in letters too large for some of us to see."

Challenges to the miraculous are not a new problem; ancient people could be incredulous as well. In the seventh century, for example, an Irish monk composed a work titled *On the Miracles of Holy Scripture*. (He wrote it using the name of the famous theologian Augustine; hence modern scholars refer to the author as "the Irish Augustine.") The Irish Augustine wanted to prove the Bible's miracles were feasible; and—like fellow Irishman Lewis thirteen hundred years later—he did so by claiming that miracles were in accord with ordinary laws of nature. To do this he drew on the keen observations of nature and deep book-learning of his fellow Irish monks.

The Irish Augustine wrote about the Incarnation and the birth of Jesus to the "Virgin Mary." Modern scholars have questioned whether the word "virgin," which Matthew (1:23) quotes from the prophet Isaiah, is an accurate translation, but this seventh-century monk reading a Latin Bible had no reason to doubt that the word did indeed mean "virgin" with all that implies—and indeed, the Greek word "parthenos" used by the author of Matthew holds the same meaning.

So how did this ancient Celtic scholar, who firmly believed that God does not overwrite "natural" laws, defend the feasibility of Jesus' virgin birth? Like this: "Although it is indeed contrary to all human experience . . . it was not outside nature" that a virgin birth should take place. "We can point to . . . animals generating without the intercourse of parents," and he cites bees, as well as some fish and birds as examples. His science was spot on—and thirteen centuries ahead of time, for scientists today agree that bees, some species of fish, and (rarely) birds do exhibit parthenogenesis (virgin birth).

Do you believe miracles are possible? Two Irish scholars—one from the Middle Ages, the other from the twentieth century—give us reason to believe that even the greatest miracle was not "unnatural"—and these scholars' thoughts on miracles in no way threatened their faith in Jesus.

—Kenneth McIntosh

CHAPTER ONE

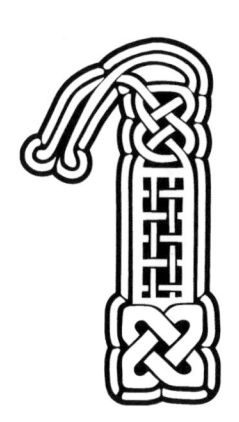

¹ The book of the genealogy of Jesus the Christ,ᵃ the son of David, the son of Abraham. ² Abraham became the father of Isaac. Isaac became the father of Jacob. Jacob became the father of Judah and his brothers. ³ Judah became the father of Perez and Zerah by Tamar. Perez became the father of Hezron. Hezron became the father of Ram. ⁴ Ram became the father of Amminadab. Amminadab became the father of Nahshon. Nahshon became the father of Salmon. ⁵ Salmon became the father of Boaz by Rahab. Boaz became the father of Obed by Ruth. Obed became the father of Jesse. ⁶ Jesse became the father of King David. David became the father of Solomon by her who had been Uriah's wife. ⁷ Solomon became the father of Rehoboam. Rehoboam became the father of Abijah. Abijah became the father of Asa. ⁸ Asa became the father of Jehoshaphat. Jehoshaphat became the father of Joram. Joram became the father of Uzziah. ⁹ Uzziah became the father of Jotham. Jotham became the father of Ahaz.

Ahaz became the father of Hezekiah. ¹⁰ Hezekiah became the father of Manasseh. Manasseh became the father of Amon. Amon became the father of Josiah. ¹¹ Josiah became the father of Jechoniah and his brothers, at the time of the exile to Babylon. ¹² After the exile to Babylon, Jechoniah became the father of Shealtiel. Shealtiel became the father of Zerubbabel. ¹³ Zerubbabel became the father of Abiud. Abiud became the father of Eliakim. Eliakim became the father of Azor. ¹⁴ Azor became the father of Zadok. Zadok became the father of Achim. Achim became the father of Eliud. ¹⁵ Eliud became the father of Eleazar. Eleazar became the father of Matthan. Matthan became the father of Jacob. ¹⁶ Jacob became the father of Joseph, the husband of Mary, from whom was born Jesus,[b] who is called the Christ. ¹⁷ So all the generations from Abraham to David are fourteen generations; from David to the exile to Babylon fourteen generations; and from the carrying away to Babylon to the Christ, fourteen generations.

¹⁸ Now the birth of Jesus Christ was like this: After his mother, Mary, was engaged to Joseph, before they came together, she was found pregnant by the Holy Breath.[c] ¹⁹ Joseph, her husband, being a righteous man, and not willing to make her a public example, intended to put her away secretly. ²⁰ But when he thought about these things, look![d] An angel of the Eternal One appeared to him in a dream, saying, "Joseph, son of David, don't be afraid to take to yourself Mary, your wife, for that which is conceived in her is of the Holy Breath. ²¹ She shall give birth to a son. You shall call his name Jesus, for it is he who shall save his people from their failures."[e]

²² Now all this has happened, that it might be fulfilled which was spoken by the Eternal One through the prophet, saying, ²³ "Pay close attention to this, the virgin shall be with child, and shall give birth to a son. They shall call his name Immanuel"; which interpreted means, "God with us."[f]

²⁴ Joseph arose from his sleep, and did as the angel commanded him, and took his wife to himself; ²⁵ and did not have sex with her until she had given birth to her firstborn son. He named him Jesus.

[a] *Messiah* (Hebrew) and *Christ* (Greek) both mean "Anointed One." Anointing with oil signified that one was chosen or set apart for a God-given role.

[b] *Jesus* means "salvation."

[c] The Greek word usually translated "spirit" means literally "breath" or "wind." We have used one of these words in many cases instead of the more familiar "spirit," because it gives a fresh and more tangible understanding of the Spirit.

[d] The Greek word used here means "look at, take notice, observe, see, or gaze at." It was often used as an interjection.

[e] The Greek word ἁμαρτία, traditionally translated as "sin" in most versions of the Bible, meant literally "missing the mark" (as when an arrow fails to hit its target). We have chosen to translate it as "failure," "mistake," "misdeed," "wrongdoing," etc., not to minimize or trivialize the seriousness of "missing the mark" but in order to focus on the original meaning of this word.

[f] This is a reference to Isaiah 7:14.

two

After Jesus is born, Matthew tells us that three magi travel to Jerusalem from the east, guided by a star, searching for the newborn "King of the Jews," whom they seek to worship. King Herod, hearing of their search, seeks to find Jesus in order to destroy him, and asks his priests and scribes the whereabouts of the child's birth. They tell Herod of a prophecy foretelling Jesus' birth in Bethlehem. King Herod calls on the foreigners to go to Bethlehem and inform him once they find the child, so that he may worship Jesus as well, he tells them. The magi travel to Bethlehem and are guided to Jesus and his mother Mary by the same star that led them to Jerusalem. Upon finding Jesus, they worship him and give him gifts of gold, frankincense, and myrrh. The travelers then return to their homeland in the east, heeding a warning from a dream to not tell King Herod of Jesus' location. Joseph, Jesus' father, is also visited by an angel while dreaming, who tells him to take Jesus and flee with Mary to Egypt where they will be safe from King Herod's plan to kill Jesus. Enraged by the magi not informing him once they'd found Jesus, Herod orders the murder of all male children under two years old in Bethlehem and the surrounding areas. After King Herod's death, an angel tells Joseph that it is safe to return from Egypt, but upon learning that Herod's son Archelaus has succeeded his father as king, Joseph, Jesus, and Mary travel to Nazareth, a city in Galilee.

WE THREE DRUIDS?

"We three kings of orient are, bearing gifts we traverse afar." When Reverend John Henry Hopkins wrote these words in 1857 he could not have guessed how many people would sing them, year after year. Unfortunately, the song's popularity also perpetuated some historical misunderstandings. The "three wise men" were not actually kings.

In Matthew's Gospel, the Greek word used for these travelers is *magos*, referring to the educated, priestly class from what is now Iran. According to historians, the Old Persian word *magush* was used to refer generically to all wise men, teachers, priests, physicians, astrologers, seers, interpreters of dreams, augurs, soothsayers, and sorcerers. In fact, the magi probably had much in common with the Celts' educated priestly class, the Druids,

Tragically, the Hebrew scriptures would have condemned people like this to death, as indicated in Leviticus 20:27: "A man or a

woman that is . . . a wizard, shall surely be put to death: they shall stone them with stones." Matthew's Gospel, however, corrected this xenophobic law. These magi—Pagan wizards once considered worthy of death—are the only people in Matthew's account of the Nativity who understand what God is doing. They are the ones who honor baby Jesus. Furthermore, they defy the Jewish king (who seeks Jesus' death) and put themselves at risk to save the newborn savior. Matthew makes this clear: religious leaders of another faith are God's good servants.

Six centuries later, when the Leinster historian Muirchu set his quill to vellum in order to chronicle the life of Saint Patrick, he wrote that when Patrick encountered Loegaire, king of the O'Neill clan, Loegaire was not surprised, because *magi* had advised him of Patrick's coming. Why this odd use of an archaic Persian word in the tale of an Irish saint, when you'd think he would have used the word "druid," which would have been far more familiar to his readers? Muirchu is sending a signal to his readers: just as God used Pagan sorcerers to honor and serve the baby Jesus, in the same way God used the pre-Christian Druids to anticipate the coming of the Gospel. As Thomas O'Loughlin explains in his book *Celtic Theology*, "It is not a case of Christianity walking into a void—into a place where God is not, where religion is not, culture is not—nor into a place where the Spirit has not been at work." God was already there.

Many Christians do not expect God to be at work in the lives of people who do not profess Christ. They doubt that God's Spirit could be working in religions outside of Christianity. The Gospel of

Matthew, however, portrays God using Pagan sorcerers to welcome and protect the Christ, and in the same way Celtic historian Muirchu used the word *magi* to show God at work in his Druid ancestors. If we take the Gospel as seriously as did the Celtic Christians, then we will recognize and honor God's Spirit, whether the Spirit works in Pagan or Christian; in Buddhist, Hindu, or Muslim; in Jew, atheist, or agnostic. Who are we to set boundaries on the universality of God?

—Kenneth McIntosh

[1] Now when Jesus was born in Bethlehem of Judea in the days of King Herod, behold, sages from the east came to Jerusalem, saying, [2] "Where is the one who is born King of the Jews? For we saw his star in the east, and have come to worship him." [3] When King Herod heard it, he was troubled, and all Jerusalem with him. [4] Gathering together all the chief priests and scribes of the people, he asked them where the Christ would be born. [5] They said to him, "In Bethlehem of Judea, for this is written through the prophet,

[6] 'You Bethlehem, land of Judah,
are in no way least among the rulers of Judah:
for out of you shall come a governor,
who shall shepherd my people, Israel.'" [a]

⁷ Then Herod secretly called the sages, and learned from them exactly what time the star appeared. ⁸ He sent them to Bethlehem, and said, "Go and search diligently for the young child. When you have found him, bring me word, so that I also may come and worship him."

⁹ They, having heard the king, went their way; and behold, the star, which they saw in the east, went before them, until it came and stood over where the young child was. ¹⁰ When they saw the star, they rejoiced with exceedingly great joy. ¹¹ They came into the house and saw the young child with Mary, his mother, and they fell down and worshiped him. Opening their treasures, they offered to him gifts: gold, frankincense, and myrrh. ¹² Being warned in a dream not to return to Herod, they went back to their own country another way.

¹³ Now when they had departed, behold, an angel of the Eternal One appeared to Joseph in a dream, saying, "Arise and take the young child and his mother, and flee into Egypt, and stay there until I tell you, for Herod will seek the young child to destroy him."

¹⁴ He arose and took the young child and his mother by night, and departed into Egypt, ¹⁵ and was there until the death of Herod; that it might be fulfilled which was spoken by the Eternal One through the prophet, saying, "Out of Egypt I called my son." ᵇ

¹⁶ Then Herod, when he saw that he was mocked by the sages, was exceedingly angry, and sent out, and killed all the male children who were in Bethlehem and in all the surrounding countryside, from two years old and under, according to the exact time which he had learned from the sages. ¹⁷ Then that which was spoken by Jeremiah the prophet was fulfilled, saying,

> [18] "A voice was heard in Ramah,
> lamentation, weeping and great mourning,
> Rachel weeping for her children;
> she wouldn't be comforted,
> because they are no more." [c]

[19] But when Herod was dead, behold, an angel of the Eternal One appeared in a dream to Joseph in Egypt, saying, [20] "Arise and take the young child and his mother, and go into the land of Israel, for those who sought the young child's life are dead."

[21] He arose and took the young child and his mother, and came into the land of Israel. [22] But when he heard that Archelaus was reigning over Judea in the place of his father, Herod, he was afraid to go there. Being warned in a dream, he withdrew into the region of Galilee, [23] and came and lived in a city called Nazareth; that it might be fulfilled which was spoken through the prophets: "He will be called a Nazarene." [d]

---

[a] Micah 5:2
[b] Hosea 11:1
[c] Jeremiah 31:15
[d] Matthew's statement here is puzzling, since nowhere in the Hebrew scriptures is there any reference to the Messiah being called a Nazarene. Some biblical scholars believe that this was actually a play on words that has been lost in the translation, since the literal meaning of Nazareth is "little branch," and the Hebrew scriptures refer to the Messiah as a Branch (Isa. 11:1, 60:21; Jer. 23:5, 33:15; Zech. 3:8, 6:12).

CHAPTER THREE

three

While Jesus remains safe in Galilee, John the Baptist preaches in Judea of a coming savior. John baptizes people in the Jordan River, hearing their confessions of wrongdoing. When he sees that Pharisees and Sadducees, members of strict Jewish sects that dutifully adhered to the written law over oral tradition, are coming to him for baptism in the Jordan, he becomes angry at what he sees as religious hypocrisy. He speaks to them of a coming savior who will judge them if they do not truly change their lives.

Soon, Jesus travels from Galilee to be baptized by John. At first, John protests, telling Jesus that he should baptize John, not the other way around. Jesus explains to John that his baptism will serve as a lesson to others, and John is convinced. Upon Jesus' baptism, the Holy Spirit appears as a dove and the voice of God speaks from the heavens, claiming Jesus as the son of God.

John the Baptist is a wild and wooly figure, the incendiary preacher who is clad in skins and lives off the land. In today's world, he would be the long-haired, bearded hippie who wanders out of the wilds into a city square. Though John is a fascinating character, he remains a minor one when compared to the center of Matthew's story: Jesus. In church art, John the Baptist is always portrayed pointing—to Christ, whom he baptizes. In Matthew, John the Baptist declares, "He who comes after me is mightier than I" (3:11).

⊠ A NEW VIEW OF GOD'S MERCY ⊠

In the seventh century, a brilliant Irish monk attained a new perspective on God's mercy from John's statement about Jesus in verse 11. Cummian the Tall, who had his own library of more than forty manuscripts, including two Latin Bibles and writings by both Augustine and Pelagius, was aware of the controversy between these two great theologians: both Augustine and Pelagius agreed that God was strictly just and inclined to punish transgressors, but they disagreed as to the method of attaining salvation. Augustine believed that God forgave people who received baptism and confirmation, thus adhering to the Church. According to this perspective, the Church was like a boat; those outside would drown in damnation but those chosen by God would ride to safety in the vessel. In contrast to Augustine, Pelagius believed that those outside of the Church could attain salvation by adhering to God's moral demands. The way up the steep mountain of salvation was to follow the path of God's rules, but a slip on the hard route of righteousness could result in a tumble all the way to hell.

Neither theology could entirely be characterized as "good news." Augustine's God was good to those who happened to agree with the doctrines and rituals of the Church—but what of the many outside the church who could never hope for salvation? Pelagius's God was an equal-opportunity Saver-of-Souls, but still strict in demanding obedience. Cummian looked at these two options and wondered what hope could there be for someone who fell into lust or anger.

Cummian, practicing the multilayered Celtic way of reading the Bible, interpreted Scripture expecting to see both the literal meaning and the deeper, mystical sense of each verse. As he pondered John's declaration, "The one who is coming after me is mightier than I," Cummian had an insight that took him beyond the views of both Augustine and Pelagius—Jesus is "mightier" than John because Jesus' Good News is based on pure *mercy*. The "mightier" mercy of Jesus, said Cummian, springs forth from God's inclination to forgive. Jesus' strength is not one of violence or aggression but of love.

John the Baptist was angry with the hypocrites he encountered (vss. 7–12), just as we too grow angry when we see people in authority who claim to be something they clearly are not. John recognized, however, that Jesus offers strength we cannot possess on our own. Seven centuries after Cummian, the English mystic Julian of Norwich reached a similar conclusion. "The Spirit works in us," she wrote, "creating peace and comfort, helping us to become once more aligned with the Divine Will, pliant and supple to the Spirit's wind. This is mercy." She continued:

> This is how our Protector continually leads us, as long as we are here in this changeable life. I saw no wrath, except on humanity's part, and God forgives us for it. Wrath merely puts us off course from the straight roadway that leads toward God;

it makes us at odds with peace; it separates us from love. Anger springs up in our minds when we lack strength or wisdom, when we are fragmented and unfocused—but these failures are only in ourselves, not in God. Our sin turns us into outcasts from peace and love; it separates us from them. But God's face is always turned toward us. For love is the foundation of mercy, and mercy's action keeps us safe in love.

Does your view of God have more to do with wrath and judgment—or with mercy? Do you think of God primarily as an enforcer—or as a forgiver? Many of us have grown up with answers to these questions that are quite different from the ones that Cummian and Julian found. These are important questions, not ones to be set aside easily or quickly. Think about it: how does your view of God's nature influence your life? And how might your life be changed if you were to open yourself to the sense of the "mightier mercy" of Jesus?

—Kenneth McIntosh

CHAPTER THREE

¹ In those days, John the Baptizer came, preaching in the wilderness of Judea, saying, ² "Change your lives, for the Reign of Heaven is at hand!" ³ For this is the one who was spoken of by Isaiah the prophet, saying,

> "'The voice of one crying in the wilderness,
> make ready the way of the Eternal One.
> Straighten the pathways.'" [a]

⁴ Now John himself wore clothing made of camel's hair, with a leather belt around his waist. His food was locusts and wild honey. ⁵ Then people from Jerusalem, all of Judea, and all the region around the Jordan went out to him. ⁶ They were baptized by him in the Jordan, confessing their mistakes.

⁷ But when he saw many of the Pharisees and Sadducees coming for his baptism, he said to them, "You offspring of vipers, who warned you to flee from the wrath to come? ⁸ Therefore produce fruit worthy of changed lives! ⁹ Don't think to yourselves, 'We have Abraham for our father,' for I tell you that God is able to raise up children to Abraham from these stones.

¹⁰ "Even now the ax lies at the root of the trees. Therefore every tree that doesn't produce good fruit is cut down, and cast into the fire. ¹¹ I indeed baptize you in water as a sign of how you are changing your lives, but the one who is coming after me is mightier than I, whose shoes I am not worthy to carry. He will baptize you in the Holy Breath and with fire. ¹² His winnowing fork is in his hand, and he will thoroughly cleanse his threshing floor. He will gather his wheat into the barn, but the chaff he will burn up with unquenchable fire."

¹³ Then Jesus came from Galilee to the Jordan River to John, to be baptized by him. ¹⁴ But John would have hindered him, saying, "I need to be baptized by you, and you come to me?"

¹⁵ But Jesus, answering, said to him, "Allow it now, for this is the fitting way for us to fulfill all righteousness." Then he allowed him. ¹⁶ Jesus, when he was baptized, went up directly from the water: and behold, the heavens were opened to him. He saw the Breath of God descending as a dove, and coming on him. Suddenly, a voice out of the heavens said, "This is my beloved Son, with whom I am well pleased."

ᵃ Isaiah 40:3

CHAPTER FOUR

four

The temptation of Jesus is a familiar story. After Jesus' baptism, the Spirit leads him into the wilderness where he fasts for forty days and nights. At the end of this time, Matthew writes that the Devil comes to Jesus to tempt him with three tests. First, the Devil taunts Jesus by saying if he were God's son, he could turn rocks into bread. Jesus resists the Devil's temptation to work a miracle to satisfy his hunger. Next, the Devil takes Jesus to the top of the Temple in the city of Jerusalem and says if Jesus really were the son of God, he could jump from the Temple and be carried to safety by angels. Jesus again resists the Devil's urgings. Finally, the Devil takes Jesus to the top of a mountain to show him the riches of the world, telling Jesus that all that wealth could be his if he'd only bow down and serve the Devil. Once more Jesus refuses and tells the Devil that he only worships God. And the Devil leaves him.

After this experience, Jesus goes to Capernaum, a city by the sea in Galilee, where he begins to call his disciples. He then travels

102   THE GOSPEL OF MATTHEW

throughout Galilee, teaching and speaking, as well as healing the sick. Upon hearing of Jesus' healing sicknesses and diseases, people travel from far and wide to seek and follow him, to be healed and to hear his message.

⌘ Temptation ⌘

All of us—even Jesus—have faced the temptation to seek our own way, to put our needs before the needs of others, to place ourselves at the center of the world. Matthew's account of Jesus' temptation emphasizes the interior nature of temptation: physical hungers, worldly power, and financial riches trigger our selfish desires. Nowhere, though, does Matthew's story indicate that Jesus perceived food, power, or riches to be evil in and of themselves. The problem that Jesus recognizes if he were to yield to these temptations is that they would take his focus away from God. They would replace God's place in his heart.

We're not always so wise—nor were the Celtic saints, as is clear in the story of the temptation of Saint Kevin of Glendalough, as told by John O'Hanlon in his book, *Lives of the Irish Saints*. The story goes that when Kevin was "in the bloom of youth" he was already a monk living in a monastery. One day a "youthful and beautiful maiden" saw Kevin and "conceived a particular attraction to him." So, she set out to win his affection, or, as O'Hanlon so poetically puts it, "she endeavoured to engage the love of this holy youth, by her looks, her words, and sometimes, by her messages." But Kevin rejected it all.

One day, however, when the monks left to go work in the wood, the maiden followed them. As she watched and waited, Kevin went off by himself and she approached him. With "words of affections" and "blandishments" the young maiden sought to make Kevin forget his holy vows. But, making the sign of the cross, Kevin ran away and hid. The young maiden chased after him and found Kevin hiding in the nettles.

Kevin retained his celibacy, but in the process, he doesn't seem so pious. When the maiden found him, Kevin, the "holy youth," took a bundle of nettles and began to "strike her several times." Clearly, instead of acknowledging his physical urge to use this woman sexually, Kevin projected his own shortcomings onto her. He put the blame on her.

Before we dismiss this as merely a tale indicative of medieval misogyny, we might want to examine our own hearts. When we are angry, do we acknowledge our interior selfishness—or do we blame the person who "made" us angry? Do we take responsibility for what we put inside our minds, instead of allowing them to be sponges, soaking up the perspectives we see and hear on television, social media, and elsewhere? Do we recognize that sin can take many forms, because it can be anything that comes between God and ourselves? Do we understand that temptation is something that happens inside us, rather than something we can project onto others?

When Kevin was older, he is said to have had a vision of another monk beating a woman with nettles—and Kevin urged him to stop. Perhaps by then Kevin had realized that violence is never the Way of Jesus. Like us, the Celtic saints learned and grew.

Sometimes, even our lowest points—the moments when we are at our weakest and most unlovely, as Kevin was with the young woman—turn out to be the very place where, when we look back, we will see we turned a corner. We would do well to remember that Jesus emerged from his time of temptation ready to begin teaching and serving others. It could be that the moments we feel most tempted to turn from God are the very times at which God is preparing us for a new level of service.

—Jack Gillespie

CHAPTER FOUR

¹ Then Jesus was led by the Wind into the wilderness to be tempted by the devil. ² When he had fasted forty days and forty nights, he was hungry afterward. ³ The tempter came and said to him, "If you are the Son of God, command that these stones become bread."

⁴ But he answered, "It is written, 'We shall not live by bread alone, but by every word that proceeds out of the mouth of God.'" [a]

⁵ Then the devil took him into the holy city, set him on the pinnacle of the temple, ⁶ and said to him, "If you are the Son of God, throw yourself down, for it is written, 'God will command the angels concerning you,' and, 'On their hands they will bear you up, so that you don't dash your foot against a stone.'" [b]

⁷ Jesus said to the devil, "Again, it is written, 'You shall not test the Sovereign, your God.'" [c]

⁸ Again, the devil took him to an exceedingly high mountain, and showed him all the nations of the world, and their glory. ⁹ Satan said to

him, "I will give you all of these things, if you will fall down and worship me."

¹⁰ Then Jesus said to the devil, "Go away, Satan! For it is written, 'You shall worship the Sovereign your God, and you shall serve God alone.'" ᵈ

¹¹ Then the devil left him, and behold, angels came and served him.

¹² Now when Jesus heard that John was delivered up, he withdrew into Galilee. ¹³ Leaving Nazareth, he came and lived in Capernaum, which is by the sea, in the region of Zebulun and Naphtali, ¹⁴ that it might be fulfilled which was spoken through Isaiah the prophet, saying,

¹⁵ "The land of Zebulun and the land of Naphtali,
toward the sea, beyond the Jordan, Galilee of the Gentiles,
¹⁶ the people who sat in darkness saw a great light,
to those who sat in the region and shadow of death,
to them light has dawned." ᵉ

¹⁷ From that time, Jesus began to preach, and to say, "Change your lives! For the Reign of Heaven is at hand."

¹⁸ Walking by the sea of Galilee, he saw two brothers: Simon, who is called Peter, and Andrew, his brother, casting a net into the sea; for they made their living by fishing. ¹⁹ He said to them, "Come after me, and I will make you fishers for people."

²⁰ They immediately left their nets and followed him. ²¹ Going on from there, he saw two other brothers, James the son of Zebedee, and John his brother, in the boat with Zebedee their father, mending their nets. He called

them. ²² They immediately left the boat and their father, and followed him.

²³ Jesus went about in all Galilee, teaching in their synagogues, preaching the Good News of the Reign of Heaven, and healing every disease and every sickness among the people. ²⁴ The report about him went out into all Syria. They brought to him all who were sick, afflicted with various diseases and torments, possessed with demons, epileptics, and paralytics; and he healed them. ²⁵ Great crowds from Galilee, Decapolis, Jerusalem, Judea and from beyond the Jordan followed him.

[a] Deuteronomy 8:3
[b] Psalm 91:11–12
[c] Deuteronomy 6:16
[d] Deuteronomy 6:13
[e] Isaiah 9:1–2

five

Jesus, seeing a crowd gathering, climbs a mountain and speaks to his disciples. He tells them that the poor, the cast off, the hungry, the persecuted—all the world's outcasts and downtrodden—are blessed in the eyes of God. He goes on to say that his disciples must share his messages and glorify God. He also says, however, that he has not come to destroy or remake the laws of the land and the Hebrew scripture, and in fact he exhorts his followers to adhere to the law, to obey the commandments of the Torah. Jesus also expands on these commandments, saying, for example, that not only must his followers obey the commandment "You shall not murder," but also refrain from anger and hatred, even against those who have wronged them. Jesus tells his followers that they must make amends with their enemies, that they must remain faithful to their spouses in body and mind, and that any lie is wrong. He commands his followers to open themselves to those in need, to give freely to friend, enemy, and stranger alike. In what has come to be known as the Sermon on the Mount, Jesus outlines the tenets of a righteous, faithful life, emphasizing the importance of empathy, giving, forgiveness, honesty, and openheartedness.

⋈ BLESSED ARE THE POOR IN SPIRIT ⋈

The word "poor" isn't one that appeals to most of us. Few people wish to be poor. Most of us wish we could make more money than we do; wouldn't life be easier with a better income? And although we may not admit it, even to ourselves, we tend to look down on the poor—or we look at those wealthier than ourselves and ask, "Why can't I have that?" So when Jesus tells us that the poor are blessed, his words seem paradoxical.

"Poor in spirit," the phrase Jesus uses in Matthew 5:3, has been equated with humility, and for most of us, humility is no more desirable than poverty. We connect it to the similar word "humiliated"—and no one wishes to be humiliated. We'll pass up opportunities, make excuses, and go out of our way rather than face the risk of being humbled publicly.

Franciscan spiritual master Richard Rohr says he "prays for one good humiliation daily"—but that's what makes him a spiritual guru, I suspect, while most of us are not. So what do we do with this chapter, where Jesus lauds the "poor in spirit"? Instead of thinking of his words as a vague spiritual recommendation, how can we use them as the foundation of a practical way of life?

The Celts found their answer in monasticism, which arose in the Celtic regions not long after the conversion of the Irish, Scots, Picts, and Northumbrian Angles to Christianity. During those early centuries, life was often harsh and violent. For some, the way to avoid violent and cruel transactions in society was to withdraw into a lonely spot, surrounded by Nature, and become a hermit. According to Benedicta Ward in *High King of Heaven*, the Celtic hermit "deliberately chose to live at the limits of existence, a human person containing both heaven and earth." Other Celts gathered together in monastic settlements. These were like small villages where people could pray and work together. Within these communities of faith, men and women could experience a reality "lived on the edge of things, on the very margins of life," according to Timothy Joyce, author of *Celtic Christianity*. Living the simple life, they could avoid the temptations of wealth. At the same time, these communities also became centers of art, education, and charitable work—and yet, even while creating great artistic and intellectual riches, their members were also "poor in spirit." They followed the advice of Saint Comgall of Bangor, who said, "Shun wealth, remain close to the Heavenly King, and be gentle to all people."

The example of these Celtic monastics may seem remote from our time, but their witness still calls to us. Retreating to a hermitage or joining a modern-day version of a monastery may not be an option for most of us—but might we nevertheless find ways to "contain heaven and earth" in our lives? What would "living on the margins" look like in the modern world? Would being "poor in spirit" mean finding ways to step outside our privilege and comfort, in order to identify with those who are "marginalized," those who, for one reason or another, have been pushed off to the edges of our society?

The Community of Aidan and Hilda, a modern neomonastic Celtic community, calls for its members to practice "simplicity, purity, and obedience." Mahatma Gandhi said, "Live simply that others may simply live." In a world where Western nations, particularly the United States, consume far more than their fair share of the planet's resources, "living simply" has environmental as well as spiritual implications. (The Celts would have said that the two cannot be separated—and we would be wise to consider their perspective.)

When Jesus blesses the "poor in spirit," he calls us to consider: How can we pare down our material lives in order to share with others less fortunate? The Celtic monastics found a radical answer that could be lived out in their day. Our twenty-first-century answer will not be the same as theirs. But what *will* it be? How can we live out—in specific, practical ways—Saint Comgall's plea to "shun wealth, remain close to the Heavenly King, and be gentle to all people"?

—Teresa Cross

5

¹ Seeing the crowds, he went up onto the mountain. When he had sat down, his disciples came to him. ² He opened his mouth and taught them, saying, ³ "Blessed are the poor in spirit, for theirs is the Realm of Heaven. ⁴ Blessed are those who mourn, for they shall be comforted. ⁵ Blessed are the gentle, for they shall inherit the earth. ⁶ Blessed are those who hunger and thirst after justice, for they shall be filled. ⁷ Blessed are the merciful, for they shall obtain mercy. ⁸ Blessed are the pure in heart, for they shall see God. ⁹ Blessed are the peacemakers, for they shall be called children of God. ¹⁰ Blessed are those who have been persecuted for righteousness's sake, for theirs is the Realm of Heaven. ¹¹ "Blessed are you when people reproach you, persecute you, and say all kinds of evil against you falsely, for my sake. ¹² Rejoice, and be exceedingly glad, for great is your reward in heaven. For that is how they persecuted the prophets who were before you.

¹³ "You are the salt of the earth, but if the salt has lost its flavor, with what will it be salted? It is then good for nothing, but to be cast out and

trodden under the feet of others. ¹⁴ You are the light of the world. A city located on a hill can't be hidden. ¹⁵ Neither do you light a lamp, and put it under a basket, but on a stand; and it shines to all who are in the house. ¹⁶ Even so, let your light shine before all people; that they may see your good works, and glorify your Abba God who is in heaven.

¹⁷ "Don't think that I came to destroy the law or the prophets. I didn't come to destroy, but to fulfill. ¹⁸ For most certainly, I tell you, until heaven and earth pass away, not even one smallest letter, not one tiny pen stroke, shall in any way pass away from the law, until all things are accomplished. ¹⁹ Whoever, therefore, shall break one of these least commandments, and teach others to do so, shall be called least in the Realm of Heaven; but whoever shall do and teach them shall be called great in the Realm of Heaven. ²⁰ For I tell you that unless your righteousness exceeds that of the scribes and Pharisees, there is no way you will enter into the Realm of Heaven.

²¹ "You have heard that it was said to the ancient ones, 'You shall not murder;' and 'Whoever murders will be in danger of the judgment.' ²² But I tell you, that everyone who is angry with their neighbor will be in danger of the judgment; and whoever says to their neighbor, 'Idiot!' will be in danger of the council; and whoever says, 'You fool!' will be in danger of the fire of Gehenna.

²³ "If therefore you are offering your gift at the altar when you remember that your neighbor has anything against you, ²⁴ leave your gift there before the altar, and go your way. First be reconciled to your neighbor, and then come and offer your gift. ²⁵ Agree with your adversary quickly, while you are together on the way; lest perhaps the prosecutor deliver you to the judge, and the judge deliver you to the officer, and you be cast into prison. ²⁶ Most certainly I tell you, you shall by no means get out of there, until you have paid the last penny.ᵃ

²⁷ "You have heard that it was said, 'You shall not commit adultery;' ²⁸ but I tell you that all who gaze at others with lust have already committed adultery in their heart. ²⁹ If your right eye causes you to stumble, pluck it out and throw it away from you. For it is better for you to lose a body part, than for your whole body to be cast into Gehenna.[b] ³⁰ If your right hand causes you to stumble, cut it off, and throw it away from you. For it is better overall to lose a single body part, than for your whole body to be cast into Gehenna.

³¹ "It was also said, 'Whoever shall put away his wife, let him give her a writing of divorce,' ³² but I tell you that whoever puts away his wife, except for the cause of sexual immorality, makes her an adulteress; and whoever marries her when she is put away commits adultery.

³³ "Again you have heard that it was said to the ancient ones, 'You shall not make false vows, but shall perform to the Eternal One your vows, ³⁴ but I tell you, don't swear at all: neither by heaven, for it is the throne of God; ³⁵ nor by the Earth, for it is the footstool of the Eternal One, nor by Jerusalem, for it is the city of our great Ruler. ³⁶ Neither shall you swear by your head, for you can't make one hair white or black. ³⁷ But let your 'Yes' be 'Yes' and your 'No' be 'No.' Whatever is more than these is of the evil one.

³⁸ "You have heard that it was said, 'An eye for an eye, and a tooth for a tooth.' ³⁹ But I tell you, don't resist those who are evil; but whoever strikes you on your right cheek, turn to them the other also. ⁴⁰ If anyone

sues you to take away your coat, offer your cloak also. ⁴¹ Whoever compels you to go one mile, go with them two. ⁴² Give to those who ask you, and don't turn away those who want to borrow from you.

⁴³ "You have heard that it was said, 'You shall love your neighbor and hate your enemy.' ⁴⁴ But I tell you, love your enemies, bless those who curse you, do good to those who hate you, and pray for those who mistreat you and persecute you, ⁴⁵ that you may be children of your Abba who is in heaven. For God makes the sun to rise on the evil and the good, and sends rain on the just and the unjust. ⁴⁶ For if you love those who love you, what reward do you have? Don't even the tax collectors do the same? ⁴⁷ If you only greet your friends, what more do you do than others? Doesn't everybody do the same? ⁴⁸ Therefore you shall be perfect, just as your Abba in heaven is perfect.

> ᵃ Literally, *kodrantes*, a small copper coin worth about two *lepta* (widow's mites)—not enough to buy very much of anything.
> ᵇ In the Hebrew Bible, Gehenna, the valley of Hinnom adjacent to Jerusalem, was a place where children were sacrificed by fire to Gentile gods (2 Chr. 28:3, 33:6). Thereafter it was considered cursed (Jer. 7:31, 19:2–6). In Jesus' day Gehenna may have been comparable to the city dump. According to author Rob Bell, "There was a fire there, burning constantly to consume the trash," a metaphor for the terrible consequences of rejecting "the good and true and beautiful life that God has for us."

six

In this chapter, the author continues his account of the Sermon on the Mount. He describes Jesus telling his followers that when they do good for others, pray, or fast, they must not do so merely for the sake of being seen, because true love and spiritual practices are their own rewards. Jesus also teaches his followers what we often call the "Lord's Prayer" or the "Our Father," and commands them to freely give their wealth to others, advising against amassing treasure for its own sake. He warns of the dangers of worshipping the acquisition of wealth, speaks about the anxiety that the pursuit of material pleasures causes, and the true fulfillment of the devoted life. Rather than worry about money, fashion, status, external validation for doing good or acting piously, Jesus pushes his followers to consider living lives dedicated to God, to helping and sharing with others.

CHAPTER SIX

▧ THE CELTS AND THE PRAYER THAT JESUS TAUGHT ▧

Seventh- and eighth-century Irish missals show that the prayer Jesus taught (verses 9 through 13 of this chapter) held a central role in Celtic churches' order of worship, a part of every Eucharist celebration and every sacrament. For the Celts—and for many other ancient Christian communities—this prayer summed up in a few short sentences everything that happened during the mass, from the "Sanctus" (where God's holiness is proclaimed) through God's meeting our daily physical needs (in the communion Host), intertwined with the reenactment of Christ's sacrifice (where we are forgiven), alongside the reminder that we not partake of the Lord's Table if we have not forgiven others. Finally, in the words of Nicholas Ayo (author of *The Lord's Prayer: A Survey Theological and Literary*), the final portion of the prayer "yearns for that condition of peace and absence of evil" that increases the experience of "eucharistic communion in one's life and that of the entire human community."

Like Catholic, Protestant, and many Orthodox churches today, the Celts also included at the end of the prayer what's known as an "embolism." Today we usually think of an embolism as being a rather nasty medical crisis—a clot in a blood vessel—but its usage here refers to a short additional prayer that's been inserted at the end of verse 13. The Protestant embolism is this: "For thine is the kingdom, the power, and the glory forever"; the Catholic version begins, "Deliver us, Lord, from every evil, and grant us peace in our day. . . ." We're so accustomed to these prayers that we may forget that Jesus didn't actually conclude his prayer with those extra words.

Early Irish churches' embolism went like this:

Free us, O Lord, from every evil—past, present, and to come—and through the intercessions on our behalf of Your blessed Apostles Peter, Paul, and Patrick, give us life-giving peace in our time, that helped by the strength of Your mercy, we may be always free of misdeeds and safe from all turmoil, through our Lord Jesus Christ Who reigns with You and the Holy Spirit, God throughout all ages of ages.

Why did the Celts (like so many other Christians) feel the need to add these extra words to the prayer that Jesus taught? Perhaps we can get a clue from even older meanings of "embolism." In Greek, an *embolos* was a bottle stopper or something that plugged up a hole; these extra prayer sentences may have worked as a spiritual "stopper," ensuring that the power of Christ's prayer would remain in the Celts' hearts, not leak out and be lost in the tumult of everyday life. The Latin *embolus* gives us an even more dynamic image: the piston in a pump. If the Celts' thought of their embolism in this way, then it may have helped them transfer the power of Christ's prayer into action. It was a reminder that Christ's prayer is not meant to be recited so much as *lived*.

—Ellyn Sanna

CHAPTER SIX

¹ Be careful that you don't do your acts of righteousness where others can see them, or else you have no reward from your Abba who is in heaven. ² Therefore when you do merciful deeds, don't sound a trumpet before yourself, as the hypocrites do in the synagogues and in the streets, that they may get glory from those who witness their deeds. Most certainly I tell you, they have received their reward. ³ But when you do merciful deeds, don't let your left hand know what your right hand does, ⁴ so that your merciful deeds may be in secret. Then your Abba who sees in secret will reward you openly.

⁵ "When you pray, don't be like the hypocrites, for they love to stand and pray in the synagogues and on the street corners, that they may be seen by others. Most certainly, I tell you, they have received their reward. ⁶ But you, when you pray, enter into your inner room, and having shut your door, pray to your Abba who is in secret, and your Abba who sees in secret will reward you openly.

⁷ "In praying, don't use empty repetitions, as others do; for they think that they will be heard simply because they talk so much. ⁸ Don't be like them, for your Abba knows what things you need, before you ask for them.

⁹ "Pray like this: 'Abba in heaven, may your name be kept holy. ¹⁰ Let your Reign come. Let your will be done on earth the same as it is in heaven. ¹¹ Give us today our daily bread. ¹² Forgive us what we owe, as we also forgive those who owe us. ¹³ Bring us not into temptation, but deliver us from the evil one.'

¹⁴ "For if you forgive people their missteps, God your Abba will also forgive you. ¹⁵ But if you don't forgive others when they go astray, neither will Abba forgive you when you do.

¹⁶ "Moreover when you fast, don't be like the hypocrites, wearing sad faces. For they neglect their appearance, so that others will be able to recognize that they are fasting. Most certainly I tell you, they have received their reward. ¹⁷ But you, when you fast, comb your hair and wash your face; ¹⁸ so that no one can tell that you are fasting, only your Abba who is in secret—and your Abba, who sees in secret, will reward you.

¹⁹ "Don't lay up treasures for yourselves on the earth, where moth and rust consume, and where thieves break in and steal; ²⁰ but lay up for yourselves treasures in heaven, where neither moth nor rust consume, and where thieves don't break in and steal; ²¹ for where your treasure is, there your heart will be also.

²² "The lamp of the body is the eye. If therefore your eye is clear, your whole body will be full of light. ²³ But if your eye is evil, your whole body will be full of darkness. If therefore the light that is in you is darkness, how great is the darkness!

²⁴ "People can't serve two rulers, for either they will hate the one and love the other; or else they will be devoted to one and despise the

other. You can't serve God and at the same time put your trust in material wealth. ²⁵ Therefore I tell you, don't be anxious for your life: what you will eat, or what you will drink; nor yet for your body: what you will wear. Isn't life more than food, and the body more than clothing? ²⁶ See the birds of the sky: they don't sow, neither do they reap, nor gather a harvest into barns. Your Abba in heaven feeds them. Aren't you much more valuable than they?

²⁷ "Which of you, by being anxious, can add one moment[a] to your lifespan? ²⁸ And why are you anxious about clothing? Consider the lilies of the field, how they grow. They don't toil, neither do they spin, ²⁹ yet I tell you that even Solomon in all his glory was not dressed like one of these. ³⁰ So if God so clothes the grass of the field, which today exists and tomorrow is thrown into the oven, won't God much more clothe you, you of little faith?

³¹ "Therefore don't be anxious, saying, 'What will we eat?' 'What will we drink?' 'How will we be clothed?' ³² For the rest of the world seeks after all these things; but God your Abba knows that you need these things. ³³ So seek first the Realm of God, and God's righteousness; and all these things will be given to you as well. ³⁴ Therefore don't be anxious for tomorrow, for tomorrow will be anxious for itself. Each day's own evil is sufficient."

[a] Literally, "cubit," an ancient unit of measurement based on the forearm length from the middle fingertip to the end of the elbow.

seven

In this chapter, Jesus tells us that we should refrain from judging others without first considering our own faults and weaknesses; he reminds us that if we judge others, soon the roles may be reversed, and he speaks out against the hypocrisy of criticizing others for having the very faults we ourselves possess. Instead, Jesus tells us, we are to open ourselves up to God and the nourishment of a spiritual life, and he compares God to a loving parent: just as a good parent would feed a hungry child, and just as God gives nourishment to us, each person must treat others in the way they would want to be treated themselves. Jesus warns of people who speak piously or act like good people outwardly but are in actuality adding to the world's woes through action or inaction. Though many may speak in a religious manner and may appear to be good people, not everyone who claims to be righteous is righteous. Those who follow his teachings, Jesus says, will be basing their lives on a solid foundation that will endure throughout hardship, akin to a house built on a rock foundation rather than one built on sand. Then Jesus finishes speaking from the mountain, leaving the crowd astonished by his teachings and powerful messages.

⋈ PSEUDO-CHRISTIANS AND AUTHENTIC LIVING ⋈

In what is commonly known as the "Sermon on the Mount," Jesus speaks about the authenticity of those who will follow him. Today, the world is sometimes confused about how to recognize Christ's followers. Government leaders may claim to be Christians for political reasons. Others have defined Christianity according to a set of external behaviors that draws boundary lines between insiders and outsiders. Both of these create what psychiatrist M. Scott Peck referred to as a "pseudo-community," a group that "attempts to purchase community cheaply by pretense. It is not an evil, conscious pretense of deliberate black lies. . . . But it is still a pretense."

In the fourth century, a Celtic theologian called Morgan, better known by his Latin name Pelagius, spoke about those who were using the name "Christian" to describe themselves but were not actually acting like Christ. In *On the Christian Life*, Morgan wrote, "It is from the sacrament of anointing, both of Christ and of all Christians . . . that the name and term [Christian] have come, which name those people have been wrongly given who imitate Christ hardly at all. How can you be called something which you are not, and falsely take another's name? But if you wish to be a Christian, then do those things that are of Christ and worthily bear the name of Christian."

What, then, are "things that are of Christ"? Jesus tells us the answer in this chapter of Matthew: not judging; treating others the way you wish to be treated; and bearing fruit as a good tree. While many who call themselves Christians today may be sincere in their goal to lead lives based on the Bible, they are overlooking the emphasis Jesus placed on these three things.

Instead of judging others (even those we consider to be pseudo-Christians!), we are to be like loving parents who give whenever they see their children in need. We are to treat others the way we would wish to be treated. And the only criteria we should use for judging are the *results* of others' actions. In other words, if people are bringing love into the world, it doesn't really matter whether they conform to our idea of what a follower of Christ should look like. Do they make the world a better place for others? Do they give of themselves in ways that improve others' lives? If the answer is yes, then they are bearing "good fruit."

Morgan goes on to say, "Perhaps you do not wish to *be* a Christian but only to be called one? Wanting to be something without actually being it is both base and wretched . . . such people are not Christ's servants at all, but rather they mock and deride him; although they declare themselves to be his servants, their service is no more than pretense." Jesus points out the consequence of this in verses 21 through 23.

If we want to attach Christ's name to ourselves, we need to live up to the challenge Jesus gave us in his Sermon on the Mount. To understand how Jesus lived, we must study his life—and then work to reflect his priorities, attitudes, and behaviors in our own lives. We must give ourselves away, just as Jesus did. If we don't want to be guilty of forming pseudo-communities, we must, as Morgan said, imitate Jesus in order to be his authentic followers—living, healthy trees, bearing fruit that nourishes others.

—David Cole

7

¹ Don't judge, so that you won't be judged. ² For with whatever judgment you judge, you will be judged; and with whatever measure you measure, it will be measured to you. ³ Why do you see the speck that is in your neighbor's eye, but don't consider the beam that is in your own eye? ⁴ Or how will you tell your neighbor, 'Let me remove the speck from your eye'; and behold, the beam is in your own eye? ⁵ You hypocrite! First remove the beam out of your own eye, and then you can see clearly to remove the speck out of your neighbor's eye.

⁶ "Don't give that which is holy to the dogs, neither throw your pearls before the pigs, lest perhaps they trample them under their feet, and turn and tear you to pieces.

⁷ "Ask, and it will be given you. Seek, and you will find. Knock, and it will be opened for you. ⁸ For everyone who asks receives. Those who seek, find. To those who knock it will be opened. ⁹ Or who is there among you,

who, if their child asks for bread, will give instead a stone? [10] Or if a child asks for a fish, who will give that child instead a serpent? [11] If you then, being evil, know how to give good gifts to your children, how much more will your Abba who is in heaven give good things to those who ask? [12] Therefore, whatever you desire for others to do to you, you shall also do to them; for this is the law and the prophets.

[13] "Enter in by the narrow gate; for wide is the gate and broad is the way that leads to destruction, and many are those who enter in by it. [14] How narrow is the gate, and restricted is the way that leads to life! Few are those who find it.

[15] "Beware of false prophets, who come to you in sheep's clothing, but inwardly are ravening wolves. [16] By their fruits you will know them. Do you gather grapes from thorns, or figs from thistles? [17] Even so, every good tree produces good fruit; but the corrupt tree produces evil fruit. [18] A good tree can't produce evil fruit, neither can a corrupt tree produce good fruit. [19] Every tree that doesn't grow good fruit is cut down, and thrown into the fire. [20] Therefore, by their fruits you will know them. [21] Not everyone who says to me, 'Exalted One, Exalted One,' will enter into the Realm of Heaven; but those who do the will of my Abba who is in heaven. [22] Many will tell me in that day, 'Exalted One, Exalted One, didn't we prophesy in your name, in your name cast out demons, and in your name do many great things?' [23] Then I will tell them, 'I never knew you. Depart from me, you lawbreakers.'

[24] "Therefore, all who hear these words of mine, and follow them, I will liken to a person of great wisdom who built a house on a rock. [25] The rain came down, the floods came, and the winds blew, and beat on that

house; and it didn't fall, for it was founded on the rock. ²⁶ Everyone who hears these words of mine, and doesn't do them will be like a fool who built a house on the sand. ²⁷ The rain came down, the floods came, and the winds blew, and beat on that house; and it fell—and great was its fall."

²⁸ When Jesus had finished saying these things, the crowds were astonished at his teaching, ²⁹ for he taught them with authority, and not like the scribes.

eight

After Jesus' sermon on the mountainside, Matthew records that he is followed by a crowd of people, one of whom is a leper who asks Jesus to heal him—and Jesus does. In Capernaum, a soldier asks Jesus to heal his paralyzed servant, saying that Jesus only need say that the servant is healed and it will be so, just as the soldier commands those who serve under him. Jesus marvels at the man's conviction and says his servant is healed. Jesus heals Peter's mother-in-law, who is sick with a fever, as well as a group of people said to be possessed by demons (perhaps ill with mysterious diseases). Jesus, seeing crowds of people coming toward him, decides to take a boat to the other side of the sea. He asks his disciples to leave their lives behind to follow him above all others, even their families. They set sail in a boat, only to be beset by a storm that threatens to destroy their craft. Jesus calms the storm, much to the astonishment of his disciples. Upon arriving on the shore, two people possessed by demons block the way for passersby. Jesus casts the demons out, forcing them to join a herd of pigs that then run into the sea. The people of the nearby city are fearful of Jesus and tell him to leave their country.

⋈ POWER OVER EVIL ⋈

If we remember that Matthew, like all authors, juxtaposed his stories in order to make a point, we can identify some common themes in this chapter: some people (the leper and the centurion) respond to Jesus with total confidence, while others, even his own disciples, are afraid. There are also several references to death (verses 22, 25, 32). In this chapter, the author demonstrates Jesus' power over disease, Nature, the forces of evil, and even death.

The Celts were an impetuous people, and after their conversion, they threw themselves headlong into Christianity. They would have identified with the leper and centurion, for their confidence in Divine power was absolute. This early prayer from a Celtic missal (written in the mid-eighth century but likely dating in practice from the mid-seventh century) expresses faith that God will overcome the dominion of evil and death.

> Everlasting God,
> break up the works of Satan;
> burst the chains of failure;
> so that we who have obtained eternal life
> through the Holy Name of Jesus
> may owe nothing to the author of death.

All of us have moments when our own mortality terrifies us, just as the storm frightened the disciples in the boat. At other times, we may be anxious about what Jesus may ask of us, as the people were when he approached their city; like them, we would rather avoid him than be confronted by his challenge to follow his example. In those fearful moments, may we be inspired by the Celts' passionate confidence in the power of God!

—Ellyn Sanna

¹ When he came down from the mountain, great crowds followed him. ² Then a leper came to him and worshiped him, saying, "Great One, if you want to, you can make me clean."

³ Jesus stretched out his hand, and touched the leper, saying, "I want to. Be made clean." Immediately the leper was cleansed. ⁴ Jesus said to the leper, "See that you tell nobody, but go, show yourself to the priests, and offer the gift that Moses commanded, as a testimony to them."

⁵ When he came into Capernaum, a centurion came to him, ⁶ saying, "Sir, my servant lies in the house paralyzed, sadly tormented."

⁷ Jesus replied, "I will come and heal him."

⁸ The centurion answered, "Sir, I'm not worthy for you to come under my roof. Just say the word, and my servant will be healed. ⁹ For I am also under authority, having under myself soldiers. I tell this one, 'Go,'

and he goes; and I tell another, 'Come,' and he comes; and I tell my servant, 'Do this,' and it is done."

[10] When Jesus heard it, he marveled, and said to those who were around him, "Most certainly I tell you, I haven't found so great a faith, not even in Israel. [11] I tell you that many will come from the east and the west, and will sit down with Abraham, Isaac, and Jacob in the Realm of Heaven, [12] but the children of the Realm will be thrown out into the outer darkness. There will be weeping and gnashing of teeth." [13] Jesus said to the centurion, "Go your way. Let it be done for you as you have believed." The centurion's servant was healed in that hour.

[14] When Jesus came into Peter's house, he saw Peter's mother-in-law lying sick with a fever. [15] Jesus touched her hand, and the fever left her. She got up and served him.

[16] When evening came, people brought to Jesus many who were possessed with demons. He cast out the evil spirits with a word, and healed all who were sick; [17] that it might be fulfilled which was spoken through Isaiah the prophet, saying, "The Servant took our infirmities, and bore our diseases." [a]

[18] Now when Jesus saw great crowds around him, he gave the order to depart to the other side of the sea. [19] A scribe came, and said to him, "Teacher, I will follow you wherever you go."

[20] Jesus replied, "The foxes have holes, and the birds of the sky have nests, but the Human One has no dwelling in which to rest."

[21] Another of his disciples said to him, "Rabbi, allow me first to go and bury my parents."

[22] But Jesus answered, "Follow me, and leave the dead to bury their own dead."

[23] When he got into a boat, his disciples followed him. [24] Then a violent storm came up on the sea, so

134 THE GOSPEL OF MATTHEW

CHAPTER EIGHT 135

much that the boat was covered with the waves, but he was asleep. ²⁵ His disciples came to him, and woke him up, saying, "Save us, Great One! We are dying!"

²⁶ He said to them, "Why are you fearful, O you of little faith?" Then he got up, rebuked the wind and the sea, and there was a great calm.

²⁷ They all marveled, saying, "What kind of man is this, that even the wind and the sea obey him?"

²⁸ When he came to the other side, into the country of the Gadarenes, two people possessed by demons met him there, coming out of the tombs, exceedingly fierce, so that nobody could pass that way. ²⁹ They cried out, saying, "What business do we have with you, Jesus, Son of God? Have you come here to torment us before the time?"

³⁰ Now there was a herd of many pigs feeding far away from them. ³¹ The demons begged him, saying, "If you cast us out, permit us to go away into the herd of pigs."

³² He said to them, "Go!"

They came out, and went into the herd of pigs: and behold, the whole herd of pigs rushed down the cliff into the sea, and died in the water. ³³ Those who fed them fled, and went away into the city, and told everything, including what happened to those who were possessed with demons. ³⁴ All the city came out to meet Jesus. When they saw him, they begged him to depart from their borders.

[a] Isaiah 53:4

nine

In this chapter, the author has gathered several stories of Jesus' healing power, allowing us to see the parallels Jesus drew between physical healing and spiritual well-being. In verse 2, when Jesus is asked to heal the young man with paralysis, Jesus' first response is to say, "Your misdeeds have been forgiven." The Greek words used here mean, literally, "Your failures have been driven away. You have been released from them." Jesus then goes on to demonstrate his authority to release the power that our past failures have over us: he also heals the man physically, indicating that physical and spiritual wholeness are interwoven. Later, when asked why he eats with people known to be "sinners," Jesus refers to himself as a physician whose entire mission is to heal the sick (vss. 12–13).

CHAPTER NINE   137

WHAT IS SIN?

In the centuries that have passed since Jesus walked the Earth, our understanding of sin has mutated away from the illness, brokenness, and failure of which Jesus spoke, into moral evil. Dealing with this definition of sin involves not healing but punishment. Although many Christians believe that the grace of Christ will allow believers to escape the ultimate punishment of hellfire, this punitive view of God's reaction to sin has infiltrated our cultural consciousness. In society as a whole, we attempt to use the same methodology for dealing with "sins"—such as drug use, violence, and theft—by making these acts illegal, punishable by law.

The early medieval Celts, however, took another approach to sin, one that was more closely aligned with the attitude Jesus demonstrates in this chapter. Their "penitentials" were texts that gave them precise instructions as to how to respond to all manner of sins, prescribing "remedies congruent with the set of maladies" (in the words of the fourth-century French theologian, John Cassian).

According to Thomas Pollock Oakley in *English Penitential Discipline and Anglo-Saxon Law*, the penitential guides originated in Wales, spread from there first to Ireland and then Britain, and eventually made their way to the Continent. In Walter J. Woods' *Walking with Faith*, he indicates that penitentials were successful at the societal level, because they eventually "helped suppress homicide, personal violence, theft, and other offenses that damaged the community and made the offender a target for revenge."

The earliest Celtic penitential that still exists is *The Penitential of Finnian*, written in the sixth century at Clonard. As Thomas O'Loughlin explains in *Celtic Theology*, "The fifty or more situations envisaged as requiring penance cover the whole range of sins.... To each crime it prescribes a specific 'penitential remedy' of a fixed quantity of prayer, fasting and alms." These penances were understood to be medicinal treatments rather than punishments. They were intended to restore the individual to wholeness and well-being.

The sixth-century British monk Gildas gives this practical penance for an inebriated monk: "If anyone because of drunkenness is unable to sing the Psalms, being stupefied and without speech, he is deprived of dinner." In general, however, the Celtic penitentials focused more on the heart than on external behaviors, as indicated in this passage from *The Penitential of Finnian*:

> If anyone is wrathful or envious or backbiting, gloomy or greedy . . . there is this penance . . . until these [attitudes] are plucked forth and eradicated from our hearts: we shall continue in weeping and tears day and night so long as these things are turned over in our heart. . . . Let us make haste . . . cleanse away the faults from our hearts and introduce virtues in their places. Patience must arise for wrathfulness; kindliness, or the love of God and of one's neighbour, for envy; for gossip, restraint of the heart and tongue; for dejection, spiritual joy; for greed, liberality.

Few modern practitioners of a form of Celtic Christianity would consider consulting the ancient penitential books with reference to theirs and others' shortcomings. But we smug moderns are often too quick to dismiss our ancestors' wisdom. In a world as a large and complex as ours is today, the Celts' exact methodologies are not practical at the societal level—but as a society, we might consider the Celts' challenge to "treat brokenness" rather then "punish crime"; we might seek ways to heal and restore more often than we adjudicate and imprison. Then, having been administered the appropriate "medicine," individuals could resume their place in society with their lives restored.

The Celtic penitentials challenge us at the individual level as well. We are freed to let go of shame over our past failures; we can "take courage" and walk forward into a healthier, fuller life. Then, when we encounter others' failures, we are asked to follow Jesus' example and let our hearts be "moved with compassion" (vs. 36). He calls us to take our place as workers in his "harvest" of healing, actively seeking the wholeness of all (vs. 37).

—Kenneth McIntosh

CHAPTER NINE

9

¹He entered into a boat, and crossed over, and came into his own city. ²And then, they brought to him a man who was paralyzed, lying on a bed. Jesus, seeing their faith, said to the paralytic, "Take courage, child! All your failures have been removed from you. Your misdeeds have been forgiven."

³Then some of the scribes said to themselves, "This man blasphemes."

⁴Jesus, knowing their thoughts, said, "Why do you think evil in your hearts? ⁵For which is easier, to say, 'Your misdeeds are forgiven;' or to say, 'Get up, and walk?' ⁶But that you may know that the Human One has authority on earth to forgive human failures—"

Then he said to the paralytic, "Get up, and take up your mat, and go to your house."

⁷The man arose and departed to his house. ⁸When the crowd saw it, they marveled and glorified God, who had given such authority to mortals.

⁹ As Jesus went on his way, he saw a man called Matthew sitting at the tax collection office. He said to him, "Follow me." Matthew got up and followed him.

¹⁰ As Jesus sat in the house, many tax collectors and wrongdoers came and sat down with Jesus and his disciples. ¹¹ When the Pharisees saw it, they said to his disciples, "Why does your teacher eat with tax collectors and wrongdoers?"

¹² When Jesus heard it, he said to them, "Those who are healthy have no need for a physician, but those who are sick do. ¹³ But you go and learn what this means: 'I desire mercy, and not sacrifice,' [a] for I came not to call the righteous but the wrongdoers."

¹⁴ Then John's disciples came to him, saying, "Why do we and the Pharisees fast often, but your disciples don't fast?"

¹⁵ Jesus said to them, "Can the friends of the bridegroom mourn, as long as the bridegroom is with them? But the days will come when the bridegroom will be taken away from them, and then they will fast. ¹⁶ No one puts a piece of unshrunk cloth on an old garment; for the patch would tear away from the garment, and a larger hole would be made. ¹⁷ Neither do people put new wine into old wineskins, or else the skins would burst, and the wine be spilled, and the skins ruined. No, they put new wine into fresh wineskins, and both are preserved."

¹⁸ While he told these things to them, a ruler came and worshiped him, saying, "My daughter has just died, but come and lay your hand on her, and she will live."

¹⁹ Jesus got up and followed him, as did his disciples. ²⁰ Suddenly a woman who had had a discharge of blood for twelve years came behind him, and touched the fringe of his

garment; ²¹ for she said within herself, "If I just touch his garment, I will be made well."

²² But Jesus, turning around and seeing her, said, "Daughter, take courage! Your faith has made you well." And the woman was made well from that hour.

²³ When Jesus came into the ruler's house, and saw the flute players, and the crowd in noisy disorder, ²⁴ he said to them, "Make room, because the girl isn't dead but sleeping."

At that, they ridiculed him. ²⁵ But when the crowd was put out, he entered, took her by the hand, and the girl arose. ²⁶ The report of this went out into all that land.

²⁷ As Jesus went on from there, two blind men followed him, calling out and saying, "Have mercy on us, Heir of David!"

²⁸ When he had come into the house, the blind men came to him. Jesus said to them, "Do you believe that I am able to do this?"

They told him, "Yes, Sir."

²⁹ Then he touched their eyes, saying, "According to your faith be it done to you." ³⁰ Their eyes were opened. Jesus strictly commanded them, saying, "See that no one knows about this." ³¹ But they went out and spread abroad his fame in all that land.

³² As they went out, a mute man who was demon possessed was brought to him. ³³ When the demon was cast out, the man could speak. The crowds marveled, saying, "Nothing like this has ever been seen in Israel!"

³⁴ But the Pharisees said, "He must be the ruler of the demons, if he casts out demons."

³⁵ Jesus went about all the cities and the villages, teaching in their synagogues, preaching the Good News of the Reign of Heaven, and healing

every disease and every sickness among the people. ³⁶ When he saw the crowds, he was moved with compassion for them, because they were harassed and scattered, like sheep without a shepherd. ³⁷ Then he said to his disciples, "The harvest indeed is plentiful, but the workers are few. ³⁸ Pray therefore that the overseer of the harvest will send out workers into the harvest."

ᵃ Hosea 6:6

Jesus calls together his twelve disciples and gives them the power to heal the sick. Then he sends his disciples out to spread his good news and heal diseases, taking no money or other recompense. Jesus warns them that they may face hardship, scrutiny, even harassment at the hands of those who don't believe in his message. They may be arrested or even offered up to the authorities by family and friends. Though they may face all these trials, including betrayal by those closest to them, Jesus assures them they will be rewarded for persevering. He goes on to explain that he has not come to make the world perfectly peaceful, but instead to push people beyond the comfort of conformity, to make them question received wisdom and see life anew, regardless of what their family, society, or old religion is telling them to believe.

❈ SPIRIT WORDS ❈

All of us have felt nervous at one time or another when we have been called on to speak. In this chapter, Jesus foretells a time when his disciples "will be brought before governors and kings for my sake, for a testimony to them and to the nations" (vs. 18). How's that for daunting? In the next verse, however, he goes on to comfort the disciples by telling them: "But when they deliver you up, don't be anxious how or what you will say, for it will be given you in that hour what you will say."

The life of Saint Patrick illustrates God's Spirit continuing to speak through human lives. After escaping slavery in Ireland, Patrick was called back there to bring the people the Good News of Jesus, because, he wrote, he heard the Spirit praying "in my inner man." Later, he was summoned back to Britain on false charges of heresy. Crushed in his soul, Patrick was saved from despair when he "heard divine revelation" that reassured him he was God's chosen vessel. He returned to Ireland, able to continue his mission because of his experience with the still-speaking Spirit of God.

Patrick's *Confessions* make clear that although the Spirit speaks directly to our souls, God also relies on human mouths and human language. We are called to speak on God's behalf, Patrick wrote, and then he quoted Scriptures to support this statement. "Wisdom is recognized through the tongue, and knowledge and learning by the word of the wise," Patrick quoted from Sirach, and then from Tobit: "It is a matter of honor to reveal and speak the works of God." (Patrick's Bible, like that of all the Celtic saints, contained what we now

CHAPTER TEN

know as the Apocrypha, including the books of Wisdom, Sirach, and Tobit.)

Patrick went on to explain:

> That is why I cannot be silent—nor would it be good to do so—about such great blessings and gifts that the Lord so kindly gave to me in the land of my captivity. This is how we can repay such blessings, when our lives change and we come to know God, to praise and speak out about the great wonders of God.

Patrick also made clear that we should take seriously our ability to speak. God has little use for babbling small talk and gossip; our words must have integrity. Quoting from the Psalms, Patrick wrote, "You destroy those who speak lies" (5:7), from the Book of Wisdom, "A mouth that lies kills the soul" (1:11), and then from a later verse in Matthew, "I tell you that every empty word that people speak, they will one day be called to give account of it" (12:36).

Patrick's *Confessions* indicate the connection between listening to God's voice and being able to speak Divine truth ourselves. He recorded a time in his life when he was once again full of despair—and then was inspired and strengthened by the Spirit's presence in the natural world: "The splendor of the sun fell on me; and immediately, all that weight was lifted from me. I believe that I was helped by Christ the Lord, and that his Spirit cried out for me. I trust that it will be like this whenever I am under stress." Patrick went on to quote from verse 20 in this chapter of Matthew: "It is not you speaking, but the Spirit of your Abba who speaks in you."

After years of slavery, Patrick found courage and identity in his Spirit-given powers of speech. "I was a silent stone," he wrote, "unable to speak, lying squashed in the mud, when the Mighty and Merciful God came, dug me out, and set me on top of the wall. Therefore, I praise him." As we listen to God's voice, speaking to us in Nature, in Scripture, through others, and through our own hearts and minds, we too can find a new, more courageous, and more authentic form of speech. "What I tell you in the darkness," Jesus says in verse 27, "speak in the light; and what you hear whispered in the ear, proclaim on the housetops."

—Kenneth McIntosh

10

¹ He called to himself his twelve disciples, and gave them authority over unclean spirits, to cast them out, and to heal every disease and every sickness.

² Now the names of the twelve apostles are these: the first, Simon, who is called Peter; Andrew, his brother; James the son of Zebedee; John, his brother; ³ Philip; Bartholomew; Thomas; Matthew the tax collector; James the son of Alphaeus; Thaddaeus; ⁴ Simon the Canaanite; and Judas Iscariot, who also betrayed him.

⁵ Jesus sent these twelve out, and commanded them, saying, "Don't go among the Gentiles, and don't enter into any city of the Samaritans. ⁶ Rather, go to the lost sheep of the house of Israel. ⁷ As you go, preach, saying, 'The Reign of Heaven is at hand!' ⁸ Heal the sick, cleanse the lepers, and cast out demons. Freely you received, so freely give. ⁹ Don't take any gold, silver, or brass in your money belts. ¹⁰ Take no bag for your journey, neither two coats, nor shoes, nor staff: for laborers are worthy of their food. ¹¹ Into whatever city or village you enter, find an

appropriate house in which to stay; and stay there until you go on. ¹² As you enter into the household, greet it. ¹³ If the household is worthy, let your peace come on it, but if it isn't worthy, let your peace return to you. ¹⁴ Whoever doesn't receive you nor hear your words, as you go out of that house or that city, shake the dust off your feet. ¹⁵ Most certainly I tell you, it will be more tolerable for the land of Sodom and Gomorrah in the day of judgment than for that city.

¹⁶ "Pay careful attention now, I send you out as sheep among wolves. Therefore be wise as serpents, and harmless as doves. ¹⁷ But beware of others: for they will deliver you up to councils, and in their synagogues they will scourge you. ¹⁸ Yes, and you will be brought before governors and rulers for my sake, for a testimony to them and to the nations. ¹⁹ But when they deliver you up, don't be anxious how or what you will say, for it will be given you in that hour what you will say. ²⁰ For it is not you speaking, but the Breath of your Abba who speaks in you.

²¹ "Brother will deliver up brother to death, and the father his child. Children will rise up against parents, and cause them to be put to death. ²² You will be hated by others for my name's sake, but those who endure to the end will be saved. ²³ But when they persecute you in this city, flee into the next, for most certainly I tell you, you will not have gone through the cities of Israel, until the Human One has come.

²⁴ "Disciples are not above their teachers, nor are servants above their superiors. It is enough for disciples to be like their teachers, and servants like their superiors. If they have called the owner of the house Beelzebul, how much more those of the household! ²⁶ Therefore don't be afraid of them, for there is nothing covered that will not be revealed; and hidden that will not be known. ²⁷ What I tell you in the darkness, speak in the light; and what you

hear whispered in the ear, proclaim on the housetops. ²⁸ Don't be afraid of those who kill the body, but are not able to kill the soul. Rather, fear the one who is able to destroy both soul and body in Gehenna.

²⁹ "Aren't two sparrows sold for a single coin[b]? Not one of these birds falls on the ground apart from your Abba's will, ³⁰ and the very hairs of your head are all numbered. ³¹ Therefore don't be afraid. You are of more value than many sparrows. ³² Everyone therefore who confesses me before others, I will also confess before my Abba who is in heaven. ³³ But whoever denies me before others, I will also deny before my Abba who is in heaven.

³⁴ "Don't think that I came to send peace on the earth. I didn't come to send peace but a sword. ³⁵ For I came to set a man at odds against his father, and a daughter against her mother, and a daughter-in-law against her mother-in-law. ³⁶ People's foes will be those of their own household. ³⁷ Anyone who loves father or mother more than me is not worthy of me; or who loves son or daughter more than me isn't worthy of me. ³⁸ Those who don't take up their crosses and follow after me, are not worthy of me.

³⁹ "Those who seek their life will lose it; and any who lose their life for my sake will find it. ⁴⁰ All who receive you receive me, and all who receive me receive the Eternal One who sent me. ⁴¹ Those who receive a prophet in the name of a prophet will receive a prophet's reward. Those who receive a righteous person in the name of a righteous person will receive a righteous person's reward. ⁴² Whoever gives one of these little ones just a cup of cold water to drink in the name of a disciple, most certainly will in no way lose their reward."

[a] Literally, Lord of the Flies, a Hebrew name for one of the demons of hell.
[b] Literally, *assarion*, approximately the wages of one half hour of agricultural labor.

CHAPTER ELEVEN 153

eleven

After sending his disciples to spread his message, Jesus continues preaching. John the Baptist is in prison, where he hears of Jesus' teachings and sends two of his disciples to find Jesus and ask if he is the messiah whose coming is foretold in the Hebrew scriptures. Jesus sends John's disciples back to him after telling them of his healing and preaching, and he praises John for his faithful life and perseverance. Jesus then criticizes the cities in which he's been speaking and teaching, telling the citizens that more immoral cities would have reacted with greater awe and faith to his miraculous healing of the sick. Jesus praises God, thanking God for showing the hypocrisy of seemingly faithful people to him and his followers. He asks those listening to follow him, learn from him, and let him help them carry their heavy burdens.

BURDENS

In this chapter, Jesus seems to have a harsh edge to his voice as he first complains that people are never satisfied with the messengers

154   THE GOSPEL OF MATTHEW

CHAPTER ELEVEN   155

they're sent (vss. 16–19) and then denounces those who have rejected him (vss. 20–24). Then his tone changes, becomes gentle and loving. In verse 28, he promises to give rest to those who are tired, who work hard, who feel burdened.

We could assume that Jesus was speaking in this chapter to three different groups of people—first, those who are never satisfied; second, those from the various cities who did not accept him and his message; and third, the "good people" who are willing to hear what he has to say. Matthew's account does not make clear whether this is the case, and yet when we read this chapter, we tend to take to heart the promise of rest, identifying ourselves with those listeners, while we separate ourselves from the long-ago people who were in groups one and two. People like to quote verses 28 through 30, finding comfort in Jesus' words, but we seldom hear anyone applying these words to their own lives: "Wisdom is justified by action" (vs. 19) or, "Woe to you" (vs. 21).

As relative newcomers to Matthew's Gospel, the Celts, however, did not skip over Jesus' harsher words while memorizing only his words of comfort, nor did they set themselves apart from Jesus' historical listeners. They took the totality of Jesus' message, integrated it, and applied it to their own lives.

This Celtic prayer (translated from the Lorrha, a seventh- to eighth-century Irish missal) acknowledges that we, like the people of Jesus' day, are hypocrites who often lack self-understanding. We are no better than the people who rejected Christ. In the same breath, however, this prayer also expresses total confidence in God's love, gentleness, and willingness to help us.

You know, O Lord,
all that we commit with our inner thoughts.
We are unafraid to mentally commit

what we would blush to say aloud.
We yield ourselves to You in words only
We deceive ourselves
within our own hearts,
but by our deeds we prove the falseness
of what we say we intend.
Spare us, O Lord; forgive us;
have mercy upon us.
Because my self-understanding is so weak,
call forth, O Lord—
who receives with a gentle heart the words I speak—
from Your own Self
and bestow forgiveness upon us.

The Jesus who denounced the people of his day is the same person who extended to them his offer to help them. He understood that sometimes the greatest burdens we carry are our own arrogance, our hypocrisy, and our failures to be the people we'd like to be—and he promised to lighten our loads.

—Ellyn Sanna

CHAPTER ELEVEN

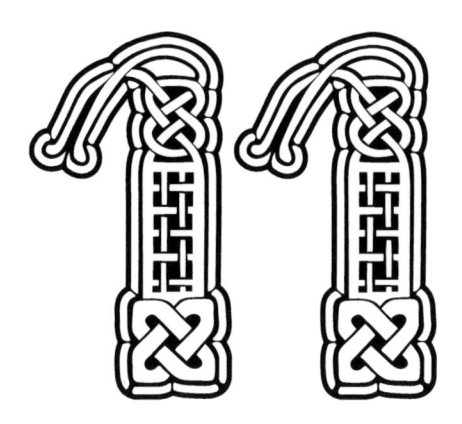

¹ When Jesus had finished giving directions to his twelve disciples, he departed from there to teach and preach in other cities. ² Now when John heard news of this from prison, he sent two of his disciples ³ to ask Jesus, "Are you the One we have been waiting for—or should we look for another?"

⁴ Jesus answered them: "Go and tell John the things which you hear and see: ⁵ the blind receive their sight, the lame walk, the lepers are cleansed, the deaf hear, the dead are raised up, and the poor have good news preached to them. ⁶ Blessed are those who find no occasion for stumbling in me."

⁷ As John's disciples went their way, Jesus began to say to the crowds concerning John, "What did you go out into the wilderness to see? A reed shaken by the wind? ⁸ But what did you go out to see? Someone in soft clothing? But those who wear soft clothing are in rulers' houses. ⁹ But why did you go out? To see a prophet? Yes, I tell you, and much

more than a prophet. ¹⁰ For this is the one, of whom it is written, 'See this, I send my messenger before your face, who will prepare your way before you.' ᵃ ¹¹ Most certainly I tell you, among those who are born of women there has not arisen anyone greater than John the Baptizer; yet those who are least in the Realm of Heaven are greater than he. ¹² From the days of John the Baptizer until now, the Realm of Heaven suffers violence, and the violent plunder it. ¹³ For all the prophets and the law prophesied until John. ¹⁴ If you are willing to receive it, this is Elijah, who is to come. ¹⁵ Those who have ears to hear, let them hear.

¹⁶ "But to what shall I compare this generation? It is like children sitting in the marketplaces, who call to their companions ¹⁷ and say, 'We played the flute for you, and you didn't dance. We mourned for you, and you didn't lament.' ¹⁸ For John came neither eating nor drinking, and they say, 'He has a demon.' ¹⁹ The Human One came eating and drinking, and they say, 'Look at that, a glutton and a drunkard, a friend of tax collectors and wrongdoers!' But wisdom is justified by action."

²⁰ Then Jesus began to denounce the cities in which most of his mighty works had been done, because they didn't change. ²¹ "Woe to you, Chorazin! Woe to you, Bethsaida! For if the mighty works had been done in Tyre and Sidon which were done in you, they would have repented long ago in sackcloth and ashes. ²² But I tell you, it will be more tolerable for Tyre and Sidon on the day of judgment than for you. ²³ You, Capernaum, who are exalted to heaven, you will go down into the realm of the dead. For if the mighty works had been done in Sodom which were done in you, it would have remained until today. ²⁴ But I tell you that it will

be more tolerable for the land of Sodom, on the day of judgment, than for you."

²⁵ At that time, Jesus answered, "I thank you, Abba, Ruler of Heaven and Earth, that you hid these things from those who are clever and educated, and reveal them to children. ²⁶ Yes, Abba, for this was your kind intention. ²⁷ All things have been given to me by my Abba. No one recognizes the Son, except Abba God, and no one recognizes Abba God, except the Son and those to whom the Son has chosen to reveal Abba.

²⁸ "Come to me, all you who labor and are heavily burdened, and I will give you rest. ²⁹ Take my yoke upon you, and learn from me, for I am gentle and humble in heart; and you will find rest for your souls. ³⁰ For my yoke is easy, and my burden is light."

[a] Malachi 3:1

twelve

In this chapter, the author indicates that the conflict between Jesus and the religious authorities is intensifying. When they question his right to pick grain and heal on the Sabbath. Jesus explains to them that he is the "Ruler of the Sabbath," and then indicates he does not support a legalist view. The Pharisees also accuse Jesus of working with Satan. He questions their logic, and says that his healing is instead evidence of the coming of the Realm of God. In this chapter, Jesus again reinforces his message that we can judge people only by the fruits their lives produce, rather than holding them up to any legalistic standard. When the Pharisees then ask to see a sign of Jesus' power, he refuses, saying the only sign they will have is his own resurrection after three days, comparing it to the three days Jonah was trapped in the belly of the whale. While Jesus speaks to the crowd, his mother and siblings are listening outside, hoping to talk with him. Jesus responds by gesturing to his followers, saying that they are his family, that in fact anyone who follows God is Jesus' true family.

CHAPTER TWELVE

WHAT SHALL WE MAKE OF THE SABBATH?

In Exodus 20:8, God commanded that the Sabbath be kept as a holy day of rest. The meaning of that commandment has plagued those in the Judeo-Christian traditions for centuries. Is the Sabbath a day of restriction or of celebration? Many later forms of Christianity came to emphasize restriction, turning the Sabbath into a day when nothing "frivolous"—including children's games—was allowed. "There is probably no worse way of keeping the Lord's Day than the old-fashioned Calvinistic way, under whose yoke groaned suffering childhood," wrote a contributor to *The Scottish Guardian* in 1872.

In this chapter of Matthew's Gospel, the author frames the Sabbath question as a polemical dispute between Jesus and a group of religious leaders. The Pharisees first complain that Jesus' disciples are eating grain from a field, saying they are "harvesting" (doing work) on the Sabbath. These legalistic leaders then accuse Jesus of again breaking the Sabbath by healing a man's hand. Jesus' answer to their criticisms is this: "It is lawful to do good on the Sabbath Day?" (vs. 12). He makes clear that what God wants from us is "mercy and not sacrifice" (vs. 7). In the Gospel of Mark's account of this incident, Jesus says that the Sabbath was made to meet human needs, rather than humans made to meet the requirements of the Sabbath (2:27).

By the nineteenth century, the stern formal religion of Scotland had lost any sense of the Sabbath being intended to benefit human beings. The earliest Celtic Christians, however, were closer to the original meaning of Sabbath as a day of rest. Their cultural understanding that time is a sacred circle, with each season, each day, and even each hour having sacramental meaning, meant that the Sabbath would intuitively have made sense to them.

With their affinity for Jewish practices, the Celts observed Saturday (the seventh day) as the Sabbath, rather then Sunday (the day Jesus rose from the dead). According to medievalists A. O. and M. O. Anderson, *Adomnan's Life of Columba*, written by an abbot of Iona, indicates that in both Columba's day (the sixth century) and Adomnan's (the seventh century), the Sabbath (Saturday) was observed as a day of rest, while the "Lord's Day" (Sunday) was a day for community-wide worship. By the ninth century, however, there were contrasting beliefs on this matter, and as the Roman church came into prominence in the British Isles, the Sabbath and the Lord's Day were conflated.

The day of the week considered to be the Sabbath is less important, however, than what the Sabbath is understood to be. Medieval Celts had varying perspectives. One text, "The Law of Sunday," enumerated strict penalties to be doled out to those who performed ordinary work on Sunday. In contrast to this, an Irish preaching text titled "The Lord's Day" provided a long list of the wonderful works of God, from the Hebrew scriptures up to the author's time, which God performed on this special day. Rather than a dour experience, Sundays for this author were a day to connect with the extravagant generosity of God.

In the centuries since then, Christians have continued to have various concepts of the Sabbath, some healthy and joyful, some less so. Nowadays, with our busy lives structured around the demands of work

CHAPTER TWELVE

and family, we are unlikely to distinguish any day as being sacred.

Discarding the old Sunday traditions seems to make sense given the demands of modern life. We might want to reconsider, though, what we have lost. If we were to reclaim the earliest Celtic understanding of the Sabbath, it might be akin to what modern-day Jewish author Tracey Rich describes as the Orthodox perspective:

> It is a precious gift from G-d, a day of great joy eagerly awaited throughout the week, a time when we can set aside all of our weekday concerns and devote ourselves to higher pursuits . . . a day of rest and spiritual enrichment.

How might we reclaim a sense of Sabbath in the modern world? What if we decided to speak only gratitude on Sundays and made a conscious effort to refrain from complaints of any sort? Or perhaps we could set aside one day a week to disconnect from all electronic screens, both big and small. Could our Sundays become sacred time to write poems, draw pictures, and make music that reflect God's splendorous works? What would rest our souls—and draw us closer to the Creator?

Translated from the Gaelic Lorrha Missal, which would have been used during Sabbath worship, this ninth-century prayer challenges us to create positive Sabbath experiences—spaces of time where we make room in our hearts and lives for God's love and blessing.

> O God Who did prepare unseen good things
> for those who are devoted to You,
> send forth an attitude of love into our hearts,
> that we may follow You in all things,
> and above all things pursue Your promises,
> which are so attentive to our needs,

> surpassing all our expectations.
> Through our Lord Jesus Christ
> Who reigns with You and the Holy Spirit
> throughout all divisions of time.

May we gain a new sense of the Sabbath as a time that strengthens us to do the will of our Abba here on earth, so that we too will be the mothers, fathers, sisters, and brothers of Jesus (vs. 50).

—Kenneth McIntosh

12

¹ At that time, Jesus went on the Sabbath day through the grain fields. His disciples were hungry and began to pluck heads of grain and to eat. ² But the Pharisees, when they saw it, said to him, "Look at that, your disciples do what is not lawful to do on the Sabbath."

³ But he said to them, "Haven't you read what David did, when he was hungry, and those who were with him; ⁴ how he entered into God's house, and ate the showbread, which was not lawful for him to eat, neither for those who were with him, but only for the priests? [a] ⁵ Or have you not read in the law, that on the Sabbath day, the priests in the temple profane the Sabbath, and are guiltless? ⁶ But I tell you that one greater than the temple is here. ⁷ But if you had known what this means, 'I desire mercy, and not sacrifice,' [b] you wouldn't have condemned the guiltless. ⁸ For the Human One is Ruler of the Sabbath."

⁹ He departed there, and went into their synagogue. ¹⁰ And behold there was a man with a withered hand. They asked him, "Is it lawful to

heal on the Sabbath day?" that they might accuse him.

¹¹ He said to them, "Who is there among you, who has one sheep, and if this one falls into a pit on the Sabbath day, won't that person grab on to it, and lift it out? ¹² Of how much more value then is a person than a sheep! Therefore, it is lawful to do good on the Sabbath day." ¹³ Then he told the man, "Stretch out your hand." He stretched it out; and it was restored whole, just like the other. ¹⁴ But the Pharisees went out, and conspired against him, how they might destroy him.

¹⁵ Jesus, perceiving that, withdrew from there. Great crowds followed him; and he healed them all, ¹⁶ and commanded them that they should not make him known: ¹⁷ that it might be fulfilled which was spoken through Isaiah the prophet, saying,

> ¹⁸ "Pay attention to my servant whom I have chosen;
> my beloved in whom my soul is well pleased:
> I will put my Breath on him.
> He will proclaim justice to the nations.
> ¹⁹ He will not strive, nor shout;
> neither will anyone hear his voice in the streets.
> ²⁰ He won't break a bruised reed.
> He won't quench a smoking flax,
> until he leads justice to victory.
> ²¹ In his name, the nations will hope." ᶜ

²² Then one possessed by a demon, blind and mute, was brought to him and he healed him, so that the blind and mute man both spoke and saw. ²³ All the crowd were amazed, and said, "Can this be the promised heir of David?" ²⁴ But when the Pharisees heard it, they said, "This man does not cast out demons, except by Beelzebub, the ruler of the demons.

²⁵ Knowing their thoughts, Jesus said to them, "Every empire divided against itself is brought to desolation, and every city or house divided against itself will not stand. ²⁶ If Satan casts out Satan, the dominion of the evil one is divided against itself. How then will Satan's dominion stand? ²⁷ If I by Beelzebub cast out demons, by whom do your children cast them out? Therefore they will be your judges. ²⁸ But if I by the Breath of God cast out demons, then the Dominion of God has come upon you. ²⁹ Or how can thieves break in and plunder a house unless they first subdue and bind the people inside?

³⁰ "Those who are not with me are against me, and those who don't gather with me will be scattered. ³¹ Therefore I tell you, every failure and double-talk will be forgiven, but double-talking about the Breath of God will not be forgiven. ³² Whoever speaks a word against the Human One it will be forgiven, but whoever speaks against the Holy Breath, it will not be forgiven; neither in this age, nor in that which is to come.

³³ "Either make the tree good, and its fruit good, or make the tree corrupt, and its fruit corrupt; for the tree is known by its fruit. ³⁴ You offspring of vipers, how can you, being evil, speak good things? For out of the abundance of the heart, the mouth speaks. ³⁵ Good people out of their good nature bring out good things, and evildoers out of the evil nature of their heart bring out evil things. ³⁶ I tell you that every empty word that people speak, they will one day be called to give account of it. ³⁷ For by your words you will be justified, and by your words you will be condemned."

³⁸ Then certain of the scribes and Pharisees answered, "Teacher, we want to see a sign from you."

³⁹ But he answered them, "An evil and adulterous generation seeks after a sign, but no sign

will be given to it but the sign of Jonah the prophet. ⁴⁰ For as Jonah was three days and three nights in the belly of the whale, so will the Human One be three days and three nights in the heart of the earth. ⁴¹ The people of Nineveh will stand up in the judgment with this generation, and will condemn it, for they changed their ways at the preaching of Jonah; and behold, someone greater than Jonah is here. ⁴² The ruler of the south will rise up in the judgment with this generation, and will condemn it, for that ruler came from the ends of the earth to hear the wisdom of Solomon; and behold, someone greater than Solomon is here.

⁴³ When an unclean spirit has gone out of someone, they pass through waterless places, seeking rest and cannot find it. Then they say, 'I will return to my house from which I came out,' and when they come back, they find it empty, swept, and put in order. Then they return and bring with them seven other spirits more evil then they are, and enter in and dwell there, and that person's last state becomes worse than the first. Even so will it be also to this evil generation."

⁴⁶ While he was yet speaking to the crowds, behold, his mother and his brothers stood outside, seeking to speak to him. ⁴⁷ One said to him, "Look, your mother and your brothers stand outside, seeking to speak to you."

⁴⁸ But he answered, "Who is my mother? Who are my siblings?" ⁴⁹ He stretched out his hand towards his disciples, and said, "Observe my mother and my siblings! ⁵⁰ For whoever does the will of my Abba who is in heaven, is my brother, and sister, and mother."

ᵃ 1 Samuel 21:3–6
ᵇ Hosea 6:6
ᶜ Isaiah 42:1–4

CHAPTER THIRTEEN

thirteen

One day a group gathers as Jesus sits near the sea, so he gets into a boat to speak to the crowd on the shore. He tells the group a number of parables, stories with deep meaning he wishes to impart to the people. When questioned as to why he speaks to his followers in stories, Jesus explains that stories hold a power to convey truths difficult to perceive by normal means. Jesus continues to speak to his followers in images and stories, and when he is finished, he returns to Nazareth to teach in the city's synagogue, to the shock and amazement of the people, who cannot understand how a man from his ordinary background can have so many truths to share. When the people take offense at Jesus' teachings, Jesus remarks that a prophet cannot be understood and accepted by the people from his home.

MYSTICAL MEANINGS IN SECRET STORIES

Storytelling has been an intrinsic aspect of humanity since it began. Ever since we could communicate, we have been telling stories to one another. Ancient civilizations had stories as part of their identities, and different civilizations told similar stories slightly differently to distinguish them from their neighbors. This included the Babylonians' Epic of Gilgamesh (c. 2100 BCE), and the Jewish stories we find in the Hebrew scriptures from a similar time. Many of the greatest spiritual teachers through the ages have used storytelling as a way of getting across deep and sometimes almost unfathomable truths. Every culture and spirituality has its stories. We still feel the appeal of a good story, although these days we are more likely to find our stories in movie theatres, on television, or in novels.

Jesus used allegory and illustrations from real life to express and expand his message. The parables that he told, such as the ones in this chapter, are as important to his teaching as anything else he said. This chapter holds eight different stories that Jesus told to enable us to understand what the Reign of Heaven is like.

Celtic nations had these stories too, and stories of heroes and warriors were important to their folklore. The eighth-century historian Bede tells in *The Ecclesiastical History of the English People* of the ancient Celtic tradition of the "Passing of the Harp," where communities would gather in the mead hall, or other communal space, and tell stories through the evenings around a fire, with food and drink flowing. This tradition was continued in the Celtic monastic communities, such as the one in Whitby, where Bede makes mention of it.

The first person to write Bible stories in the English language was Cædmon, who is the main character in Bede's expansion of the Passing of the Harp tradition. Cædmon had divine dreams of Scripture, which he wrote in the common language of the Angles (the first Angle-ish dialect), bringing Bible stories to life. This is what storytelling is all about—connecting deep truths with ordinary lives to make those lives extraordinary.

The medium of storytelling may have changed over the years from the oral tradition with the Passing of the Harp, to reading books, and on to making feature films and television programs, but the art of storytelling is within our DNA; it is a part of who we are. Stories help us to fathom out who we are and our place in the greater scheme of things; they enable us to learn from our past so that we can better step into the future; they allow us to be inspired by people who came before us through hero sagas, allegory, and true-life accounts.

The Celts have always understood the powerful properties of stories to speak hidden truths. For them, stories were sacred, capable of revealing God to us in new and surprising ways, and Jesus used parables in the same way. As he quoted from the prophet Isaiah, through stories, we hear "things hidden from the foundation of the world" (vs. 35), so that we might perceive with our eyes, hear with our ears, understand with our hearts, and turn again to God to be healed.

—David Cole

13

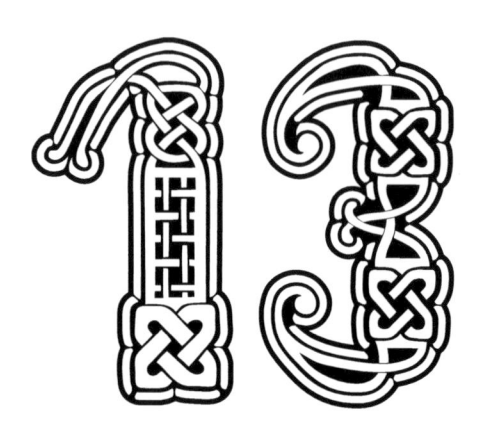

¹ On that day Jesus went out of the house, and sat by the seaside. ² Great crowds gathered around him, so he boarded a boat, where he sat while the crowd stood on the beach. ³ He spoke to them many things in parables, saying, "Pay close attention now, a farmer went out to sow. ⁴ As the farmer sowed, some seeds fell by the roadside, and the birds came and devoured them. ⁵ Others fell on rocky ground, where they didn't have much soil, and immediately they sprang up, because they had no depth of earth. ⁶ When the sun had risen, they were scorched. Because they had no root, they withered away. ⁷ Others fell among thorns. The thorns grew up and choked them. ⁸ Others fell on good soil, and yielded fruit: some one hundred times as much, some sixty, and some thirty. ⁹ "Those who have ears to hear, let them hear."

¹⁰ The disciples came, and said to him, "Why do you speak to them in parables?"

[11] He answered them, "To you it is given to know the mysteries of the Reign of Heaven, but it is not given to them. [12] For whoever has, to them will be given, and they will have abundance, but whoever doesn't have, from them will be taken away even that which they have. [13] Therefore I speak to them in parables, because though they can't see, they will see, and though they can't hear, they will hear, neither do they understand. [14] In them the prophecy of Isaiah is fulfilled, which says,

'You will hear,
but you will not understand;
You will see,
but you will not perceive:
[15] for this people's heart has grown callous,
their ears are dull of hearing,
they have closed their eyes;
or else perhaps they might perceive with their eyes,
hear with their ears,
understand with their heart,
and would turn again;
and I would heal them.' [a]

[16] "But blessed are your eyes, for they see; and your ears, for they hear. [17] For most certainly I tell you that many prophets and righteous people desired to see the things that you see, and didn't see them; and to hear the things that you hear, and didn't hear them.

[18] "Hear, then, the parable of the farmer. [19] When anyone hears the word of the Reign of Heaven and doesn't understand it, the evil one comes, and snatches away that which has been sown in their heart. This

is what was sown by the roadside. ²⁰ What was sown on the rocky places, these are the ones who hear the message of the Reign of Heaven, and immediately with joy receive it; ²¹ yet have no root in themselves, but they endure for a while. When oppression or persecution arises because of the message of the Reign, immediately they stumble. ²² What was sown among the thorns, these are the ones who hear the word, but the cares of this age and the deceitfulness of riches choke the message of the Reign, and they become unfruitful. ²³ What was sown on the good ground, these are the ones who hear the message of the Reign and understand it, who most certainly bear fruit and produce, some one hundred times as much, some sixty, and some thirty."

²⁴ He set another parable before them, saying, "The Reign of Heaven is like someone who sowed good seed in a field, ²⁵ but while people slept, an enemy came and sowed darnel weeds[b] also among the wheat and went away. ²⁶ But when the blades sprang up and produced fruit, then the darnel weeds appeared also. ²⁷ The servants came and said to the householder, 'Sir, didn't you sow good seed in your field? Where did these darnel weeds come from?'

²⁸ "The householder said to them, 'An enemy has done this.'

"The servants asked, the householder, 'Do you want us to go and gather them up?'

²⁹ "But the householder said, 'No, since while you gather up the darnel weeds, you might uproot the wheat with them. ³⁰ Let both grow together until the harvest, and in the harvest time I will tell the reapers, "First, gather up the darnel weeds, and bind them in bundles to burn them; but gather the wheat into my barn."'"

³¹ He set another parable before them, saying, "The Reign of Heaven is like a grain of mustard seed, which someone took and sowed in a field; ³² which indeed is smaller than all seeds. But when it is grown, it is

greater than the other garden plants and becomes a tree, so that the birds of the air come and lodge in its branches."

³³ He spoke another parable to them: "The Reign of Heaven is like yeast, which was hidden in three measures[c] of meal, until it was all leavened."

³⁴ Jesus spoke all these things in parables to the crowds; and without a parable, he didn't speak to them, ³⁵ that it might be fulfilled which was spoken through the prophet, saying,

"I will open my mouth in parables;
I will utter things hidden from the foundation of the world." [d]

³⁶ Then Jesus sent the crowds away, and went into the house. His disciples came to him, saying, "Explain to us the parable of the darnel weeds of the field."

³⁷ He answered them, "The one who sows the good seed is the Human One, ³⁸ the field is the world; and the good seed are the children of the Realm of Heaven; and the darnel weeds are the children of the evil one. ³⁹ The enemy who sowed them is the devil. The harvest is the end of the age, and the reapers are angels. ⁴⁰ As therefore the darnel weeds are gathered up and burned with fire; so will it be at the end of this age. ⁴¹ The Human One will send forth the angels, and they will gather out of the Realm of Heaven all things that cause stumbling and those who do evil, ⁴² and will cast them into the furnace of fire. There will be weeping and the gnashing of teeth. ⁴³ Then the righteous will shine like the sun in the Realm of their Abba. Those who have ears to hear, let them hear.

⁴⁴ "Again, the Realm of Heaven is like treasure found hidden in a field. In joy, the one who found it sold all and purchased that field.

⁴⁵ "Again, the Realm of Heaven is like a merchant seeking fine pearls, ⁴⁶ who having found one pearl of great price, went and sold all he had and purchased it.

⁴⁷ "Again, the Realm of Heaven is like a dragnet, that was cast into the sea, and gathered everything in its way, ⁴⁸ which, when it was filled, they drew up on the beach. They sat down and gathered what was useful into containers, but the useless things they threw away. ⁴⁹ So will it be when this time span has been accomplished. The angels will come and separate the worthless from among the righteous, ⁵⁰ and will cast them into the furnace of fire. There will be the weeping and the gnashing of teeth."

⁵¹ Jesus said to them, "Have you understood all these things?"

They answered him, "Yes, Sir."

⁵² He said to them, "Therefore every scribe who has been made a disciple in the Heavenly Realm is like a householder, bringing out of treasure both old and new things."

⁵³ When Jesus had finished these parables, he departed from there. ⁵⁴ Coming into his own country, he taught them in their synagogue, so that they were astonished, and said, "Where did this man get this wisdom, and these mighty works? ⁵⁵ Isn't this the carpenter's son? Isn't his mother called Mary, and his brothers, James, Joses, Simon, and Judah? ⁵⁶ Aren't all of his sisters with us? Where then did this man get all of these things?" ⁵⁷ They were offended by him.

But Jesus said to them, "A prophet is not without honor, except in his own country, and in his own house." ⁵⁸ He didn't do many mighty works there because of their unbelief.

    ᵃ Isaiah 6:9–10
    ᵇ Darnel is a weed grass that looks very much like wheat until it is mature, when the difference becomes very apparent.
    ᶜ Literally, three sata, which is about 39 liters or a bit more than a bushel
    ᵈ Psalm 78:2

fourteen

In this chapter, Matthew gives us the story of Herod and his relationship with his brother's wife, Herodias. On Herod's birthday, Herodias' daughter dances for Herod, pleasing the king so much that he offers to bring the girl anything she wishes. She asks for John's head on a platter and Herod, though hesitant to execute a man whom many believe to be a prophet, complies. Jesus hears of John's death and leaves on a boat to be alone, but when a crowd follows him, he feels compassion for them and heals the sick among them. When night falls, Jesus' disciples tell him to send the crowd away so the people can get something to eat in town. Jesus then miraculously feeds the multitude from five fishes and three loaves. After he dismisses the crowd, he sends his disciples in the boat across the sea and leaves by himself to pray on the mountainside. Later, a storm arises, and Jesus walks across the water to his disciples. Seeing him, the disciples are afraid, but Jesus calls out to them, reassuring them—and then calls Peter to walk on the water as well.

CHAPTER FOURTEEN

THE OTHERWORLD

The miracles Jesus performs in this chapter may strain our modern credulity. The Celts, however, were quite comfortable with stories of the impossible being possible. They lived in a world where the Otherworld was so interwoven with this world that nothing surprised them. Another reality could easily overlap with everyday reality, causing all sorts of strange things to happen.

In the old stories, Celtic saints perform miracles with a matter-of-fact air, as though these feats are a normal part of life. Brigid, for example, regularly multiplied milk, butter, bread, and ham for the benefit of the hungry; Saint Abban walked on water to prove to his mentor, Saint Ibar, that he was ready to go on pilgrimage; and Columba spoke often with angels. Many of these miraculous acts benefited someone in need but not always. Brigid, the story goes, was once observed hanging her cloak on a shaft of sunlight, as though in the reality where she moved, light was as substantial as a coat rack. We can imagine Brigid coming in from the outdoors, so busy with some household task that when she takes off her cloak, she absent-mindedly hooks it over the nearest thing available. This utilitarian miracle served no purpose other than convenience.

But what is significant about these miracles is that they were retold again and again, indicating that they meant something important to the Christian Celts. The same is true of Jesus' miracles. Matthew recorded them for a reason: they held meaning for the story he was telling about Jesus. For Matthew—as for the Celts—miracles were signs, pointing toward something deeper than the surface circumstances.

The miracle itself was not as important as what that event said about the individuals involved. Jesus' miracles paralleled the stories in the Hebrew scriptures of Moses, Abraham, and Elijah, indicating to his followers that he was indeed the Chosen One they had been promised. The Celtic Christians' miracle stories served a similar purpose:

CHAPTER FOURTEEN

they indicated that their saints shared both the power of Jesus and the compassion of Jesus. Just as Jesus' miracles aligned him with an ancient tradition, turning a familiar belief system into a living, breathing reality, the Celtic saints' miracles joined them with Jesus, proving that he was alive and real in their lives.

What do these stories—both Jesus' and the Celtic saints'—say to us as modern readers? If we focus on the meaning of these events rather than the events themselves, we can step away from questions as to whether these stories are *factual* and instead look at the *truths* they convey. They tell us that Jesus has the power to meet our needs, even when our resources seem far too scarce (vss. 19–21). They say that he can empower us to do what we never believed we could, even when all circumstances indicate that we are in mortal peril (vss. 29–31). And they promise that Jesus requires no elaborate formal ceremony or specific action on our part; all we need to do to be whole is to touch even the "fringe" of his garment (vss. 35–36).

Modern-day quantum physicists tell us that reality is not what we see, and other dimensions are not mere fantasies. We may not believe that cloaks can hang from sunbeams—but the scientific nature of light is just as mysterious, just as radically amazing, existing as both "particles" and "waves," with its reality dependent in part upon our perceptions. Recently, scientists at Harvard, Princeton, and MIT have even found that light can indeed become a solid (upon which it would be actually possible to hang a cloak).

The Celtic Christians, however, did not waste their time being amazed, incredulous, or frightened by glimpses into another reality. For them, that wasn't the point. Instead, like the author of Matthew, they were more concerned with the message coming to them from the Otherworld, a message that said, in effect: "Things may look bad—but there's more going on here behind the scenes than you can perceive. You don't need to be afraid. There's another world, a world you can't see, and it's at work in the world you do see, in ways you can't really understand." Ultimately, the message of all these stories (both in the Gospel account and in the Celtic traditions) is summed up by these words of Jesus: "Take courage" (vs. 27).

The prayer that follows, attributed to Saint Columba, expresses the Celts' confidence in Divine care:

> Alone with none but You, my God,
> I journey on my way.
> What need I fear when You are near,
> O Ruler of night and day?
> More safe am I within Your hand
> than if a host should round me stand.
> My life I yield to Your decree,
> and bow to Your control in peaceful calm,
> for from Your arm
> no power can wrest my soul.
> The child of God can fear no ill,
> God's chosen dread no foe;
> we leave our fate with You,
> and wait Your bidding when to go.
> It's not from chance our comfort springs.
> You are our trust, O King of kings.

When we feel oppressed by the world's darkness rising around us, we too can take comfort and be grateful for the same assurance that Jesus called to his frightened disciples: "Don't worry, I'm here—even in this place where you'd least expect to see me. I have things under control in ways you can't understand right now. Don't be scared."

—Ellyn Sanna

14

¹ At that time, Herod the tetrarch[a] heard the report concerning Jesus, ² and said to his servants, "This is John the Baptizer. He is risen from the dead. That is why these powers work in him." ³ For Herod had captured John, and bound him, and put him in prison for the sake of Herodias, his brother Philip's wife. ⁴ For John said to him, "It is not lawful for you to have her." ⁵ When Herod would have put John to death, he feared the crowd, because they thought of John as a prophet. ⁶ But when Herod's birthday came, the daughter of Herodias danced among them and pleased Herod. ⁷ Whereupon he promised with an oath to give her whatever she should ask. ⁸ She, being prompted by her mother, said, "Give me here on a platter the head of John the Baptizer."

⁹ The king was grieved, but for the sake of his oaths and of those who sat at the table with him, he commanded it to be given, ¹⁰ and he sent and

CHAPTER FOURTEEN ☨ 185

beheaded John in the prison. ¹¹ His head was brought on a platter and given to the young woman; and she brought it to her mother.

¹² John's disciples came and took the body, and buried it; and they went and told Jesus. ¹³ Now when Jesus heard this, he withdrew from there in a boat, to a deserted place to be alone. When the crowds heard it, they followed him on foot from the cities.

¹⁴ Jesus went out, and he saw a great crowd. He had compassion on them and healed their sick. ¹⁵ When evening had come, his disciples came to him, saying, "This place is deserted, and the hour is already late. Send the crowds away, that they may go into the villages and buy themselves food."

¹⁶ But Jesus said to them, "They don't need to go away. You give them something to eat."

¹⁷ They told him, "We only have here five loaves and two fish."

¹⁸ He said, "Bring them here to me." ¹⁹ He commanded the crowds to sit down on the grass; and he took the five loaves and the two fish, and looking up to heaven, he blessed, broke, and gave the loaves to the disciples, and the disciples gave them to the crowds. ²⁰ All who were there ate and were satisfied. They gathered up twelve baskets full of that which remained left over from the broken pieces. ²¹ Those who ate were about five thousand men, in addition to women and children.

²² Immediately, Jesus made the disciples get into the boat, to go ahead of him to the other side, while he sent the crowds away. ²³ After he had sent the crowds away, he went up into the mountain by himself to pray. When evening had come, he was there alone. ²⁴ But the boat was now in the middle of the sea, distressed by the waves, for the wind was contrary. ²⁵ In the fourth watch of the night,[b] Jesus came to them, walking on the sea. ²⁶ When the disciples saw him walking on the sea, they were upset, saying, "It's a ghost!" and they cried out in fear. ²⁷ But immediately Jesus spoke to them, saying, "Take courage! It's me![c] Don't be afraid."

²⁸ Peter answered him and said, "Great One, if it is you, command me to come to you on the waters."

²⁹ Jesus said, "Come!"

Peter stepped down from the boat, and walked on the waters to come to Jesus. ³⁰ But when he saw that the wind was strong, he was afraid and beginning to sink, he cried out, saying, "Great One, save me!"

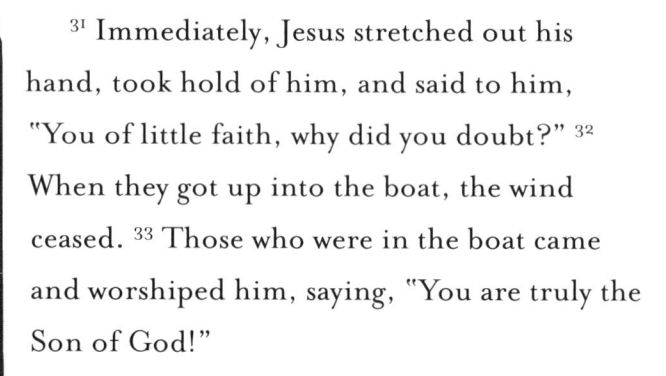

³¹ Immediately, Jesus stretched out his hand, took hold of him, and said to him, "You of little faith, why did you doubt?" ³² When they got up into the boat, the wind ceased. ³³ Those who were in the boat came and worshiped him, saying, "You are truly the Son of God!"

³⁴ When they had crossed over, they came to the land of Gennesaret. ³⁵ When the people of that place recognized him, they sent into all the surrounding region and brought to him all who were sick; ³⁶ and they begged him that they might just touch the fringe of his garment. Everyone who touched it were made whole.

ᵃ A tetrarch ruled over a fourth of a region, making him a similar to a governor.
ᵇ The night was equally divided into four watches, so the fourth watch is approximately 3:00 a.m. to sunrise.
ᶜ Or, "I AM!" the same words that God spoke to Moses (Exodus 3:14).

fifteen

The Pharisees come to Jesus and ask why his disciples disregard traditional customs. Jesus retorts that the Pharisees are following tradition over God. He asks them if they understand that their traditions are in contradiction of the commandments from the Hebrew scriptures, and he accuses them of hypocrisy, of saying one thing and doing another. The Pharisees are offended that Jesus' disciples eat without washing their hands, but Jesus disregards the criticism, explaining that what people say is much more reflective of what they think and believe, reflective of their true selves. Jesus compares the Pharisees to the blind guiding the blind unknowingly to ruin, and he continues to work miracles of healing.

Matthew also describes in this chapter yet another occasion when Jesus miraculously feeds a crowd of thousands of people. Sounding like a good hostess who's concerned for her guests' well-being, Jesus doesn't want to send his listeners home hungry, and so he and the disciples find food for them all. Bible scholars speculate that there may have actually been two miraculous feeding incidents—one in this chapter and one in chapter 14—or that the story is told twice for symbolic reasons.

A TWOFOLD MEANING

If we go with the symbolic interpretation for the double stories, it works like this: In the first miraculous feeding in Matthew chapter 14, where Jesus and his disciples are in a Jewish region, the twelve leftover baskets represent Divine sustenance to the Jews' twelve tribes. The miracle that takes place now in chapter 15, however, is slightly different. It occurs in a "Gentile" area, and this time there are seven leftover baskets rather than twelve. In the Bible, the number seven symbolizes wholeness—Divine fullness and totality—perhaps indicating that Jesus' Good News is for all peoples, bringing us all to the completion that God intends.

Like the people in Bible times, the Pagan Celts believed that numerals could convey deep spiritual wisdom, and the number seven also had a special significance for them. In Irish mythology, the hero Cuchulain has seven fingers on each hand, seven toes on each foot, and seven pupils in each eye. The number seven recurs again and again throughout his story, as well as in other Celtic myths, including tales of King Arthur. For the Pagan Celts, seven was a sign pointing to the Otherworld, a place with seven doors and seven levels, indicating that Cuchulain (and other Celtic heroes) gained their power from their connection to another reality. In *Shakespeare and the Stars*, Priscilla Costello explains that the medieval mind, building on this and other ancient traditions, continued to associate the number seven with that which is outside the visible, everyday world. All this meant that when the Celts read the story in chapter 16 of Matthew's account of the Good News, they would have immediately grasped a symbolic meaning that escapes us modern readers. They would have understood that the number seven was not coincidental; it pointed their attention to another world.

Because of Jesus' compassion (vs. 32), he broke and blessed the seven loaves, then gave then to the disciples to give to the people (vs. 36). Then every single person in that huge crowd ate and was satisfied, and there were seven baskets left over (vs. 37). In *The Celtic Way of Prayer*, Esther De Waal describes the importance that Celtic Christians, up through the early twentieth century, placed on this story. References to it recur in many Celtic blessings, stressing that God is the "Great Giver of the Open Hand."

As modern readers, when we read these stories of miraculous feeding, we are likely to see a reassuring symbolism that speaks to us of God's ability to meet our needs, to multiply our meager resources so that we have enough. The Christian Celts also read this meaning into the story, but unlike us, they focused on the disciples' role as well. For them, the story had a twofold meaning, speaking of Otherworldly providence while equally emphasizing that humans are to do their share in this Divine work. "The good of the loaves and fishes," says one blessing, "as God divided them. . . . Good fortune from the King who made the division, on our share and on our co-division."

According to De Waal, the Celts saw the Gospel story as a lesson about our role as co-workers with God. As followers of Jesus, they believed, it is our job to do the practical legwork, carrying Divine nourishment out into the world. Hospitality—sharing physical food with hungry people—takes on spiritual meaning. Ordinary manual jobs—earning a living, planting and harvesting crops, cooking, making butter, sewing clothes—are all "baskets" that Jesus shares, allowing us to participate in the work of Creation. Earthly work gains new significance, because it is the means by which we participate in blessing our world, bringing the miraculous and bountiful Otherworld into everyday physical reality.

We are nourished—and we are meant to nourish others. Both are deeply spiritual acts. De Waal offers a traditional Celtic blessing that indicates this double perspective:

> Bless, O Lord, the food we are about to eat,
> and we pray you, O God,
> may it be good for our body and our soul,
> and if there are any poor creatures hungry or thirsty
> walking the roads, may God send them in to us
> so that we can share the good with them—
> just as God shares with all of us.

We who have been fed from the Otherworld are now called to use our physical and mental strength to actively engage in bringing abundance into this world. Just as he did with his disciples, Jesus has given us food to share.

—Ellyn Sanna

CHAPTER FIFTEEN

[1] Then Pharisees and scribes came to Jesus from Jerusalem, saying, [2] "Why do your disciples disobey the tradition of the elders? For they don't wash their hands when they eat bread."

[3] He answered them, "Why do you also disobey the commandment of God because of your tradition? [4] For God commanded, 'Honor your father and your mother,' and, 'Those who speak evil of father or mother, let them be put to death.' [5] But you say, 'Whoever may tell their father or mother, "Whatever help you might otherwise have gotten from me is a gift devoted to God," [6] they shall not honor their father or mother.' You have made the commandment of God void because of your tradition. [7] You hypocrites! Well did Isaiah prophesy of you, saying:

[8] "'These people draw near to me with their mouth,
and honor me with their lips;

> but their heart is far from me.
> ⁹ And in vain do they worship me,
> teaching as doctrine rules made by people.'" ᵃ

¹⁰ He summoned the crowd, and said to them, "Hear, and understand. ¹¹ That which enters into the mouth doesn't defile the person; but that which proceeds out of the mouth, this defiles the person."

¹² Then the disciples came, and said to him, "Do you know that the Pharisees were offended when they heard this saying?"

¹³ But he answered, "Every plant which God my Abba didn't plant will be uprooted. ¹⁴ Leave them alone. They are blind guides of the blind. If the blind guide the blind, both will fall into a pit."

¹⁵ Peter said to him, "Explain the parable to us."

¹⁶ So Jesus said, "Do you also still not understand? ¹⁷ Don't you understand that whatever goes into the mouth passes into the belly, and then out of the body? ¹⁸ But the things that proceed out of the mouth come out of the heart, and they defile the person. ¹⁹ For out of the heart come evil thoughts, murders, adulteries, sexual immorality, thefts, false testimony, and blasphemies. ²⁰ These are the things that defile people; but to eat with unwashed hands doesn't defile them."

²¹ Jesus went out from there, and withdrew into the region of Tyre and Sidon. ²² Suddenly a Canaanite woman came out from those borders, and cried out, saying, "Have mercy on me, Sovereign One, heir of David! My daughter is severely possessed by a demon!"

²³ But Jesus answered her not a word.

His disciples came and begged him, saying, "Send her away; for she cries after us."

²⁴ But he answered, "I wasn't sent to anyone but the lost sheep of the house of Israel."

²⁵ But she came and worshiped him, saying, "Great One, help me."

²⁶ But he answered, "It is not appropriate to take the children's bread and throw it to the dogs."

²⁷ But she said, "Yes, Sir, but even the dogs eat the crumbs that fall from their owner's table."

²⁸ Then Jesus answered her, "Woman, great is your faith! Be it done to you even as you desire." And her daughter was healed from that hour.

²⁹ Jesus departed from there, and came near to the sea of Galilee; and he went up into the mountain, and sat there. ³⁰ Great crowds came to him, having with them the lame, blind, mute, maimed, and many others, and they put them down at his feet. He healed them, ³¹ so that the crowd wondered when they saw the mute speaking, the injured healed, the lame walking, and the blind seeing—and they glorified the God of Israel.

³² Jesus summoned his disciples and said, "I have compassion on the crowd, because they continue with me now three days and have nothing to eat. I don't want to send them away fasting, or they might faint on the way."

³³ The disciples said to him, "Where should we get so many loaves in a deserted place as to satisfy so great a crowd?"

³⁴ Jesus said to them, "How many loaves do you have?"

They said, "Seven, and a few small fish."

³⁵ He commanded the crowd to sit down on the ground; ³⁶ and he took the seven loaves and the fish. He gave thanks and broke them, and

gave to the disciples, and the disciples to the crowds. ³⁷ They all ate, and were filled. They took up seven baskets full of the broken pieces that were left over. ³⁸ Those who ate were four thousand men, in addition to women and children. ³⁹ Then he sent away the crowds, got into the boat, and came into the borders of Magdala.

ᵃ Isaiah 29:13

sixteen

In this chapter, Jesus again runs into conflict with the religious leaders of his day. He also continues his use of bread as an analogy for the spiritual world, and he refers back to his feeding miracles in chapters 14 and 15. Then Jesus asks his disciples who the people believe him to be, and then what they themselves believe. When Peter says he believes Jesus to be God's Chosen One, Jesus praises Peter's faith and tells his disciples that this faith will be the foundation of those who follow him. He goes on to explain that he will go to Jerusalem and face persecution and death at the hands of the authorities of the time, but he will return from the dead after three days. When Peter protests, Jesus pushes back, explaining that Peter's denial of the truth is not God's perspective. Jesus calls his disciples to sacrifice their lives in order to follow him.

⋈ BEARING THE CROSS FOR CREATION ⋈

Early Celtic Christians interpreted Jesus' call to "take up the cross" (vs. 24) in practical ways that we may find overly literal. Irish monks would often pray with their arms straight out from their sides in the shape of a cross, sometimes praying for hours in this uncomfortable pose atop a windswept hill or in the waters of a lake or stream. This was known as the Cross-Vigil, a practice that the monks believed allowed them to obey Jesus' challenge in verse 24. For us, this seems like an extreme interpretation, but the Celtic saints were enacting the Gospel with their physical bodies.

One day, the story goes, as Saint Kevin was praying the Cross-Vigil in his cell, with his arms outstretched and a hand resting on the windowsill, a blackbird perched on his palm and then began constructing

CHAPTER SIXTEEN　　　197

her nest there. Kevin held perfectly still while she finished her nest and settled down to lay her eggs. Kevin was so filled with tenderness for the bird, we are told, that he remained immobile, his hand outstretched, until the eggs hatched and the nestlings ventured forth. This event is memorialized by a stone sculpture of Kevin and the blackbird beside the stone foundation of his cell at Glendalough, the lovely lake-filled Irish valley where Kevin built his monastic community so he could be close to the plants and animals he loved.

Mary Low, in the book *Celts and Christians*, points out that the story of Kevin and the blackbird turns Christ's call to take up the cross in a direction few Christians today consider, linking it "with positive, considerate relationships towards other creatures, and the rest of the natural world." She goes on to say that Kevin, arms upraised in Cross-Vigil, is "Christ crucified" for the sake of a nonhuman neighbor.

Modern Christianity is accustomed to applying Jesus' teaching in the final verses of this chapter from a spiritual perspective. The Celts, however, made no division between the spiritual and the physical worlds—and as a result, Jesus' words were seen to have far-reaching, physical implications. Like most indigenous peoples, the Celts knew that human life and the well-being of the natural world cannot be separated. The physical and spiritual worlds do not exist in two boxes, allowing us to set one aside whenever we choose to concentrate on the other. What Jesus calls us to do in one must be done in both.

In light of our current reality, where humankind has caused so much suffering and extinction to our planet's creatures, what might it mean if we were to heed Christ's call to "take up the cross" and live sacrificially for all those around us, human and otherwise? Would we be willing to inconvenience ourselves, as Kevin did? Could we conserve resources on behalf of the natural world, foregoing certain products and accepting restrictions of comforts to which we have become accustomed?

If we are not willing to do these things, we may find that the questions Jesus asks have an all-too-real meaning in the physical world: "For what does it profit those who gain the whole world, and forfeit their lives? Or what will someone give in exchange for life?" (vs. 26). We are not being "overly literal" if we make the connection that our physical well-being means we will have to make changes in our lifestyle; we cannot continue to act as though human life can be separated from the planet's.

When Jesus calls us to start focusing "on that which comes from of God," rather than seeing our world purely in the light of "human desire" (vs. 27), he challenges us to think and act differently—to allow ourselves to be changed spiritually in ways that will have radical implications for our physical lives.

Are we willing to listen?

—Kenneth McIntosh

16

¹ The Pharisees and Sadducees came, and testing him, asked him to show them a sign from heaven. ² But he answered them, "When it is evening, you say, 'It will be fair weather, for the sky is red.' ³ In the morning, 'It will be foul weather today, for the sky is red and threatening.' Hypocrites! You know how to discern the appearance of the sky, but you can't discern the signs of the times! ⁴ An evil and adulterous generation seeks after a sign, and there will be no sign given to it, except the sign of the prophet Jonah."

He left them, and departed. ⁵ The disciples came to the other side and had forgotten to take bread. ⁶ Jesus said to them, "Take heed and beware of the yeast of the Pharisees and Sadducees."

⁷ They reasoned among themselves, saying, "We brought no bread."

⁸ Jesus, perceiving it, said, "Why do you reason among yourselves, you of little faith, 'because you have brought no bread?' ⁹ Don't you

yet perceive, neither remember the five loaves for the five thousand, and how many baskets you took up? ¹⁰ Nor the seven loaves for the four thousand, and how many baskets you took up? ¹¹ How is it that you don't perceive that I didn't speak to you concerning bread? But beware of the yeast of the Pharisees and Sadducees."

¹² Then they understood that he didn't tell them to beware of the yeast of bread, but of the teaching of the Pharisees and Sadducees.

¹³ Now when Jesus came into the parts of Caesarea Philippi,ᵃ he asked his disciples, saying, "Who do people say that I—the Human One—am?"

¹⁴ They said, "Some say John the Baptizer, some, Elijah, and others, Jeremiah, or one of the prophets."

¹⁵ He said to them, "But who do you say that I am?"

¹⁶ Simon Peter answered, "You are the Chosen One of God."

¹⁷ Jesus answered him, "Blessed are you, Simon Bar Jonah, for flesh and blood has not revealed this to you, but my Abba who is in heaven. ¹⁸ I also tell you that you are Peter,ᵇ and on this rockᶜ I will build my assembly, and the gates of Hadesᵈ will not prevail against it. ¹⁹ I will give to you the keys of the Dominion of Heaven, and whatever you bind on earth will have been bound in heaven; and whatever you release on earth will have been released in heaven." ²⁰ Then he commanded the disciples that they should tell no one that he was Jesus the Christ.

²¹ From that time, Jesus began to show his disciples that he must go to Jerusalem and suffer many things from the elders, chief priests, and scribes, and be killed, and the third day be raised up. ²² Peter took him aside,

and began to rebuke him, saying, "Far be it from you, Great One! This will never be done to you."

²³ But he turned and said to Peter, "Get behind me, Satan! You are a stumbling block to me, for you are not setting your mind on that which comes from of God, but on that which comes from human desire." ²⁴ Then Jesus said to his disciples, "If any wish to come after me, let them deny themselves, and take up their cross, and follow me. ²⁵ For whoever wishes to save their life will lose it, and whoever will lose their life for my sake will find it. ²⁶ For what does it profit those who gain the whole world, and forfeit their lives? Or what will someone give in exchange for life? ²⁷ For the Human One will come in the glory of his Abba, and with the angels, and will render to everyone according to their deeds. ²⁸ Most certainly I tell you, there are some standing here who will in no way taste of death, until they see the Human One coming into his dominion."

 a Caesarea Philippi was in the northeast section of Israel (in what is now called the Golan Heights). There is a massive wall of rock there (about 100 feet tall and 500 feet wide) that may have been why the word "rock" was on Jesus' mind in verse 18.
 b Peter's name, *Petros* in Greek, is the word for a specific rock or stone.
 c Greek *petra* means a rock mass (like that found at Caesarea Philippi) or bedrock.
 d The Greek word *Hades* was a proper noun that meant literally "the unseen place," referring to the invisible realm in which all the dead reside. It was not a reference to what we think of as "hell," but rather the present dwelling place of all those who have departed this life. The word could also be used metaphorically, in the same way that we might say, "I went through hell," to describe terrible and painful circumstances.

seventeen

Jesus takes Peter, James, and John up a mountain where he seems to glow with white light. Matthew's author describes Moses and Elijah talking with Jesus, while Peter is so impressed that he asks if Jesus wants them to erect three tents, one each for Jesus, Moses, and Elijah. Then the three disciples hear a voice saying that Jesus is the Son of God and that they should listen to him. This strikes fear into them, but Jesus reassures them.

Afterward, Jesus enters the crowd that has been waiting for him, and a man asks Jesus to heal his ailing son. Jesus explains that faith is so powerful that a tiny amount can enable the seemingly impossible. Jesus then speaks about the suffering he will experience in Jerusalem, how he will die, and when he will return. Finally, in this chapter Jesus and his disciples deal with taxes.

CHAPTER SEVENTEEN ☫ 203

⋈ NATURE AND THE LIGHT OF GOD ⋈

In *Will-of-the-Land,* author Jay Hansford C. West describes the Celts' religious tradition (both Pagan and Christian versions) as "Nature Awe," a deeply sacramental perception of sun and sky, tree and earth, bird and beast, which perceived the natural world as "alive with a creative life force." Coming from this perspective, the Celts would have read this chapter of Matthew from an angle that we may miss.

In verses 1 through 5, the disciples see Jesus changed into a being of light. Unlike the disciples, who were terrified, the Celts may not have been surprised as they encountered this story for the first time. Their Pagan gods and goddesses were often creatures of light—but even more than that, the Celts perceived the sun itself, that which gives light to our planet, as a Divine image. While Roman Christianity considered this to be a Pagan perspective, this understanding continued to shape and inform the Celts' concept of God, even after their conversion to Christianity.

The *Carmina Gadelica,* a collection of traditional Celtic prayers collected by Alexander Carmichael in the nineteenth century, contains this prayer that connects the revelation of God with the sun's light:

> The eye of the great God
> The eye of the God of glory
> The eye of the King of hosts
> The eye of the King of the living
> Pouring upon us
> At each time and season
> Pouring upon us
> Gently and generously
> Glory to thee
> Thou Glorious Sun

> Glory to thee, thou Sun
> Face of the God of Life.

Carmichael described an old man he interviewed who made a practice of standing in the light of the rising sun while saying this prayer. For him, this was a sacramental act that allowed the worshipper to experience the transformation of light, just as Jesus did in this chapter.

Later in this chapter (vs. 20), Jesus uses two objects from Nature—a seed and a mountain—to illustrate the life of faith. This metaphor would have been particularly meaningful to Celtic Christians, who always had sharp eyes for perceiving God's image in the natural world, as indicated by yet another prayer from the *Carmina Gadelica*:

> There is no plant in the ground
> but is full of God's virtue.
> There is no shape on the shore
> but it is full of God's blessing.
> There is no life in the sea,
> there is not a creature in the river,
> there is nothing in the firmament
> but proclaims God's goodness.

How might we, like Christ, be transformed if we too opened ourselves to God's revelation in sunlight, in plants, in sea and sky?

—Ellyn Sanna

CHAPTER SEVENTEEN

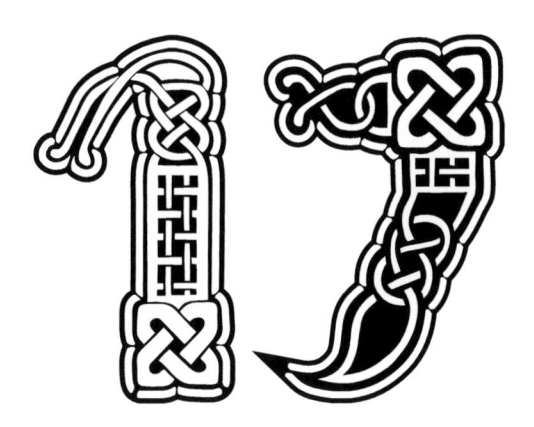

¹ After six days, Jesus took with him Peter, James, and John his brother, and brought them up into a high mountain by themselves. ² He was transformed before them. His face shone like the sun, and his clothes became as white as the light. ³ And look! Moses and Elijah appeared to them talking with him.

⁴ Peter said to Jesus, "Great One, it is a beautiful thing for us to be here. If you want, let's make three tents[a] here: one for you, one for Moses, and one for Elijah."

⁵ While he was still speaking, a bright cloud enveloped them. And then a voice came out of the cloud, saying, "This is my beloved Son, in whom I am well pleased. Listen to him."

⁶ When the disciples heard it, they fell on their faces and were very afraid. ⁷ Jesus came and touched them and said, "Get up, and don't be afraid." ⁸ Raising their eyes, they saw no one, except Jesus alone. ⁹ As they

were coming down from the mountain, Jesus commanded them, saying, "Don't tell anyone what you saw, until the Human One has risen from the dead."

¹⁰ His disciples asked him, saying, "Then why do the scribes say that Elijah must come first?"

¹¹ Jesus answered them, "Elijah indeed comes first, and will restore all things, ¹² but I tell you that Elijah has come already, and they didn't recognize him but did to him whatever they wanted to. Even so the Human One will also suffer by them." ¹³ Then the disciples understood that he spoke to them of John the Baptizer.

¹⁴ When they came to the crowd, a man came to him, kneeling down to him and saying, ¹⁵ "Great One, have mercy on my son, for he is epileptic, and suffers grievously; for he often falls into the fire and often into the water. ¹⁶ So I brought him to your disciples, and they could not cure him."

¹⁷ Jesus answered, "Unbelieving and distorted generation! How long will I be with you? How long will put up with you? Bring him here to me." ¹⁸ Jesus rebuked the demon, which left the boy, and he was cured from then on.

¹⁹ Then the disciples came to Jesus privately and said, "Why weren't we able to cast it out?"

²⁰ He said to them, "Because of your unbelief. For most certainly I tell you, if you have faith as a grain of mustard seed, you will tell this mountain, 'Move from here to there,' and it will move; and nothing will be impossible for you."

²² While they were staying in Galilee, Jesus said to them, "The Human One is about to be delivered up into the hands of the assembly, ²³ and

they will kill him, and on the third day he will be raised up." They were deeply distressed.

²⁴ When they had come to Capernaum, those who collected the tax came to Peter, and said, "Doesn't your teacher pay taxes?" ²⁵ Peter said, "Yes."

When he came into the house, Jesus anticipated him, saying, "What do you think, Simon? From whom do the rulers of the earth receive toll or tribute? From their children, or from strangers?"

²⁶ Peter said to him, "From strangers."

Jesus said to him, "Therefore the children are exempt. ²⁷ But, lest we cause them to stumble, go to the sea, cast a hook, and take up the first fish that comes up. When you have opened its mouth, you will find a coin. Take that, and give it to them for me and you."

> ᵃ Peter may be thinking here of the small tents built during the Jewish Feast of Tabernacles.

eighteen

In this chapter, Matthew describes several incidents where Jesus focuses on both wrongdoing and forgiveness. First, when the disciples ask Jesus about who is considered to be the greatest in the Realm of Heaven, he calls over a child, saying that the child exemplifies the humility and simplicity of heaven. Jesus goes on to say that anyone who leads a child astray faces serious consequences, and he then explains that God is like a shepherd who will leave his flock to find one missing sheep, equating wandering sheep with children who have gone astray.

Jesus next outlines how people should handle disagreements, emphasizing the importance of rebuilding the relationship if at all possible. He also indicates the importance of the community as a stabilizing force for relationships.

Finally, when Peter asks how many times he should forgive a person who has wronged him, Jesus says "seventy times seven," making it clear that forgiveness shouldn't be viewed as finite or quantifiable.

CHAPTER EIGHTEEN

Jesus explains, via a parable, that failure to forgive, particularly in light of God's infinite forgiveness, is an especially grave transgression.

⋈ FORGIVENESS ⋈

Filmmaker Michael Moore commented once: "I think that there's something in the American psyche, it's almost this kind of right or privilege, this sense of entitlement, to resolve our conflicts with violence. There's an arrogance to that concept if you think about it. To actually have to sit down and talk, to listen, to compromise, that's hard work." We may not all resort to physical violence, but the pattern of going from disagreement to bitter dispute is a common one, rooted in our egoic need to have our own way. Self-righteous indignation makes us resist compromise; we feel justified in committing a violence of the soul that refuses to listen to another perspective.

The fiery Celts were as prone to this as we are today. Even Saint Columba, often considered to be the greatest of the Celtic saints, was famous for "violent distempers." His life shows that our greatest loves—our most passionate ego attachments—can sometimes lead to our most bitter altercations. The nineteenth-century historian Count Montalembert, who drew his account from seventh-century documents, writes that Columba's passion for reading was so great that he "went everywhere in search of volumes which he could borrow or copy; often experiencing refusals which he resented bitterly"—and Columba didn't always accept no for an answer.

While visiting the Abbot Finian, Columba clandestinely copied a psalter. What resulted may have been the first copyright battle. Finian was outraged when he discovered what Columba had done, and the abbot claimed the copy also belonged to him, on the grounds that a copy made without permission ought to belong to the master of the original, since the transcription is the "son" of the original book. Columba refused to give up his work, and the question was referred to the king—who sided with Finian, pronouncing, "To every cow its calf." From there, the disagreement escalated even further. Columba went home and "immediately set to work to excite against King Diarmid the numerous and powerful clans of his relatives and friends. . . . His efforts were crowned with success," and Columba and his clansmen marched into a battle where blood was shed and lives were lost.

Clearly, despite Columba's passion for Scripture, he failed to apply the directions Jesus gives in this chapter for dealing with conflict (vss. 15–17). Nor was this an isolated incident in his life. "His excitable and vindictive character," writes Montalembert, "and above all his passionate attachment to his relatives, and the violent part which he took in their domestic disputes and their continually recurring rivalries, had engaged him in other struggles, . . . which also ended in bloody battles."

The Celtic church, like other branches of ancient Christianity, had a formalized way of handling disputes, which followed Jesus' dictates in verse 17 of this chapter: to take the matter to a meeting of the community—what they referred to as a "synod." The Greek word used in verse 17 is often translated as "assembly," and the word "synod" came from yet another Greek term meaning the same thing. Synods were meetings to settle disagreements over doctrine—and to hand out discipline, as did the synod that convened to deal with Columba's anger and violence.

In verse 17, Jesus says that if no reconciliation can be reached through a meeting of the community, the offending individual should no longer be considered to be a part of that community. This course of action may seem harsh or extreme from our modern perspective, but Jesus was showing a way in which to set healthy boundaries to protect against destructive individuals unwilling to change their ways. This was precisely the course of action that the sixth-century synod took in response to Columba's actions: they exiled him from the Irish church and sent him to Scotland.

The order in which Matthew tells his story in this chapter of his Gospel, however, frames Christ's severe recommendation on each side with other comments about forgiveness and the restoration of relationship, indicating the overall message Matthew wants us to hear Jesus saying. Forgiveness brings healing, both between individuals and between God and ourselves. Columba's life exemplifies this restoration.

While living out the rest of his life in exile, Columba built a Christian community on the island of Iona, which he used as a base to evangelize throughout all of Scotland. Montalembert writes:

> This man, whom we have seen so passionate, so irritable, so warlike and vindictive, became little by little the most gentle, the humblest, the most tender of friends and fathers. It was he, the great head of the Caledonian Church, who, kneeling before the strangers who came to Iona, or before the monks returning from their work, took off their shoes, washed their feet, and after having washed them, respectfully kissed them. But charity was still stronger than humility in that trans-

figured soul. No necessity, spiritual or temporal, found him indifferent. He devoted himself to the solace of all infirmities, all misery and pain, weeping often over those who did not weep for themselves.

In verse 11, Jesus says, "The Human One came to rescue those who were utterly destroyed." In the life of Columba we see that Divine love not only forgives our violence and anger; it also rescues us from the destruction we have wrought upon our own selves—and restores our lives to usefulness and meaning. In doing so, God's infinite forgiveness demands that we too set no limits on our willingness to work for reconciliation and peace.

—Teresa Cross

18

¹ In that hour the disciples came to Jesus, saying, "Who then is greatest in the Realm of Heaven?"

² Jesus called a little child to himself, and set the child in the middle of them, ³ and said, "Most certainly I tell you, unless you turn around and become as little children, you will in no way enter into the Realm of Heaven. ⁴ Those who humble themselves therefore as this little child, they are the greatest in the Realm of Heaven. ⁵ Whoever receives one such little child in my name receives me, ⁶ but those who cause one of these little ones who believe in me to stumble, it would be better for them if a huge millstone were hung around their neck, and that they were sunk in the depths of the sea.

⁷ "Woe to the world because of snares that cause stumbling! For such snares are inevitable, but woe to the person through whom the snare comes! ⁸ If your hand or your foot causes you to stumble, cut it off and

cast it from you. It is better for you to enter into life maimed or crippled, rather than having two hands or two feet to be cast into an age of fire. ⁹ If your eye causes you to stumble, pluck it out, and cast it from you. It is better for you to enter into life with one eye, rather than having two eyes to be cast into the fires of destruction. ¹⁰ See that you don't despise one of these little ones, for I tell you that in heaven their angels always see the face of my Abba who is in heaven. ¹¹ For the Human One came to rescue those who were utterly destroyed.

¹² "What do you think? If someone has one hundred sheep, and one of them goes astray, doesn't that person leave the ninety-nine, go to the mountains, and seek the one that wandered away? ¹³ If the sheep is found, most certainly I tell you, it will cause more rejoicing than the ninety-nine that did not wander away. ¹⁴ Even so it is not the will of your Abba who is in heaven that one of these little ones should be destroyed.

¹⁵ "If your brother does wrong to you, go and show him his fault in private, just between the two of you. If he listens to you, you have gained back your brother. ¹⁶ But if he doesn't listen, take one or two others with you, so that from the mouth of two or three witnesses every fact may be confirmed. ¹⁷ If he refuses to listen to them, take the matter to a meeting of the community. If he also refuses to listen to the community, let that person be to you as a foreigner or a tax collector. ¹⁸ Most certainly I tell you, whatever things you bind on earth will have been bound in heaven, and whatever things you set

loose on earth will have been released in heaven. [19] Again, assuredly I tell you, that if two of you will agree on earth concerning anything that they will ask, it will be done for them by my Abba who is in heaven. [20] For where two or three are gathered together in my name, there I am in the middle of them."

[21] Then Peter came and said to him, "Sir, how often shall someone do me wrong, and I forgive them? Up to seven times?"

[22] Jesus said to him, "I don't tell you until seven times, but, until seventy times seven.[a] [23] Therefore the Realm of Heaven is like a certain ruler who wanted to reconcile accounts with all the servants. [24] While the accounts were being reconciled, one servant was brought forward who owed the ruler ten thousand measurements of silver.[b] [25] When the ruler learned that the servant was unable to pay the amount owed, the ruler ordered that the servant, his wife, and his children, and all that he owned be sold to recover the debt. [26] Upon hearing this, the servant fell down and knelt before the ruler, saying, 'Great One, have patience with me and I will repay all that I owe!' [27] The ruler, being moved with compassion, released the servant and forgave the debt.

[28] "But this servant, upon being released, went out and found a fellow servant who owed him one hundred small coins,[c] and grabbed that servant by the throat, saying, 'Pay me what you owe!' [29] So the servant fell down at his feet and begged him, saying, 'Have patience with me and I will repay you!' [30] But the servant whose own debt had just been forgiven, refused to show mercy and had that servant cast into prison until all that was due should be paid back. [31] When the other servants saw what had happened, they were deeply grieved, and they went and told the ruler all that had happened. [32] The ruler had the servant Brought forward and said to him, 'You wicked servant! I forgave you all your debt because you pleaded with me. [33] Shouldn't you also have shown mercy to your fellow

servant, even as I showed mercy to you?' ³⁴ Then the ruler had the servant seized and cast into prison until the debt should be repaid in full. ³⁵ So my Abba will also do to you, if you don't each forgive your neighbors from your heart for their misdeeds."

> ᵃ In many ancient cultures, the number seven signified completeness and perfection. As a figure of speech, it was often used in order to be emphatic. Peter's question indicates that he understands that forgiveness should not be limited, but Jesus' reply goes even further—he is emphatically emphatic. Jesus' teaching style often made use of hyperbole (overstatement to make a point).
> ᵇ Literally, 10,000 (about 300 metric tons of silver), which represented an extremely large sum of money, equivalent to about 60,000,000 denarii. One denarius was typical for one day's wages for agricultural labor.
> ᶜ Literally, 100 denarii, which was about one-sixtieth of a talent, or about 500 grams (1.1 pounds) of silver.

nineteen

Jesus leaves Galilee and travels to Judea, Matthew tells us, where a crowd gathers, asking for Jesus' healing. When some Jewish religious leaders ask Jesus if divorce is lawful, he pushes them to go to a far deeper level regarding marriage. In response to continued questions from his disciples, Jesus makes several comments about marriage and sexuality, indicating that not everyone will understand what he is saying.

When children gather around Jesus, the disciples at first shoo them away, but Jesus stops them. Again, as he did in the previous chapter, he stresses that children belong to the Realm of Heaven.

Later, when a young man asks Jesus what he can do to gain eternal life, Jesus first tells him to follow the commandments of the Hebrew scriptures, and then—when the man asks what else he can do—Jesus tells him to give his wealth away and then come and join Jesus' followers. This distresses the man, and Jesus uses the moment to talk to his disciples about how wealth can hinder people from entering the

Realm of Heaven. At the same time, he stresses that God, who can do all things, is able to overcome even the forces of greed and selfishness. When Peter asks Jesus what the disciples, who have given up everything to follow Jesus, will gain, Jesus answers that everyone who has given up wealth, family connections, even personal safety, to follow him, will be rewarded accordingly in the Realm of Heaven.

⋈ BORN EUNUCHS ⋈

Buried within these familiar verses about marriage, children, and wealth are statements that Jesus makes about eunuchs (vs. 12). These references to gender are often overlooked, but the fact that Matthew included them indicates that they held some importance to him. Perhaps he knew someone who was a member of one of the three groups of eunuchs Jesus describes: first, those who were congenitally "queer"—in modern terminology—unable to fill the traditional heteronormative roles of the day by marrying and producing children, whether because they were transgender, homosexual, or asexual; second, men who had surgically had their sexuality removed, as was a custom in the ancient world for slaves as well as for men who held positions of household authority; and third, those who had chosen celibacy as a lifestyle in order to have greater freedom to serve the Divine Realm.

Ancient cultures, including the Celts', had perspectives on gender and sexuality quite different from the modern-day versions. In the Hebrew Bible, homosexual acts were labeled as *toevah*—"ritually impure" or "things that go against ceremonial regulations"—on the same level as eating non-kosher foods or mixing fabrics. Meanwhile, male homosexuality was openly accepted among the ancient Greeks and Romans. Prior to Africa's European subjugation, same-sex intercourse was allowed and even expected there, while North America's indigenous people have a long history of honoring the unique role transgender people can play in society.

220 THE GOSPEL OF MATTHEW

CHAPTER NINETEEN

Celtic mythology and stories have few direct references to homosexuality, indicating that it was considered to be a non-issue. In one instance, however, the great Irish hero Cuchulain—the personification of manly strength and valor—says to another man, "We were heart-companions once . . . we were men who shared a bed." Outsiders who observed the Celts, including Aristotle and other Greeks and Romans, recorded that the Celts openly approved of sexual relationships between men.

The Celts' conversion to Christianity did not instantly reverse their attitudes toward gender and sexuality, and Saint Patrick himself may have had a relationship tinged with homoeroticism. Tirechan, a seventh-century cleric who recorded stories about Patrick, tells of a man Patrick visited and converted to Christianity, who had a son to whom Patrick took a strong liking "because he took Patrick's feet between his hands and would not sleep with his father and mother, but wept unless he would be allowed to sleep with Patrick." Patrick baptized the boy and made him his close lifelong companion.

Many early Celtic monastic rules did, however, prescribe penances for monks who engaged in homosexual acts. These were part of the stringent asceticism often practiced by Celtic Christians, while outside the monasteries, sexual and gender differences were generally tolerated, so long as they did not interfere with the contractual rights of marriage. Even within some monasteries, homosexual relationships were acknowledged and sometimes even honored.

According to Yale history professor John Boswell, Saint Aelred, the twelfth-century abbot, was an example of a deeply spiritual Celt who had no problem with same-sex love. Aelred was the son of a married priest who was taken into the service of King David of Scotland, where he became close to the king's son and stepsons. At twenty-four, he left the court and became a monk at the Cistercian abbey of Rievaulx, gaining a reputation for his wisdom, gentleness, and deep spirituality. By the time he was thirty-eight, he had become abbot, and although he advocated chastity for his monks, he also wrote:

It is no small consolation in this life to have someone you can unite with you in an intimate affection and the embrace of a holy love, someone in whom your spirit can rest, to whom you can pour out your soul, to whose pleasant exchanges, as to soothing songs, you can fly in sorrow . . . with whose spiritual kisses, as with remedial salves, you may draw out all the weariness of your restless anxieties. A man who can shed tears with you in your worries, be happy with you when things go well, search out with you the answers to your problems, whom with the ties of charity you can lead into the depths of your heart; . . . where the sweetness of the Spirit flows between you, where you so join yourself and cleave to him that soul mingles with soul and two become one.

In the same way that the Celtic church had varying perspectives on women, their attitude toward gender and sexuality was not homogeneous either. Like Christians today, some Christian Celts were tolerant, some supportive, and some condemning. In our twenty-first century world, progressive churches welcome people who are LGBTQ (lesbian, gay, bisexual, transgender, queer), while conservative Christians believe that homosexuality is a serious sin that threatens our society's morality. Some Evangelical and Fundamentalist Christians have declared a "culture war" against LGBTQ civil rights and marriage equality. Although they claim the Bible as the foundation for their stand, would Jesus have agreed with them?

Jesus' mention of gender roles is brief (vs. 12), but he says nothing to indicate he feels disapproval. Later in this chapter, when asked by a young man about what course of action is required for eternal life (vs. 16), Jesus makes no reference to sexual immorality. If we assume that Matthew placed this story directly after

Christ's gender discussion for a reason, we might even read between the lines and wonder if the young man were himself some form of "eunuch." We have no way of knowing that, of course, but what is clear *is* that Jesus was far more condemning of people who abused and exploited society's helpless and vulnerable individuals, whether they were children (vs. 14) or the poor (vs. 21), than he was of people who violated sexual mores.

Furthermore, Jesus himself transcended gender roles. According to the modern definition, "gender-queer" people possess identities that fall outside the traditionally accepted gender binary of masculine and feminine. They are individuals whose lives challenge the rigid definitions of gender and sexuality. Jesus, who identified himself with a mother hen (Matthew 23:37) and broke his society's edicts against close associations with women, meets that definition. He referred to God as "Father"—but he also pictured the Divine as a woman seeking a lost coin (Luke 15:8–10) and as a mother giving birth (John 3:5–8). His identity and experience of God crossed traditional gender definitions.

Centuries later, medieval Christians often focused on the femininity of Christ; they were comfortable with a "gender-bending" Jesus. Many medieval spiritual authors recognized the parallels between Jesus and Sophia (Wisdom), and often understood Sophia to be Jesus' feminine face. They wrote of Jesus as the Divine Mother, who gives birth to us and nourishes us.

Today, sexuality and gender are far more difficult and divisive topics. Whatever our personal beliefs, what might we learn from the ancient world? What can we learn from Jesus?

—Teresa Cross

19

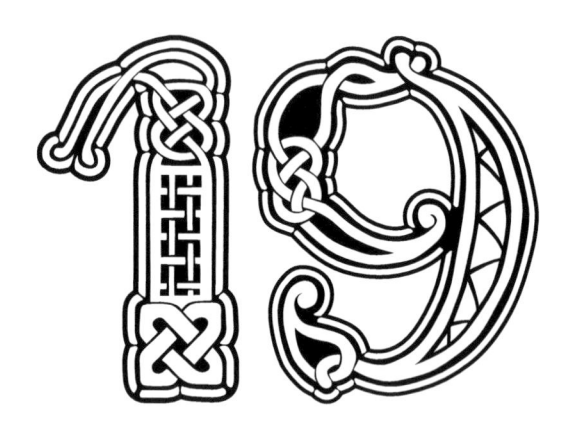

¹ When Jesus had finished these words, he departed from Galilee, and came into the borders of Judea beyond the Jordan. ² Great crowds followed him, and he healed them there. ³ Pharisees came to him, testing him, and saying, "Is it lawful for a man to divorce his wife for any reason?"

⁴ He answered, "Haven't you read that God who made them from the beginning made them male and female, ⁵ and said, 'For this cause a man shall leave his father and mother, and shall be joined to his wife, and the two shall become one flesh?' [a] ⁶ So that they are no more two, but one flesh. Therefore, what God has joined together, let no one tear apart."

⁷ They asked him, "Why then did Moses command us to give a wife a certificate of divorce and divorce her?"

⁸ He said to them, "Moses, because of the hardness of your hearts, allowed you to divorce your wives, but from the beginning it has not been

so. ⁹ I tell you that whoever divorces his wife, except for sexual immorality, and marries another, commits adultery; and he who marries her when she is divorced commits adultery."

¹⁰ His disciples said to him, "If this is the case of the man with his wife, it is better not to marry."

¹¹ But he said to them, "Not everyone can receive this saying, but those to whom it is given. ¹² For there are eunuchs who were born that way from their mother's womb, and there are eunuchs who were made eunuchs by other people; and there are eunuchs who made themselves eunuchs for the sake of the Realm of Heaven. Let those who are able to receive it, do so."

¹³ Then little children were brought to him, so that he would lay his hands on them and pray, and the disciples rebuked them. ¹⁴ But Jesus said, "Let the little children come to me, and don't hinder them, for the Realm of Heaven belongs to ones like these." ¹⁵ He laid his hands on them, and then departed from there.

¹⁶ A man came to him just then and said, "Good teacher, what good deed should I do, so that I may have eternal life?"

¹⁷ Jesus said to him, "Why do you ask me what is good? No one is good but One. But if you want to enter into life, keep the commandments."

¹⁸ "Which commandments shall I keep?" asked the youth.

Jesus said, "'You shall not murder.' 'You shall not commit adultery.' 'You shall not steal.' 'You shall not offer false testimony.' ¹⁹ 'Honor your father and your mother.' And, 'You shall love your neighbor as yourself.'"

²⁰ "All these things I have done," said the youth. "What do I still lack?"

²¹ Jesus replied, "If you want to be perfect, go, sell what you have, and give to the poor, and you will have treasure in heaven. Then come, follow me."

²² But upon hearing this, the youth, who had many possessions, turned away in sorrow. ²³ Jesus said to his disciples, "Most certainly I say to you, those who are wealthy will enter into the Realm of Heaven with difficulty. ²⁴ Again I tell you, it is easier for a camel to go through a needle's eye, than for those with great wealth to enter into the Realm of Heaven."

²⁵ When the disciples heard this, they were exceedingly astonished, saying, "Who then can be saved?"

²⁶ Looking at them, Jesus said, "With mortals this is impossible, but with God all things are possible."

²⁷ Then Peter answered, "Consider this, we have left everything, and followed you. What then will we have?"

²⁸ Jesus said to them, "Most certainly I tell you that you who have followed me, in the regeneration of the world, when the Human One will sit on the throne of glory, you also will sit on twelve thrones, judging the twelve tribes of Israel. ²⁹ Everyone who has left houses, or brothers, or sisters, or father, or mother, or wife, or children, or lands, for my name's sake, will receive one hundred times, and will inherit eternal life. ³⁰ But many will be last who are first, and first who are last."

ᵃ Genesis 2:24

CHAPTER TWENTY

twenty

In this chapter, Matthew records another parable of Jesus, this one about a landowner and his workers. The landowner hires some workers early in the day and others later in the day, but pays all of them the same amount. Jesus is making the point that God's embrace is equal for all, regardless of the breadth of our achievements.

On the way to Jerusalem, Jesus again foretells his death and resurrection. When the mother of disciples John and James asks that her sons be seated at the right and left hands of God in heaven, Jesus tells her that it is not up to him to make this decision; instead, God's choice has to do with who serves others, who does good for those in need. Jesus then explains that serving others is the only metric by which greatness is judged in heaven.

While traveling with the disciples from Jericho, Jesus heals the vision of two blind men shouting from the crowd, even after the crowd angrily bids the two be quiet.

ME FIRST

Three researchers—Jean Twenge, W. Keith Campell, and Brittany Gentile—recently used a Google search engine to count word usages in published writing from the beginning of the sixteenth century to the present. They discovered that over the centuries, words and terms appearing in print have drifted away from the usage of community-based ones toward more individual-based ideas. Terms such as "self" (combined with many other words: self-concept, self-betterment, self-esteem, self-discovery, and so on), "unique," "I come first," and "I can do it myself" have become more frequent, while terms such as "collective," "share," "band together," and "common good" are used less often. Where earlier generations emphasized values that benefited the community as a whole, the twenty-first century's zeitgeist teaches us to focus on our individual selves.

Self-esteem is a good thing, of course, and there is nothing wrong with working to learn and grow as individuals. However, this pervasive mindset can also be insidious, persuading us that a me-first perspective is healthy and justified. In this chapter, Jesus confronts this attitude. (Although it may be more common today, clearly, it has always been a part of human nature). He reminds us, both in parable form and in his words spoken to the disciples, that our need to get our fair share (vss. 1–16), to be recognized (vss. 20–23), and to be first (vss. 16, 27) can infiltrate our lives to the point that we are less useful to the Realm of Heaven.

Pagan Celts' culture, unlike our own, centered on the community, and this made them open to a Three-in-One God whose very nature was portrayed as a companionable relationship between Persons. In *The Celtic Vision*, Esther de Waal writes, "A God who is Trinity in unity challenges self-centred isolation and points instead to fellowship." For the Celtic saints, entering into a relationship with the Triune God meant to be drawn into a great, all-inclusive community that included the angelic hosts, those who had lived in the past, friends and strangers, the sick and oppressed as well as the rich, and their animal brothers and sisters. The Celtic saints took Jesus as their role model in practical ways, endeavoring to be like him by being of service rather than expecting to be served, while giving away their lives on behalf of others (vs. 28). Their devotion to all living creatures (both human and animal), to the natural world, and to creativity and the arts would not have been possible without the surrender of their egos.

Modern versions of Celtic spirituality continue this discipline of self-surrender. On the website for St. Columba of Iona Monastery, Father Peter Prebel describes the vows of this modern-day monastic community as creating a place where God's love is made manifest.

> Each monk lives within this "matrix of love," simultaneously taking from, and contributing to, the experience of the brotherhood as a whole. Living a life of total inter-dependence, where each person of the monastic family depends upon everyone else, the monk learns to surrender to the will of God at a yet more and more profound level. In return for surrendering all that he is, all that he has, and all that he might become, the monk receives all that he needs (although not necessarily all that he wants!), including a very subtle, yet essential, quality of trust in God. As this trust develops, he feels more and more able to surrender his own ego, and live in a state of total surrender, yet total security. With the surrender of the ego, the monk can even reach a level of living in which the notion of his own "wants" ceases to exert any power over him.

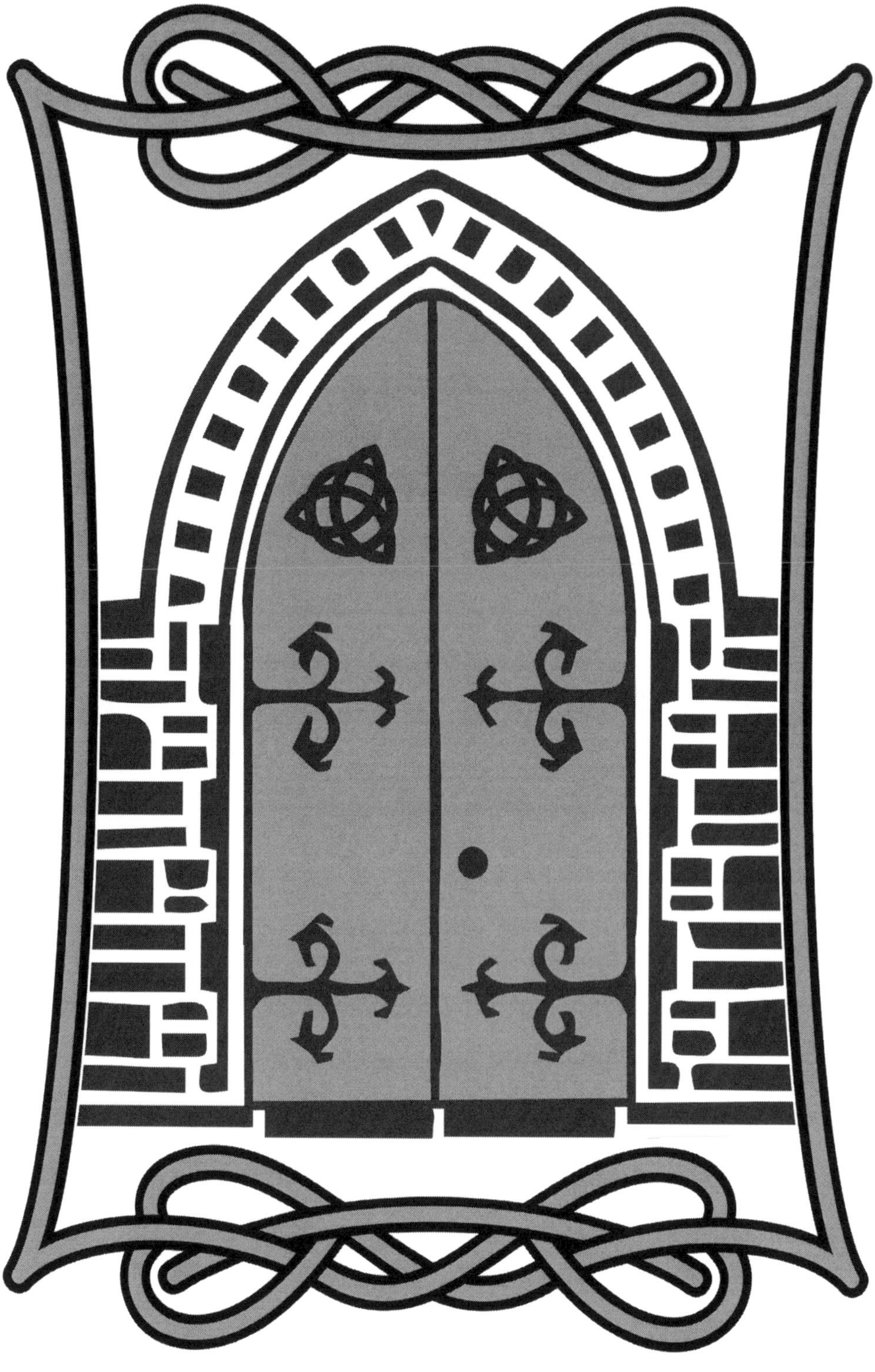

CHAPTER TWENTY 231

This level of self-surrender seems radical, even impractical, for most of us. The very thought of letting go of our "wants" is uncomfortable, frightening even. And yet Father Prebel indicates that in doing so, we might find a deeper sense of security than we have ever experienced.

Selflessness did not come any more easily to the Celtic saints than it does to us. Saint Columba, for example, clearly wrestled with his pride and ego (see the commentary for Matthew 18). His me-first mentality blinded him to the needs of others to the point that he was willing to even start a war, all so that he could have his own way. Eventually, however, he reached the place where he was able to write this prayer:

> Almighty God,
> Father, Son, and Holy Spirit,
> to me the least of saints,
> to me allow that I may keep even the smallest door,
> the farthest, darkest, coldest door,
> the door that is least used, the stiffest door,
> if only it be in Your house, O God,
> that I can see Your glory afar,
> and hear Your voice,
> and know that I am with You,
> O God.

Like Columba, we too struggle with our hubris and self-importance. We are often so focused on ourselves that we are blind to those around us. "Meanwhile," wrote Pope Francis in *The Joy of the Gospel*,

> the Gospel tells us constantly to run the risk of a face-to-face encounter with others, with their physical presence which challenges us, with their pain and their pleas, with their joy which

infects us. . . . True faith in the incarnate Son of God is inseparable from self-giving, from membership in the community, from service, from reconciliation with others. The Son of God, by becoming flesh, summoned us to the revolution of tenderness.

The struggle to surrender ourselves to God and others—this revolution of tenderness—is not one we can quickly win. It will probably take a lifetime. We can take comfort, though, that Jesus has compassion for us, even in the midst of our arrogance and selfishness. He is able to open our eyes, if we ask him, so that we can see more clearly—and follow him (vs. 34).

—Ellyn Sanna

CHAPTER TWENTY

[1] For the Realm of Heaven is like someone who was the head of a household, who went out early in the morning to hire laborers to work in the vineyard. [2] The householder agreed to pay the laborers a coin a day, then sent them into the vineyard.[a] [3] The householder went out again at about nine that morning and saw others standing idle in the marketplace. [4] These too he hired and told them they would be paid fairly for their work. [5] Again, the householder went out around noon and then at three in the afternoon to hire more laborers. [6] And then yet again, around five in the afternoon, the householder found more workers standing idle in the marketplace and said to them, 'Why are you standing idle when there is work to do?' [7] They answered, 'Because no one has hired us.' The householder said to them, 'You also go into the vineyard, and you will receive whatever is right.' [8] When evening had come, the householder said to the manager,

'Call the laborers and pay them their wages, beginning from the last to the first.'

⁹ "When those who were hired at about five in the afternoon came, they each received a coin. ¹⁰ When those who had been hired first came, they supposed that they would receive more; but they likewise each received a coin. ¹¹ When they received it, they complained against the householder, ¹² saying, 'These last have worked only an hour, and yet you have made them equal to us, who have borne the burden of the day and the scorching heat!'

¹³ "But the landowner answered one of them, 'Friend, I am doing you no wrong. Didn't you agree with me for a coin? ¹⁴ Take that which is yours, and go your way. It is my desire to give to this last just as much as to you. ¹⁵ Isn't it lawful for me to do what I want to with what I own? Or is your eye evil, because I am good?' ¹⁶ So the last will be first, and the first last. For many are called, but few are chosen."

¹⁷ As Jesus was going up to Jerusalem, he took the twelve disciples aside, and on the way he said to them, ¹⁸ "Pay careful attention now, we are going up to Jerusalem, and the Human One will be delivered to the chief priests and scribes, and they will condemn him to death, ¹⁹ and will hand him over to the Gentiles to mock, to scourge, and to crucify; and the third day he will be raised up."

²⁰ Then the mother of the sons of Zebedee came to him with her sons, kneeling and asking a certain thing of him. ²¹ He said to her, "What do you want?"

She said to him, "Command that these, my two sons, may sit, one on your right hand, and one on your left hand, in your Reign.

²² But Jesus answered, "You don't know what you are asking. Are you able to drink the cup that I am about to drink, and be baptized with the baptism that I am baptized with?"

They said to him, "We are able."

²³ He said to them, "You will indeed drink my cup, and be baptized with the baptism that I am baptized with, but to sit on my right hand and on my left hand is not mine to give; but it is for whom it has been prepared by God my Abba."

²⁴ When the ten heard it, they were indignant with the two brothers.

²⁵ But Jesus summoned them, and said, "You know that the rulers of the nations abuse their power over the people, and their great ones exercise strict authority over them. ²⁶ It shall not be so among you, but whoever desires to become great among you, shall be your servant. ²⁷ Whoever desires to be first among you shall be your servant, ²⁸ even as the Human One came not to be served, but to serve, and to give his life as a ransom for many."

²⁹ As they went out from Jericho, a great crowd followed him. ³⁰ Two blind beggars were sitting by the road; when they heard that Jesus was passing by, cried out, "Have mercy on us, Heir of David!" ³¹ The crowd rebuked them, telling them that they should be quiet, but they cried out even more, "Have mercy on us, Heir of David!"

³² Jesus stood still, and called them, and asked, "What do you want me to do for you?"

³³ They told him, "Great One, that our eyes may be opened."

³⁴ Jesus, being moved with compassion, touched their eyes; and immediately their eyes received their sight, and they followed him.

[a] Literally, a denarius, a silver Roman coin that was a common wage for a day of farm labor.

twenty-one

As Jesus approaches Jerusalem, he tells two disciples to travel to a nearby town, find a donkey and her colt, and bring it to him, so that he may ride into Jerusalem on the donkey. These verses are a little confusing, since it sounds as though Jesus will be riding both the donkey and her colt at the same time. The Hebrew scripture spoke of "on a colt, the foal of a donkey," a traditional form of parallelism, describing the same animal in two different ways, but Matthew apparently mistook this passage to refer to two separate animals—and in applying the scripture to Jesus, he added a second animal to the narrative. The other three Gospels refer to a single animal only.

Jesus' entry into Jerusalem is celebrated with cheering and palm branches, and here Matthew again underlines the role of Jesus as the Anointed One. The Gospel's author then makes a sharp distinction between the Jewish Jesus—who is the fulfillment of Hebrew scriptures—and the corruption of the religious establishment. Matthew makes clear that Judaism, as represented by Jesus, is a religion of compassion, while he portrays the religious leaders of his day as exemplifying a false piety, one that is exploitive and hypocritical.

The Jesus we see in this chapter is fiery and passionate in his defense of the marginalized, with no tolerance for deceit and sanctimonious guile. He physically throws out people who are seeking to profit financially from worshippers in the Temple; he reminds the religious leaders that God is pleased with the simple, wordless worship of babies and those with intellectual disabilities; he curses an unfruitful fig tree, a symbol of the religious establishment that has failed to live up to its potential of life-nourishing fruitfulness; and he says that prostitutes and tax collectors will enter the Realm of Heaven before the corrupt and hypocritical religious leaders.

✠ THE MARGINALIZED AND THE REALM OF HEAVEN ✠

Stories about the Celtic saints portray these men and women as having a similar concern as Jesus did for individuals who were considered to have little value. Saint Brigid in particular is described as demonstrating an active compassion for those who were the most rejected in her society. According to tradition, she welcomed lepers into her monastery, she gave sanctuary to animals pursued by hunters, she fed and clothed the poor, and she cared for women who had been abused by men.

In our world, those who are marginalized are still vulnerable, just as they were in Jesus' day and in Brigid's. Corruption and exploitation remain all too common, and people who are different in some way still face discrimination, injustice, and violence. "We will not find the Lord unless we truly accept the marginalized," Pope Francis has said. "Truly the Gospel of the marginalized is where our credibility is found and revealed!"

In the face of rising tides of prejudice and hatred, what action can we take to enter the Realm of Heaven? The "Peacekeepers' Promise," which began circulating on social media during 2016, offers some suggestions:

> If you wear a hijab, I'll sit with you on the train.
> If you're trans, I'll go to the bathroom with you.
> If you're a person of color, I'll stand with you if the cops stop you.
> If you're a person with disabilities, I'll hand you my megaphone.
> If you're LGBTQ, I won't let anybody tell you you're broken.
> If you're a woman, I'll fight by your side for all your rights.
> If you're an immigrant, I'll help you find resources.
> If you're a survivor, I'll believe you.

CHAPTER TWENTY-ONE

If you're a Native American, I'll stand with you to protect your water, your burial grounds, and your people.
If you're a refugee, I'll make sure you're welcome.
... If you need me, I'll be with you.

These are just some of the actions we can take to welcome Jesus into our world. They are a way to shout, "Hosanna!"

—Ellyn Sanna

21

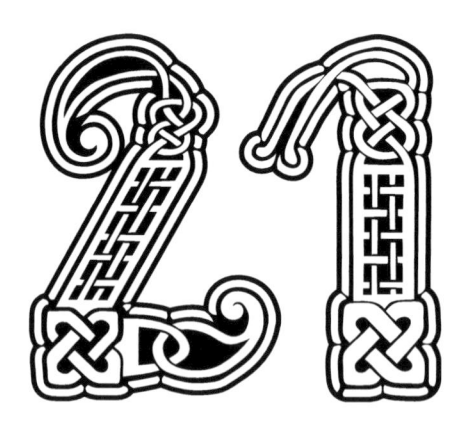

¹ When they came near to Jerusalem, and came to Bethphage, to the Mount of Olives, Jesus sent two disciples, ² saying to them, "Go into the village that is opposite you, and immediately you will find a donkey tied, and a colt with her. Untie them, and bring them to me. ³ If anyone says anything to you, you shall say, 'The Rabbi needs them,' and they will send them right away."

⁴ All this was done, that it might be fulfilled which was spoken through the prophet, saying,

> ⁵ "Tell the daughter of Zion,
> behold, your Sovereign comes to you,
> humble, and riding on a donkey,
> on a colt, the foal of a donkey." [a]

⁶ The disciples went, and did just as Jesus commanded them, ⁷ and brought the donkey and the colt, and laid their clothes on them; and he sat on the clothes. ⁸ A very great crowd spread their clothes on the road. Others cut branches from the trees, and spread them on the road. ⁹ The crowds who went in front of him, and those who followed, kept shouting, "Hosanna[b] to the heir of David! Blessed is he who comes in the name of the Exalted One! Hosanna in the highest!"

¹⁰ When he had come into Jerusalem, all the city was stirred up, saying, "Who is this?" ¹¹ The crowds said, "This is the prophet, Jesus, from Nazareth of Galilee."

¹² Jesus entered into the temple of God, and drove out all of those who sold and bought in the temple, and overthrew the moneychangers' tables and the seats of those who sold the doves. ¹³ He said to them, "It is written, 'My house shall be called a house of prayer,'[c] but you have made it a den of robbers!"

¹⁴ The blind and the lame came to him in the temple, and he healed them. ¹⁵ But when the chief priests and the scribes saw the wonderful things that he did, and the children who were crying in the temple and saying, "Hosanna to the heir of David!" they were indignant, ¹⁶ and said to him, "Do you hear what these are saying?"

Jesus said to them, "Yes. Did you never read, 'Out of the mouth of those who are simpleminded and nursing you have made ready your praise?'"[d]

¹⁷ He left them, and went out of the city to Bethany, and camped there. ¹⁸ Now in the morning, as he returned to the city, he was hungry. ¹⁹ Seeing a fig tree by the road, he came to it, and found nothing on it but leaves. He said to it, "Let there be no fruit from you forever!"

Immediately the fig tree withered away. ²⁰ When the disciples saw it, they marveled, saying, "How did the fig tree immediately wither away?"

²¹ Jesus answered them, "Most certainly I tell you, if you have faith, and don't doubt, you will not only do what was done to the fig tree, but even if you told this mountain, 'Be taken up and cast into the sea,' it would be done. ²² All things, whatever you ask in prayer, believing, you will receive."

²³ When he had come into the temple, the chief priests and the elders of the people came to him as he was teaching, and said, "By what authority do you do these things? Who gave you this authority?"

²⁴ Jesus answered them, "I also will ask you one question, which if you tell me, I likewise will tell you by what authority I do these things. ²⁵ The baptism of John, where was it from? From heaven or from mortals?"

They reasoned with themselves, saying, "If we say, 'From heaven,' he will ask us, 'Why then did you not believe John?' ²⁶ But if we say, 'From mortals,' we fear the crowd, for all hold John as a prophet." ²⁷ They answered Jesus, and said, "We don't know."

He also said to them, "Neither will I tell you by what authority I do these things. ²⁸ But what do you think? A man had two sons, and he came to the first, and said, 'Son, go work today in my vineyard.' ²⁹ He answered, 'I will not,' but afterward he changed his mind and went. ³⁰ He came to the second, and said the same thing. He answered, 'I'm going, sir,' but he didn't go. ³¹ Which of the two did the will of his father?"

They said to him, "The first."

Jesus said to them, "Most certainly I tell you that the tax collectors and the prostitutes are entering into the Realm of God before you. ³² For John came to you in the way of righteousness, and you didn't believe him, but the tax collectors and the prostitutes believed him. When you saw it, you didn't even change afterward, that you might believe him.

³³ "Hear another parable. There was a farm owner who planted a vineyard, set a hedge about it, dug a winepress in it, built a tower, leased it out to farmers, and went into another country. ³⁴ When the season for the fruit came near, the owner sent servants to the farmers to receive the fruit. ³⁵ The farmers took the servants, beat one, killed another, and stoned another. ³⁶ Again, the farm owner sent other servants more than the first: and they treated them the same way. ³⁷ But afterward the owner sent to them his son, saying, 'They will respect my son.' ³⁸ But the farmers, when they saw the son, said among themselves, 'This is the heir. Come, let's kill him, and seize his inheritance.' ³⁹ So they took him, and threw him out of the vineyard, and killed him. ⁴⁰ When therefore the owner comes, what will happen to those farmers?"

⁴¹ They replied, "Those evil people will be destroyed, and the owner will lease out the vineyard to other farmers, who will hand over the proper portion of the fruit at harvest."

⁴² Jesus said to them, "Did you never read in the Scriptures,

> 'The stone which the builders rejected,
> the same was made the head of the corner.
> This was from the Eternal One.
> It is marvelous in our eyes?' ᵉ

⁴³ "Therefore I tell you, the Realm of God will be taken away from you, and will be given to a nation producing its fruit. ⁴⁴ Those who fall

on this stone will be broken to pieces, but on whomever it falls, it will scatter them as dust." ᶠ

⁴⁵ When the chief priests and the Pharisees heard his parables, they perceived that he spoke about them. ⁴⁶ When they sought to seize him, they feared the crowd, because they considered him to be a prophet.

ᵃ Zechariah 9:9
ᵇ Hosanna is a Hebrew word that literally means "save us," which came to be used as an expression of praise.
ᶜ Isaiah 56:7
ᵈ Psalm 8:2
ᵉ Psalm 118:22–23
ᶠ Some manuscripts do not include verse 44.

Twenty-Two

In this chapter, Matthew shows us Jesus once more engaged with the local leaders. First, Jesus tells the Pharisees a parable about a wedding feast, which makes the point that religion alone does not justify spiritual complacency. This parable has often been interpreted to mean that not everyone will be allowed into a heavenly afterlife, but when Jesus talks about the Realm of Heaven, it is always a here-and-now reality.

Next, the Pharisees and the Herodians (people who supported Herod as the Roman governor of Galilee) ask Jesus if it is right to pay tax to Rome. If he says yes, then he is tacitly acknowledging a foreign and Gentile rule over Israel—but if he says no, then he is stating his rebellion against Rome. Jesus doesn't allow himself to be trapped, but instead answers in a way that separates religion from civic duty.

After this, the Sadducees come to Jesus with a complicated question about how marital law will apply to the afterlife. The Sadducees were the conservatives of their day, believing that only the Pentateuch (the first five books of the Hebrew Bible) should be considered Scripture. Unlike the Pharisees, who believed in the resurrection of the body after death, and the surrounding Greek culture, which understood the soul to be immortal, the Sadducees did not believe in any form of afterlife. Their question is meant to trap Jesus into responding in a way that will prove that the concept of an afterlife is illogical. Jesus' answer tells them that they misunderstand the entire idea; the resurrection he promises is not a literal rising from the dead on earth but a new life in heaven. He then responds directly to the real question—does Jesus believe in an afterlife?—by using the Sadducees' own scriptures, where the use of the present tense indicates that "God is not the God of the dead, but of the living" (vs. 32).

Finally, a scholar of the Hebrew law asks Jesus what he believes to be the most important commandment of the Hebrew scriptures. Jesus answers that loving God and others sums up all the other commandments.

Jesus then asks the Pharisees a question of his own, about their understanding of the Jewish Messiah (the Chosen One), and goes on to explain that his identity as the Chosen One does not contradict the Hebrew scriptures. His comments reflect the ongoing conflict between the traditions of the past and the concept of a new, never-before-seen Divine action (a conflict that still continues today). In verse 44, Jesus quotes from Psalm 110, implying that since David refers to the Messiah as "Sovereign," Jesus is greater than the religious traditions of the past.

⋈ TRICKSTER JESUS ⋈

In this chapter, the religious leaders who confront Jesus discover that trying to grab hold of him is like attempting to grasp a ray of sunlight in your fist: the light is real, it's right there in front of you where you can clearly see it—but no matter how much you try, you will never be able to catch it in your hand.

Like so many of us, the scholarly and religious men of Jesus' day are accustomed to thinking in terms of a binary reality: that which is true according to their religious traditions versus that which is not true; that which is legal versus that which is illegal; and that which is right versus that which is wrong. They are certain they can catch Jesus in their traps, forcing him to either be proven wrong or else admit that they are right. Instead, Jesus slips through their snares. He makes clear that he is talking about a living reality that lies beyond their simplistic dualism, one that cannot be constrained by traditions and laws, nor by time and death. The Reign of Heaven is a joyous feast (vs. 2), to which absolutely everyone is invited (vs. 9). It is ruled by love not law—and love is undying and always new.

Saint Brigid, perhaps the most beloved of all Celtic saints, had much in common with Jesus. Many of the stories about Brigid describe the ways in which she was able to outwit the male authority figures who tried to control her. With total disregard for property law, she gave away her father's belongings to the poor; she tricked the King of Leinster into giving her a large portion of land for her monastery; and she regularly gave to the poor from the farms and kitchens where she worked. Despite her constant mischief for good, Brigid always evades the grasp of the stingy authority figures. Like Jesus, she taps into a supernatural stream of power, but also like him, she demonstrates plenty of human intelligence, insight, and craftiness.

Brigid is like Jesus in another way. In verse 32, Jesus indicates that God is a God of the present tense—and God's people also exist in that same Holy Now. The Reign of Heaven that Jesus describes is not something that lies in the future; it cannot be considered the *after*-life, for it is the *now*-life. In the old stories, Brigid has a similar disregard for the boundaries of time. She slips into the past (and around the

248   ⚭   THE GOSPEL OF MATTHEW

CHAPTER TWENTY-TWO 249

globe) to act as Mary's midwife and Jesus' babysitter; she also travels more than three centuries forward in time to chat with a dying man, comforting him during his last hours.

Cultural scholar Lewis Hyde describes certain figures in world mythology as "boundary crossers"—tricksters who refuse to be limited by either physical or societal rules. Hyde says in *Trickster Makes This World: Mischief, Myth, and Art* that these tricksters violate the understood principles of social and natural order. They disrupt normal life and then put it back together again in a new configuration. Jesus and Brigid are tricksters in this sense of the word.

They both slip through the hard-and-fast categories we've established in our minds. They show us a wider, deeper, mysterious, and living world that lies beneath and beyond the laws we believe govern our lives. The only rule that governs that world is this: "You shall love the Eternal One with all your heart, with all your soul, and with all your mind" (vs. 37) and "You shall love your neighbor as yourself" (vs. 39).

—Ellyn Sanna

22

¹ Jesus answered and spoke to them again in parables, saying, ² "The Reign of Heaven is like a certain ruler, who prepared a wedding feast for the ruler's heir, ³ and ordered the servants to call those who were invited to the marriage feast, but they would not come. ⁴ Again this ruler sent out other servants, saying, 'Tell those who are invited, "Now look, I have prepared a feast. My cattle and my fattened livestock have been butchered, and everything is ready. Come to the wedding feast!"' ⁵ But they paid no attention and went their way, each to their own farms or businesses, ⁶ and the rest grabbed the servants and mistreated them and killed them. ⁷ When the ruler learned of this, he was enraged and sent his soldiers to kill those who murdered the servants and to burn their city.

⁸ "The ruler then said to the servants, 'The wedding is ready, but those who were invited weren't worthy. ⁹ Go therefore to all the main roads in town, and as many as you may find, invite to the wedding

feast.' ¹⁰ Those servants went out into streets and gathered together as many as they found, both bad and good. The wedding was filled with guests.

¹¹ "But when the ruler came in to see the guests, there was a guest who didn't have on wedding clothing. ¹² The ruler asked, 'Friend, how did you come in here not wearing wedding clothing?' The guest had no answer. ¹³ Then the ruler ordered that the guest be bound hand and foot and thrown into the outer darkness where there would be weeping and grinding of teeth. ¹⁴ For many are called, but few are chosen."

¹⁵ Then the Pharisees went and took counsel how they might entrap him in his talk. ¹⁶ They sent their disciples to him, along with the Herodians, saying, "Teacher, we know that you are honest, and teach the way of God in truth, no matter whom you teach, for you aren't partial to anyone. ¹⁷ Tell us therefore, what do you think? Is it lawful to pay taxes to Caesar, or not?"

¹⁸ But Jesus perceived their malice, and said, "Why do you test me, you hypocrites? ¹⁹ Show me the tax money."

They brought to him a coin.[a]

²⁰ He asked them, "Whose is this image and inscription?"

²¹ They said to him, "Caesar's."

Then he said to them, "Give therefore to Caesar the things that are Caesar's, and to God the things that are God's."

²² When they heard his answer, they marveled, and they left him and went away.

²³ On that same day, Sadducees (those who say that there is no resurrection) came to him. They asked him, ²⁴ saying, "Teacher, Moses said, 'If a man dies, having no children, his brother shall marry his wife, and have children in his brother's place.'[b] ²⁵ Now there were seven brothers with us. The first married and died, and having no children, he left his wife to his brother. ²⁶ In the same way, the second also died, and then

the third, all the way down to the seventh. ²⁷ Last of all, the woman died. ²⁸ So in the resurrection, whose wife will she be of the seven? For they all had her."

²⁹ But Jesus answered them, "You are mistaken, not knowing the Scriptures, nor the power of God. ³⁰ For in the resurrection, they neither marry, nor are given in marriage, but are like the angels in heaven. ³¹ But concerning the resurrection of the dead, haven't you read that which was spoken to you by God, saying, ³² 'I am the God of Abraham, and of Isaac, and of Jacob?' ᶜ God is not the God of the dead, but of the living."

³³ When the crowds heard it, they were astonished at his teaching. ³⁴ But the Pharisees, when they heard that he had silenced the Sadducees, gathered themselves together. ³⁵ One of them, a scholar of the law, asked him a question, testing him. ³⁶ "Teacher, which is the greatest commandment in the law?"

³⁷ Jesus replied, "'You shall love the Eternal One with all your heart, with all your soul, and with all your mind.' ᵈ ³⁸ This is the first and greatest commandment. ³⁹ A second likewise is this, 'You shall love your neighbor as yourself.' ᵉ ⁴⁰ The whole law and the prophets depend on these two commandments."

⁴¹ Now while the Pharisees were gathered together, Jesus asked them a question, ⁴² saying, "What do you think of the Messiah? Whose son is he?"

They said to him, "Of David."

⁴³ He said to them, "How then does David in the Spirit call him Sovereign,

saying, ⁴⁴ 'The Eternal One said to my Sovereign, sit on my right hand, until I make your enemies a footstool for your feet?' ⁴⁵ If then David calls him Sovereign, how is he his son?" ⁴⁶ No one was able to answer him a word, neither did they dare ask him any more questions from that day forward.

    ^a Literally, a denarius.
    ^b Genesis 38:8
    ^c Exodus 3:6
    ^d Deuteronomy 6:5
    ^e Leviticus 19:18

twenty-three

Here, Matthew describes Jesus lambasting those who portray themselves as righteous for the sake of attention, the benefits of high status, and power over others. He warns against hypocritical religious leaders, saying that the smallest individuals will be raised up, while those who consider themselves important will find themselves diminished. Then Matthew depicts Jesus outlining the ways in which the Pharisees fall tragically short of what they should be: they use religious legalism to make life more difficult for the faithful; they adhere to traditional customs over actual spirituality; and they seek to present themselves as ultra-righteous, without the substance of their lives matching the presentation. Here again Matthew highlights Jesus' insistence that hypocrisy is a primary hindrance to the Reign of Heaven.

CHAPTER TWENTY-THREE

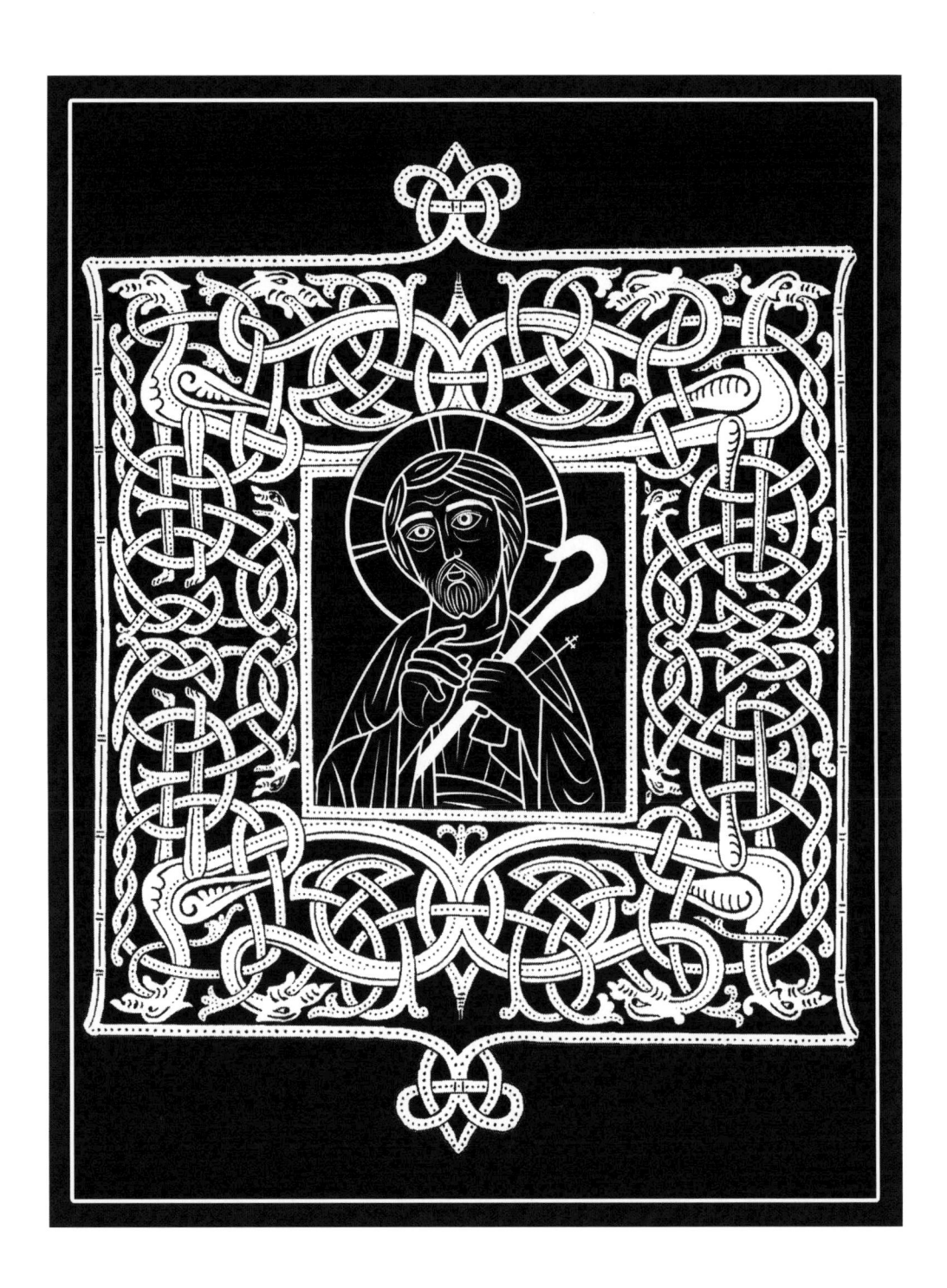

CURSING?

We love to read Matthew's list of beatitudes (5:3–12), in which Jesus blesses the meek, the gentle, the hungry, the seeking. "Happy are you," Jesus says about these folks. We're far less fond, however, of the verses found in chapter 23, where Jesus talks instead about the woes certain people bring upon themselves and into the world.

The Greek word used for woe refers to sadness and grief; it's a word similar to "alas!"—a cry of pain and lamentation. In other words, Jesus isn't pronouncing judgment on the Pharisees so much as he is expressing his dismay and sorrow at their behaviors. Instead of being happy and blessed, they will experience grief and affliction, with their woe stemming from three sources: their hypocrisy (they don't practice what they preach); legalism (they put unreasonable demands on those seeking God); and pride (they love to impress others with their clothes and their ostentatious righteousness).

When we identify the hypocrisy and failures of others, our next thought is often to curse them—to wish them ill. Jesus condemns hypocrisy more than any other human failing, but in this chapter he is not wishing ill on the religious leaders; instead, he is expressing his grief and frustration at what they themselves have created out of their lives. What we hear is not an angry Jesus so much as a sorrowful one. "It didn't have to be like this!" he's saying. "You could have taken another route. You could have made other choices. And now you're going to have to suffer the consequences of your own actions." And still we hear the love in his voice when he says he would have gathered them together under his wings, like a mother hen with her chicks, if only they had let him (vs. 39).

CHAPTER TWENTY-THREE

The Celtic saints, like us, sometimes found it easier to condemn others rather than recognize their own hypocrisy, to curse wrongdoers rather than sorrow over them. In some cases, not only did they wish ill on others, but the old stories record that they also used supernatural power to bring disaster to others. Saint Cadog, for example, saw to it that a barn burned down with a man inside, that a pigkeeper was struck down and killed, that thieves were swallowed up by the earth, and that several kings were blinded. Saint Patrick is said to have cursed into slavery the sons of the man who stole his horse, cursed a druid so that he was consumed by fire, and even made a horse drop dead because it ran through Patrick's field. These are Celtic tales we don't like to tell, the dark side of a spirituality we love to describe as tolerant and accepting.

We may, however, be attributing modern emotions to a culture that perceived things far differently from what we do today. To us, the Celtic saints' curses seem vengeful and spiteful, but in *Anger's Past: The Social Uses of Emotions in the Middle Ages*, Wendy Davies points out that in the ancient hagiographies, anger and hatred are never ascribed to the saints when they are cursing. In fact, when Cadog burned down the barn with the man inside, Cadog is explicitly described as "gentle." In the oldest Celtic tales, the saints' curses are seldom the result of any emotion whatsoever. According to Davies, for the early-medieval Celts, cursing was simply a matter-of-fact way to enact the proper consequences when boundaries of honor and ownership had been crossed. Perhaps the ancient Celts were not quite as vindictive as they appear at first glance.

In today's culture, however, cursing is not simply enacting the natural consequences of wrongdoing; it's actively wishing that bad things will happen to someone who makes us angry. Often, cursing comes to us far more easily than blessing. We may not call down fire from heaven to destroy those who anger us—but if we're honest, we sometimes wish we could!

In any case, the message conveyed to us in this chapter is not that we are entitled to curse those we perceive to be in the wrong, nor even that we should sit in judgment on the Pharisees. Jesus' condemnation of the religious leaders of his day has sometimes been used to justify anti-Semitism, but as Tim Beach-Verhey comments, "The point of this passage concerns the true nature of discipleship, rather than a condemnation of a particular people or religion." If we try to point fingers at the Pharisees, or at anyone we label as being like them, we may find that the fingers are pointing straight back at us! We're far happier seeing the Pharisees as terrible people—"Thank goodness we're not like *them*" (vs. 30)—rather than recognizing ourselves in their behaviors.

We defend ourselves against the niggling fear that we too may be hypocrites by projecting our judgment outward, onto others (whether they be our family and friends or the politicians who run our country), and then, rather than sorrowing over the hypocrisy in the world, as Jesus did, we work ourselves into a rage over it. We wish ill on those who practice it. In the process, we exalt ourselves, rather than humble ourselves (vs. 12); we are so busy cleaning the outside of the cup that we forget the grime that clings to the inside of our hearts (vs. 26); and we run around slapping at gnats *out there*, when all the while we're digesting an entire camel down inside our own bellies (vs. 24).

So as we read this chapter, we need to rethink our understanding: Jesus isn't talking to *them*; he's talking to *us*.

—Ellyn Sanna

CHAPTER TWENTY-THREE

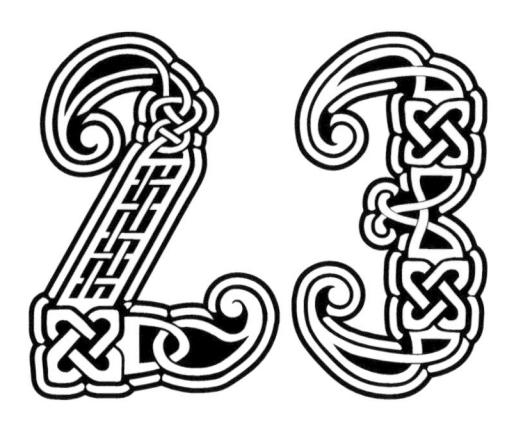

¹ Then Jesus spoke to the crowds and to his disciples, ² saying, "The scribes and the Pharisees have put themselves in Moses' seat, ³ so whatever they tell you to do, go ahead and do, but don't imitate their actions, for they don't live the way they talk. ⁴ They tie together heavy burdens and place them on people's shoulders, and then they don't lift a finger to help them. ⁵ Instead, all their works they do to be seen by others. They make their phylacteries[a] broad, lengthen the fringes of their garments, ⁶ and love the place of honor at feasts, the best seats in the synagogues, ⁷ the respectful greetings in the marketplaces, and to be called 'Rabbi, Rabbi' by others. ⁸ But don't you be called 'Rabbi,' for only one is your teacher, and you are all siblings to

each other. ⁹ Call no one in this world your parent, for you have but one parent,ᵇ the one who is in Heaven. ¹⁰ Neither be called leaders, for only one is your leader, the Chosen One. ¹¹ But the one who is greatest among you will be your servant. ¹² Those who exalt themselves will be humbled, and those who humble themselves will be exalted.

¹³ "Woe to you, scribes and Pharisees, hypocrites! For you close the door to the Realm of Heaven against others; you don't enter in yourselves, nor do you allow those who are who want to go in to enter. ¹⁵ Woe to you, scribes and Pharisees, hypocrites! For you devour widows' houses, and then you pretend to make long prayers. Therefore the case against you will be far greater. Woe to you, scribes and Pharisees, hypocrites! For you travel over sea and land seeking a convert, and when someone does convert, you make that person twice as much a child of Gehennaᶜ as yourselves.

¹⁶ "Woe to you, you blind guides, who say, 'Whoever swears by the Temple, that means nothing; but whoever swears by the gold of the Temple is obligated.' ¹⁷ You blind fools! For which is greater, the gold or the Temple that sanctifies the gold? ¹⁸ And then you say, 'Whoever swears by the altar, that means nothing; but whoever swears by the gift that is on the altar is obligated' ¹⁹ You blind fools! For which is greater, the gift or the altar that sanctifies the gift? ²⁰ Those who swear by the altar, swear by it and by everything on it. ²¹ Those who swear by the Temple, swear by it and by the One who lives in it. ²² Those who swear by Heaven, swear by the throne of God, and by the One who sits on it.

²³ "Woe to you, scribes and

Pharisees, hypocrites! For you tithe mint, dill, and cumin, and have left undone the weightier matters of the law: justice, mercy, and faith. But you ought to have done these, and not to have left the other undone. [24] You blind guides, who strain out a gnat and swallow a camel!

[25] "Woe to you, scribes and Pharisees, hypocrites! For you clean the outside of the cup and the platter, but inside they are full of robbery and self-indulgence. [26] You blind Pharisee, first clean the inside of the cup and the platter, so that its outside may become clean also.

[27] "Woe to you, scribes and Pharisees, hypocrites! For you are like whitewashed tombs, which outwardly appear beautiful but inwardly are full of dead bones and decay. [28] In the same way, you outwardly appear righteous to others, but inwardly you are full of hypocrisy and lawlessness.

[29] "Woe to you, scribes and Pharisees, hypocrites! For you build the tombs of the prophets and decorate the tombs of the righteous, [30] and say, 'If we had lived in the days of our ancestors, we wouldn't have been partners with them in shedding the blood of the prophets.' [31] And so you bear witness against yourselves that you are children of those who killed the prophets. [32] Fill up, then, the measure of your ancestors. [33] You serpents, you offspring of vipers, how will you escape the judgment of Gehenna? [34] Therefore, look—I'm sending you prophets, sages, and scribes. Some of them you will kill and crucify; and some of them you will scourge in your synagogues and persecute from city to city; [35] that on you may come all the righteous blood shed on the Earth, from the blood of righteous Abel to the blood of Zachariah son of Barachiah, whom you killed between the sanctuary and the altar. [36] Most certainly I tell you, all these things will come upon this generation.

[37] "Jerusalem, Jerusalem, who kills the prophets, and stones those who are sent there! How often I would have gathered your children

together, the way a hen gathers her chicks under her wings, but you weren't willing! ³⁸ Look—your house is being left to you empty and desolate. ³⁹ For I tell you, you will not see me from now on, until you say, 'Blessed are those who come in the name of the Eternal One!'"

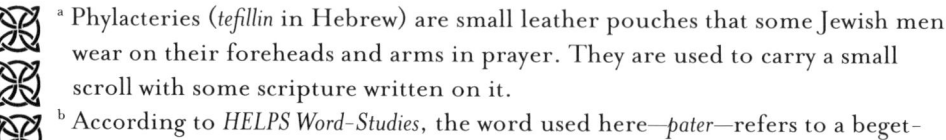

^a Phylacteries (*tefillin* in Hebrew) are small leather pouches that some Jewish men wear on their foreheads and arms in prayer. They are used to carry a small scroll with some scripture written on it.
^b According to *HELPS Word-Studies*, the word used here—*pater*—refers to a begetter, originator, progenitor—one in "intimate connection and relationship," one who imparts life and is committed to it; who brings into being and passes on the potential for likeness.
^c See note for Matthew 5:29.

Chapter Twenty-Four

Twenty-four

In chapter 24, Matthew records a long monologue in which Jesus warns the disciples of a coming time of ever-growing tragedy, chaos, lies, and disasters. The placement of this material immediately after his diatribe against the religious leaders in chapter 23 indicates that what he is describing in chapter 24 is a further explanation of the "woe" he predicted for the Pharisees in the previous chapter. During this time of war and deception, Jesus says, the disciples must hold true to their faith and continue to spread the Good News, avoiding false prophecies about Christ's coming.

This is a confusing chapter, for Matthew seems to conflate the destruction of the Temple (at the fall of Jerusalem in 70 CE) with the end-of-the-world apocalypse. The disciples may have assumed that they were asking a single question—"When will the woes you are predicting happen and when will you come back?"—since they had no way of knowing that some two thousand years later, Christians would still be waiting for Christ's return.

Matthew uses the word *parousia* here, which meant "advent," "arrival," or "presence." Jesus compares the sudden and unforeseen nature of his "parousia" to the great flood of Noah's time, a thief entering a house unseen at night, and an employer returning from time away to find one employee attending to his work while another takes advantage of the employer's absence.

⊠ THE BLOOMING OF GOD'S REALM ⊠

Eschatology—the study of "last" things—is a hard subject to comprehend, and this chapter is no exception. It contains the longest address we have from Jesus, starting at verse 4 and concluding at the end of chapter 25, a long monologue that must have been nearly as difficult for the disciples to understand as it is for us today. "Be careful that no one leads you astray," Jesus warns the disciples (vs. 4). During this time of "oppression" (vs. 29), he encourages them to hold true to their faith and continue to spread the Good News of God's Realm.

There are various views and interpretations about this chapter (as is true of most of the eschatological passages in the Christian scriptures). In the last thousand years or so, many biblical experts have come to see two separate events depicted here—the destruction of the Temple (which took place roughly forty years after Jesus) and the end of the world. But the dividing line between the two events are as various as the interpretations; some put the beginning of the next section at verse 29 and others at verse 36 (and there are other ideas besides these about where the "divide" occurs).

A more ancient view, however (that's still held by many streams of Christianity today), sees the whole chapter as relating only to the destruction of the Temple. This idea is based on a number of things. First, is Matthew's use of the word "generation." Throughout his Gospel, Matthew used the word almost exclusively to describe the people who are alive at that moment in time when Jesus is speaking, his contemporaries. (See, for example, Matthew 11:16; 12:39, 41–45; 16:4; 17:17; and 23:36.) Another factor is the use of the word "you." Throughout this chapter, Jesus uses the word "you" about twenty-four times (before and after the "divide" that some Bible students have identified), indicating that he's speaking directly to the disciples. The last reason to see all of Matthew 24 as applicable to one event is the parallel passage in Luke 17. There, many of the things Jesus talks about here in Matthew are in a different order. For example, in Matthew 24, when Jesus says, "As the days of Noah were, so will be the coming of the Human One" (vs. 37), it comes after the so-called divide, which, many Bible scholars have assumed, must mean Jesus was referring to the end of the world. But in Luke 17, that phrase is close to the beginning of the passage (vs. 26). And in Matthew 24:28 (which some say refers to the destruction of the Temple), Jesus says, "Wherever the carcass is, that is where the vultures (or eagles) gather together." But Luke places this saying at the end of the passage (vs. 37). These differences, along with several others, led the ancient church to see Matthew 24 as all one event—the war between the Jews and the Romans that led to the destruction of Jerusalem and the Temple in 70 CE.

So, again, eschatology is a hard subject and can be very confusing. I know; I've studied it for over twenty-five years and can still get dizzy trying to piece it all together! But I think the Celts had a way of approaching eschatology that can be quite beneficial to us today. They were less concerned with a global eschatology regarding the ultimate end of the cosmos than many churches are today. For the Celts, the presence of God's Realm was not a cataclysmic event that ended the world but a growing presence *within* creation.

As we mentioned earlier, Jesus uses the word *parousia* to refer to his "coming" (vss. 27, 39, for example)—his presence, his arrival. This is reminiscent of something Luke records in his Gospel: "God's Realm is in your midst" (or "within you," 17:21), says Jesus. Building from this understanding, the Celts' focus, then, was with a *realized* eschatology, a *personal* eschatology: the coming of the Reign of Heaven to each individual, both in this life and the next. The Celts' love of pilgrimage—as seen in many Celtic stories, such as the tale of Saint Brendan's voyage to the Isle of the Blessed—was an expression of their sense that the human experience was meant to be both a journey toward Heaven (in the next life) and at the same time an ushering in and an ongoing experience of Heaven (in this life).

In his book, *Listening for the Heartbeat of God,* John Philip Newell put it this way: "There is not in the Celtic way of seeing a great gap between heaven and earth. Rather, the two are seen as *inseparably intertwined.*" He goes on to say that the early Celtic Christians "permitted [the gospel] to work its *mystery of transformation* in the life and culture of the people" (emphasis added).

Adomnán, the seventy-century Abbot of Iona who wrote a biography of Saint Columba, was especially interested in the "mystery of transformation" in the saint's life, describing the ways in which the Realm of Heaven grew and "blossomed" in Columba. According to Alexander Souter, the Scottish author of a glossary of medieval Latin, the word Adomnán used for "blossom" implies the full manifestation of a plant's nature, the crowning achievement of its existence and the promise of it bearing fruit. This was what *parousia* meant to Adomnán—the presence of Heaven revealed through human beings. So when he wrote that Columba's robes were decorated with "flowers of every color," Adomnán wasn't simply making mention of an interesting detail about Columba's clothes; he was suggesting the rich abundance of Christ's presence and the manifestation of God's Realm in Columba's life.

James Bruce, author of *Prophecy, Miracles, Angels, and Heavenly Light? The Eschatology, Pneumatology, and Missiology of Adomnán's Life of St. Columba*, notes that, for Adomnán, the Reign of God was embodied in the here-and-now, "the in-breaking of the rule of God . . . by direct action." Adomnán portrayed Columba living out God's Realm in the present moment in a variety of ways: his kindness and good morals, his intimate bond with animals, his conversations with angels, his powerful miracles, and the ease with which he moved in and out of the Otherworld.

To read Matthew 24, then, as a warning about the future (or the past) is to miss Jesus' central message of faithfulness. The Realm of Heaven of which he's speaking has nothing to do with streets of gold and pie in the sky. Instead, it's a place of integrity and justice, a living and practical Reality that challenges us to be true to God, to others, to the Earth, and to our own selves.

Jesus called the disciples—and us—to live faithfully in God's Realm in the here-and-now, rather than postponing our response to his challenge for some later, more convenient day. Just as he taught us to pray for God's Realm to come "on earth as it is in heaven" (Matthew 6:9–13), Jesus asks us to be faithful in living out this Reality (vs. 46).

At any moment, the Realm of Heaven can erupt into our lives. When it does, will it have room to grow and blossom?

—Jack Gillespie

24

¹ Jesus went out from the Temple, and was going on his way. His disciples came to him to show him the buildings of the Temple. ² But he answered them, "You see all of these things, don't you? Most certainly I tell you, there will not be left here one stone on another, that will not be thrown down."

³ As he sat on the Mount of Olives, the disciples came to him privately, saying, "Tell us, when will these things be? What is the sign of your coming, and of the end of the age?"

⁴ Jesus answered them, "Be careful that no one leads you astray. ⁵ For many will come in my name, saying, 'I am the Christ,' and will lead many astray. ⁶ You will hear of wars and rumors of wars. See that you aren't troubled, for all this must happen, but the end is not yet. ⁷ For nation will rise against nation, and empire against empire; and there will be famines, plagues, and earthquakes in various places. ⁸ But all these things are the beginning of birth pains. ⁹ Then they will deliver you up to oppression and

will kill you. You will be hated by all of the nations for my name's sake. ¹⁰ Then many will stumble, and will deliver up one another, and will hate one another. ¹¹ Many false prophets will arise and will lead many astray. ¹² Because evil will be multiplied, the love of many will grow cold. ¹³ But those who endure to the end will be saved. ¹⁴ This Good News of the Reign of Heaven will be preached in the whole world as a testimony to all the nations, and then the end will come.

¹⁵ "When, therefore, you see the abomination of desolation,ᵃ which was spoken of through Daniel the prophet, standing in the holy place (let the reader understand), ¹⁶ then let those who are in Judea flee to the mountains. ¹⁷ Let those who are on the housetop not go down to get things from inside the house. ¹⁸ Let those who are in the field not go back to get their clothes. ¹⁹ But woe to those who are with child and to nursing mothers in those days! ²⁰ Pray that your flight will not be in the winter, nor on a Sabbath, ²¹ for then there will be great oppression, such as has not been from the beginning of the world until now, no, nor ever will be. ²² Unless those days had been shortened, no flesh would have been saved. But for the sake of the chosen people, those days will be shortened.

²³ "Then if anyone tells you, 'Look, here is the Christ,' or, 'There,' don't believe it. ²⁴ For there will arise false messiahs and false prophets, and they will show great signs and wonders, so as to lead astray, if possible, even the chosen people.

²⁵ "Consider this, I have told you beforehand. ²⁶ So if they tell you, 'Now look, the Christ is in the wilderness,' don't go out; 'Now look the Christ is in the inner rooms,' don't believe it. ²⁷ For as the lightning flashes from the east, and is seen even to the west, so will be the coming of the Human One. ²⁸ For wherever

the carcass is, that is where the vultures gather together. ²⁹ But immediately after the oppression of those days, the sun will be darkened, the moon will not give its light, the stars will fall from the sky, and the powers of the heavens will be shaken; ³⁰ and then the sign of the Human One will appear in the sky. Then all the tribes of the earth will mourn, and they will see the Human One coming on the clouds of the sky with power and great glory. ³¹ The angels will appear with a great sound of a trumpet, and they will gather together the chosen people from the four winds, from one end of the sky to the other.

³² "Now from the fig tree learn this parable. When its branch has now become tender, and produces its leaves, you know that the summer is near. ³³ Even so you also, when you see all these things, know that it is near, even at the doors. ³⁴ Most certainly I tell you, this age will not pass away, until all these things are accomplished. ³⁵ Heaven and earth will pass away, but my words will not pass away. ³⁶ But no one knows of that day and hour, not even the angels of heaven, nor the son, but Abba God only.

³⁷ "As the days of Noah were, so will be the coming of the Human One. ³⁸ For as in those days which were before the flood they were eating and drinking, marrying and giving in marriage, until the day that Noah entered into the ship, ³⁹ and they didn't know until the flood came, and took them all away, so will be the coming of the Human One. ⁴⁰ Then two workers will be in the field: one will be taken and one will be left. ⁴¹ Two workers will be grinding at the mill: one will be taken and one will be left. ⁴² So be alert, for you don't know in what hour your Sovereign comes. ⁴³ But know this, that if the owner of the house had known what time of the night the thief was coming, a watch would have been set, and the house would not have been broken into. ⁴⁴ Therefore also be ready, for in an hour that you don't expect, the Human One will come.

CHAPTER TWENTY-FOUR

⁴⁵ "Who then is the faithful and wise servant, whom the owner of the house has set over the household, to give them their food in due season? ⁴⁶ Blessed is the servant found faithfully attending to duty when the owner returns. ⁴⁷ Most certainly I tell you that the owner of the house will give this faithful servant charge over the entire household. ⁴⁸ But if that evil servant should think, 'The owner of this house is delayed in returning,' ⁴⁹ and begins to beat the other servants, and eat and drink with the drunkards, ⁵⁰ the owner of the house will return home unexpectedly and will have this evil servant severely punished and then cast among the hypocrites where there is weeping and grinding of teeth."

ᵃ Daniel 9:27, 11:31, 12:11

twenty-five

In this chapter, Jesus continues the conversation from the previous chapter, giving his disciples more illustrations of how to live in a state of readiness for the Realm of Heaven. He begins with a parable about a wedding and its guests, some of whom are not ready when the bride and groom arrive. Jesus then tells a parable about a landowner who gives money to his servants and leaves on a trip, expecting them to continue to work and make something of what he has given them in his absence. When the landowner returns, he rewards the servants who have built on the initial investment and punishes the servant who has not used what he was given. Jesus then explicitly spells out the behaviors that will make us ready for the Reign of Heaven: feeding the hungry, giving to the poor, and welcoming the outcasts.

THE SEVEN ACTS OF MERCY

Every time we give to those in need, we are giving to Jesus. Giving to others was an ancient custom of the Celts, as well as among many peoples. It is a sure demonstration of love, not only for others but also for God. In this chapter, Jesus makes clear that the two cannot be separated. We cannot say we love God if we are not actively engaged in showing love—in concrete, practical ways—to those around us.

The *Carmina Gadelica*, the nineteenth-century collection of ancient oral traditions, contains this Scottish "rune" that echoes Jesus' words in verses 31 to 40:

> We saw a stranger yesterday.
> We put food in the eating place,
> Drink in the drinking place,
> Music in the listening place.
> And with the sacred name of the triune God
> He blessed us and our house,
> Our cattle and our dear ones.
> As the lark says in her song:
> Often, often, often, goes the Christ
> In the stranger's guise.

Stories about Saint Brigid of Kildare also demonstrate this active and down-to-earth love for others, which was also an expression of her love for God. When Brigid was young, she took her father's sword and gave it away to a poor man. Her father was so angry that he took her to the king of Leinster to sell her. When the king asked her why she gave away her father's sword, she answered, "The son of the Virgin Mary knows, if I had your power and your wealth of all of Leinster, I would give them all to the Lord of the Elements."

The king said to her father, "It is not right for us to judge this young woman because her worth before God is greater than ours," and Brigid was saved from bondage.

THE GOSPEL OF MATTHEW

CHAPTER TWENTY-FIVE

The virtues of generosity and hospitality—of which Jesus spoke in Matthew 25 and which Brigid exemplified in her life—became known as the seven corporal works of mercy:

1. Feed the hungry.
2. Give drink to the thirsty.
3. Clothe the naked.
4. Shelter the homeless.
5. Visit the sick.
6. Visit the imprisoned.
7. Bury the dead.

This list is rarely mentioned in contemporary churches. When is the last time that you heard the world "corporal" in any sermon? But it's a good word, related to Latin *corpus*, which means "body." It makes clear that the spirituality to which Jesus called his followers is to be lived out in the physical world, in ways that benefit human bodies in practical ways. In the Early Middle Ages, Celtic followers of Jesus were very mindful that they were called to being doing good with their own bodies on behalf of others' bodies.

If we were to put to put the seven corporal virtues in today's terms, they might look something like this:

1. Consider how good stewardship practices of your own food habits can benefit others who do not have those same resources. Volunteer at local soup kitchens and canteens. Give to organizations such as City Harvest, Feeding America, the Hunger Project, Action Against Hunger, and Heifer International. Show hospitality to those you encounter who don't have enough to eat—and also to those who are lonely and hungry for companionship.
2. In a world where so many people lack access to clean water, be mindful of the ways in which you use water. Support

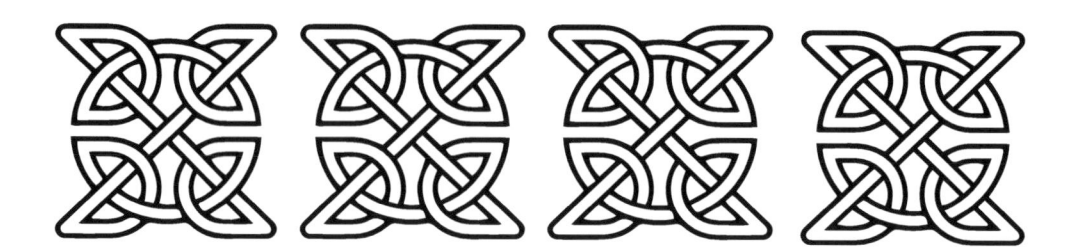

government efforts to conserve and protect water resources; get involved politically. Donate to organizations that are working to bring clean-water access to the regions of the world where it's most needed, such as Blood:Water, LifeWater.org, Splash, the Thirst Project, and Generosity.org.

3. Clean out your closets and donate what you don't need to charities such as the Salvation Army, the American Red Cross, Goodwill, and St. Vincent DePaul's. (Think in terms of giving away clothes you really don't need rather than only those that are too worn out or out of style for you to wear anymore). Consider spending less money on clothes in order to donate money to a nonprofit organization that helps provide appropriate clothing to school children or women looking for work (such as Dress for Success).

4. Homelessness is a local, national, and international crisis. You can help by volunteering with organizations like Habitat for Humanity and the National Coalition for the Homeless. Become politically involved in support of government action that welcomes international refugees. Donate to organizations such as the National Alliance to End Homelessness, Project Blanket, and StandUp for Kids (which works with homeless youth living on the streets). Practice hospitality by opening your house to those who need a place to stay.

5. Illness and disease are as real in our day as they were in Jesus'—and so is the loneliness faced by those who suffer from a chronic illness. Volunteer in nursing homes, hospitals, and

hospice programs, or sign up to cuddle babies born addicted to opioids. Donate to HIV research and become politically involved to ensure that our government continues to fund it. Donate to international health programs, such as the Carter Center's. Get involved personally by offering to assist caregivers of chronically sick family members on a one-time or periodic basis.
6. Get involved with local prison ministries. Volunteer with organizations that work with the children of inmates. Contact the Prison Activist Resource Center to see what else you could do. Take a stand politically for prison reform.
7. Our culture likes to avoid the thought of death—which means that those going through the grieving process often feel lonely and ostracized from the rest of life. Make a point of being present with friends, neighbors, and colleagues who are going through the grief process. Don't just attend the funeral; be there for the long haul. Be willing to listen; don't feel that you have to make the person's grief go away. Contact local churches and check the Internet for other opportunities.

Modern-day Christians have sometimes dismissed a "social gospel," feeling that instead we should be focused on the "spiritual needs" of those we encounter. Saint Brigid, however, never tried to convert anyone using the "Four Spiritual Laws"; she never talked about sin and hell, nor tried to persuade others to "give their hearts to Jesus." Instead, she attended to their physical needs, spreading God's love in practical ways. Her example challenges us: What are we to be doing with our body on this earth? How do we treat others and their bodies? However we answer these questions will say much about our relationship with Jesus (vs. 45).

—Teresa Cross

25

¹ Then the Realm of Heaven will be like ten wedding attendants, who took their lamps, and went out to await the arrival of the bride and groom. ² Five of them were foolish, and five were wise. ³ The foolish ones did not think to bring enough oil for their lamps, ⁴ but those who were wise brought extra oil with them to keep their lamps burning while they were waiting. ⁵ The bride and groom were delayed, and the attendants grew weary and fell asleep. ⁶ But at midnight there was a cry, 'Look! The bride and groom are coming! Come out to meet them!' ⁷ Then the attendants woke up and began to prepare their lamps. ⁸ The foolish said to the wise, 'Give us some of your oil, for our lamps are going out.' ⁹ But the wise answered, saying, 'What if there isn't enough for us and you? You must go and buy more oil for yourselves.'

¹⁰ "While they went away to buy the oil, the bride and groom came, and those who were ready went in with them to the marriage feast, and

the door was shut. ¹¹ Later, the other attendants returned, saying, 'Sir, Sir, let us in.' ¹² But the groom answered, 'Go away, for I do not know you.' 13 Be alert therefore, for you don't know the day nor the hour in which the Human One is coming.

¹⁴ "For it is like a landowner, going into another country, who called the servants together, and entrusted the household goods to them. ¹⁵ To one was given five talents,ᵃ to another two, to another one; to each according to their own ability. Then the landowner departed. ¹⁶ Immediately the servant who received the five talents went and traded with them, and made another five talents. ¹⁷ In the same way, the servant who got the two gained another two. ¹⁸ But the servant who received the one talent went away and dug in the earth, and hid the landowner's money.

¹⁹ "Now after a long time, the landowner returned and reconciled accounts with them. ²⁰ The servant who received the five talents came and brought another five talents, saying, 'Sir, you delivered to me five talents. Now look, I have gained another five talents in addition to them.'

²¹ "The landowner replied, 'Well done, good and faithful servant. You have been faithful over a few things, so I will set you over many things. Enter into my joy.'

²² "The servant also who got the two talents came and said, 'Sir, you delivered to me two talents. See, I have gained another two talents in addition to them.'

²³ "The landowner said, 'Well done, good and faithful servant. You have been faithful over a few things, I will set you over many things. Enter into my joy.'

²⁴ "But the one who had received the one talent came and said, 'Sir, I knew you that you are a hard ruler, reaping where you

didn't sow, and gathering where you didn't scatter. ²⁵ I was afraid, and went away and hid your talent in the earth. Consider this, you have what is yours.'

²⁶ "But the landowner answered, 'You wicked and lazy servant. You knew that I reap where I didn't sow, and gather where I didn't scatter. ²⁷ You ought therefore to have deposited my money with the bankers, and at my coming I should have received back my own with interest. ²⁸ Take away therefore this unfaithful servant's talent, and give it to the servant who has the ten talents. ²⁹ For to everyone who has will be given, and they will have abundance, but from those who don't have, even that which they have will be taken away. ³⁰ Throw out the unprofitable servant into the outer darkness, where there will be weeping and gnashing of teeth.'

³¹ "But the time will come when the Human One will come in glory, accompanied by the holy angels, and will sit upon the heavenly throne. ³² All the nations will be gathered before the throne and they will be separated from one another as a shepherd separates the sheep from the goats. ³³ The sheep will be set to the Human One's right, and the goats to the left. ³⁴ Then the Sovereign will say to those gathered on the right, 'Come, you whom Abba blessed from the very beginning. Inherit the Realm prepared for you of the world; ³⁵ for I was hungry, and you gave me food to eat. I was thirsty, and you gave me drink. I was a stranger, and you took me in. ³⁶ I was naked, and you clothed me. I was sick, and you visited me. I was in prison, and you came to me.'

³⁷ "Then the righteous will answer, saying, 'Exalted One, when did we see you hungry, and feed you; or thirsty, and give you a drink? ³⁸ When did we see you as a stranger, and take you in; or naked, and clothe you? ³⁹ When did we see you sick, or in prison, and come to you?'

⁴⁰ "The Sovereign will answer them, 'Most certainly I tell you, because you did it to one of the least of these my brothers and sisters, you did it

to me.' ⁴¹ Then the Sovereign will say also to those on the left hand, 'Depart from me, you cursed, into the eternal fire which is prepared for the devil and his angels; ⁴² for I was hungry, and you didn't give me food to eat; I was thirsty, and you gave me no drink; ⁴³ I was a stranger, and you didn't take me in; naked, and you didn't clothe me; sick, and in prison, and you didn't visit me.'

⁴⁴ "Then they will also answer, saying, 'Exalted One', when did we see you hungry, or thirsty, or a stranger, or naked, or sick, or in prison, and didn't help you?'

⁴⁵ "Then the Sovereign will answer them, saying, 'Most certainly I tell you, because you didn't do it to one of the least of these, you didn't do it to me.' ⁴⁶ These will go away into eternal correction, but the just will enter eternal life."

ᵃ A talent is about 30 kilograms or 66 pounds of silver.

twenty-six

In this chapter, Matthew makes the transition from Jesus' comments on the coming of the Reign of Heaven to his narrative of the betrayal that will lead to his death. The chapter describes the rejection Jesus endures: his closest friends cannot stay awake with him while he prays in the Garden of Gethsemane; Judas betrays him to the religious authorities who are plotting his death; Peter denies that he even knows Jesus; Jesus is put on trial and accused of blasphemy; the crowd curses him, spits on him, and hits him; and finally, he is sentenced to death.

⊠ THE END THAT IS THE BEGINNING ⊠

Death is the great taboo of this age. We avoid mentioning it, we postpone it as long as possible, we act as if we can be immortal if we can only get our fitness regime and diet just perfect. Not so Jesus. Matthew shows us his fear and agony in Gethsemane, but at the same time we see his matter-of-fact acceptance of imminent death. As the chief priests and elders plot to kill him, as Judas gives in to greed and betrays him, as the disciples flounder in disbelief and denial, and as Pilate plays politics to avoid possible riots, Jesus is the only one who remains totally calm and truly in control. Furthermore, Jesus not only faced physical death. He also went through the emotional death we experience when we face personal rejection—and yet he did so with equanimity, without anger or bitterness.

Tales also abound of the quiet acceptance and faith of Celtic saints in the presence of approaching death, which they often saw in advance. Their lives focused on finding their "place of resurrection," in which they could best await entry to heaven and pray for those making the same journey. In an article titled "Celtic Saints and the Ecology of Death," theologian Paul Santmire suggests that the Celts' intimate relationship with the natural world allowed them to see death as a normal and necessary point on the arc between life and rebirth.

In any case, the Celtic saints' faith allowed them to move calmly to their end, preparing and reassuring their companions, much as Jesus did. For example, Boisil, Abbot of Melrose, foretold he would die of plague, but that his protégé Cuthbert would survive; he and Cuthbert studied John's Gospel together during Boisil's last week. Columba's last day was spent blessing the monks and farm workers on Iona, and even his sorrowing horse, which knew he was about to die. Caedmon made sure he was at peace with all before his death, forgiven and forgiving. Brigid is said to have known the date of her departure from this life four years before her death—and she used the time to prepare her community, including a female companion named Dar Lugdach, with whom she shared her bed. When Dar Lugdach grieved because Brigid would soon be leaving this life, Brigid comforted her by telling her that exactly one year later she too would die. (And, according to tradition, Dar Lugdach succeeded Brigid as abbess of Kildare and then, as foretold by Brigid, she died exactly one year after her.)

We have modern examples as well of individuals who have faced death with confidence and grace. In May 2015, an interviewer marveled how Christian speaker and writer Phyllis Tickle faced her fast-approaching death from cancer. "At eighty-one you figure you're going to die of something, and sooner rather than later," she said. "I could almost embrace this, that, OK, now I know what it's probably going to be, and probably how much time there is. So you can clean up some of the mess you've made and tie up some of the loose ends."

Dietrich Bonhoeffer, who was put to death in a Nazi concentration camp at the age of thirty-nine, wrote shortly before his death:

> Why are we so afraid when we think about death? . . . Death is only dreadful for those who live in dread and fear of it. . . . Death is not bitter, if we have not become bitter ourselves. Death is grace, the greatest gift of grace that God gives . . . if only we realize that it is the gateway to our homeland, the tabernacle of joy, the everlasting kingdom of peace. How do we know that dying is so dreadful? Who knows whether, in our human fear and anguish we are only shivering and shuddering at the most glorious, heavenly, blessed event in the world?

In the Garden of Gethsemane, Jesus prays that he might be spared having to drink from the "cup" that awaits him (vss. 39, 42). Today, we have an ongoing fascination with the mythological cup Jesus drank from, known in Arthurian legend as the Grail, which has been interpreted as everything from a symbol for the Divine Feminine, to a Celtic vessel of plenty, to an archetype for individual fulfillment. Jesus' prayer in the Garden points us in a different direction. He has already shared the actual "cup" with his disciples at the Last Supper (vs. 27),

CHAPTER TWENTY-SIX 285

and the metaphorical cup he refers to now is the death that lies ahead of him. Ultimately, he accepts from his Abba the cup that is, as Bonhoeffer said as he went to his execution, "the end," which is also "the beginning of life."

—Paul Martin

CHAPTER TWENTY-SIX

26

¹ When Jesus had finished all these words, he said to his disciples, ² "You know that after two days the Passover is coming, and the Human One will be delivered up to be crucified."

³ Then the chief priests, the scribes, and the elders of the people were gathered together in the court of the high priest, who was called Caiaphas. ⁴ They took counsel together that they might take Jesus by deceit and kill him. ⁵ But they said, "Not during the feast, lest a riot occur among the people."

⁶ Now when Jesus was in Bethany, in the house of Simon the leper, ⁷ a woman came to him with alabaster jar of very expensive ointment, and she poured it on his head as he sat at the table. ⁸ But when his disciples saw this, they were indignant, saying, "Why this waste? ⁹ For this ointment might have been sold for much, and given to the poor."

¹⁰ However, knowing this, Jesus said to them, "Why do you trouble the woman? She has done a good work for me. ¹¹ For you always have the poor with you; but you don't always have me. ¹² For in pouring this ointment on

my body, she did it to prepare me for burial. [13] Most certainly I tell you, wherever this Good News is preached in the whole world, what this woman has done will also be spoken of as a memorial of her."

[14] Then one of the twelve, who was called Judas Iscariot, went to the chief priests, [15] and said, "What are you willing to give me, that I should deliver him to you?" They weighed out for him thirty pieces of silver. [16] From that time on, he sought opportunity to betray Jesus.

[17] Now on the first day of unleavened bread, the disciples came to Jesus, saying to him, "Where do you want us to prepare for you to eat the Passover?"

[18] He said, "Go into the city to a certain person, and say, 'The Teacher says, "My time is at hand. I will keep the Passover at your house with my disciples."'"

[19] The disciples did as Jesus commanded them, and they prepared the Passover. [20] Now when evening had come, he was reclining at the table with the twelve disciples. [21] As they were eating, he said, "Most certainly I tell you that one of you will betray me."

[22] They were upset, and each began to ask him, "It isn't me, is it, Rabbi?"

[23] He answered, "The one who shared this dish with me will betray me. [24] The Human One goes, even as it is written, but woe to the person through whom Human One is betrayed! It would be better if that person had not been born."

[25] Judas, who betrayed him, answered, "It isn't me, is it, Rabbi?"

Jesus replied, "You have said it."

[26] As they were eating, Jesus took bread, gave thanks for it, and broke it. He gave to the disciples, and said, "Take, eat; this is my body." [27] He took the cup, gave thanks, and gave to them, saying, "All of you drink it, [28] for this is my blood of the new covenant, which is poured out for many for the forgiveness of wrongdoing. [29] But I tell you that I will not drink

of this fruit of the vine from now on, until that day when I drink it anew with you in the Reign of Abba God." ³⁰ When they had sung a hymn, they went out to the Mount of Olives.

³¹ Then Jesus said to them, "All of you will be made to stumble because of me tonight, for it is written, 'I will strike the shepherd, and the sheep of the flock will be scattered.' ᵃ ³² But after I am raised up, I will go before you into Galilee."

³³ But Peter answered him, "Even if everyone else stumbles because of you, I will never stumble."

³⁴ Jesus said to him, "Most certainly I tell you that tonight, before the rooster crows, you will deny me three times."

³⁵ Peter said to him, "Even if I must die with you, I will not deny you." All of the disciples said the same thing.

³⁶ Then Jesus came with them to a place called Gethsemane and said to his disciples, "Sit here, while I go there and pray." ³⁷ He took with him Peter and the two sons of Zebedee, and began to be sorrowful and troubled. ³⁸ Then he said to them, "My soul is so very sad, even to death. Stay here, and watch with me."

³⁹ He went forward a little, fell on his face, and prayed, saying, "My Abba, if it is possible, let this cup pass away from me; nevertheless, not what I desire, but what you desire."

⁴⁰ He came to the disciples and found them sleeping, and he said to Peter, "What, couldn't you watch with me for one hour? ⁴¹ Watch and pray, that you don't enter into temptation. The spirit indeed is willing, but the flesh is weak."

⁴² Again, a second time he went away, and prayed, saying, "Abba, if this cup can't pass away from me unless I drink it, your desire be done." ⁴³ He came again and found them sleeping, for their eyes were heavy. ⁴⁴ He left them again, went away, and prayed a third time, saying the same

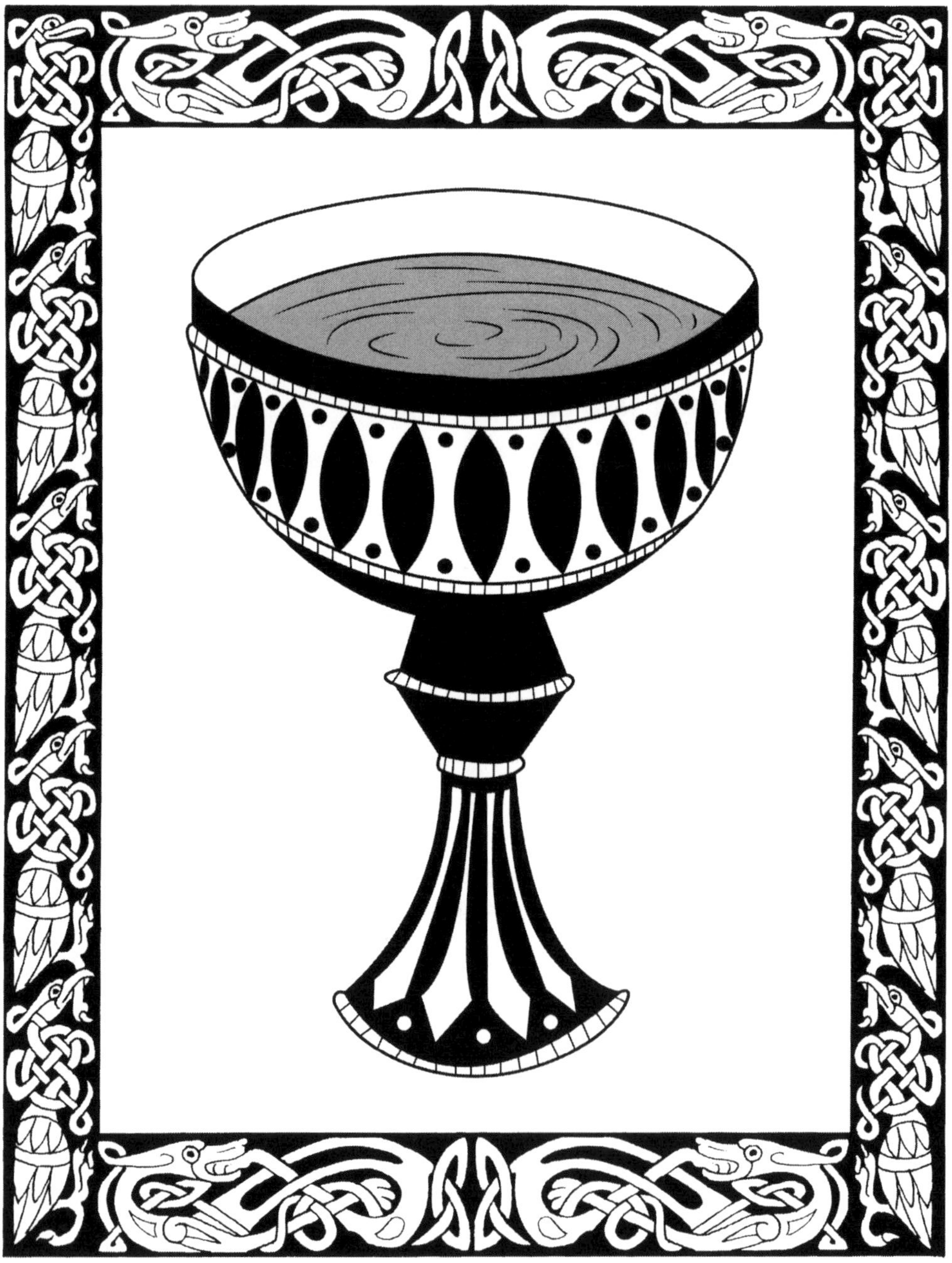

words. ⁴⁵ Then he came to his disciples, and said to them, "Sleep on now, and take your rest. Notice that the hour is at hand, and the Human One is betrayed into the hands of wrongdoers. ⁴⁶ Get up and let's be going. The one who betrays me is nearby."

⁴⁷ While he was still speaking, look!—Judas, one of the twelve, came, and with him a great crowd with swords and clubs, who came from the chief priests and elders of the people. ⁴⁸ Now he who betrayed Jesus gave them a sign, saying, "Whomever I kiss, he is the one. Seize him." ⁴⁹ Immediately Judas came to Jesus, and said, "Hail, Rabbi!" and kissed him.

⁵⁰ Jesus said to him, "Friend, why are you here?" Then they came and laid hands on Jesus and took him. ⁵¹ But one of those with Jesus drew a sword and struck off the ear of the high priest's servant. ⁵² Then Jesus said, "Put your sword back into its place, for all those who take the sword will die by the sword. ⁵³ Or do you think that I couldn't ask my Abba, who would even now send me more than twelve legions of angels? ⁵⁴ How then would the Scriptures be fulfilled that it must be so?"

⁵⁵ In that hour, Jesus said to the crowds, "Have you come out as against a robber with swords and clubs to seize me? I sat daily in the Temple teaching, and you didn't arrest me. ⁵⁶ But all this has happened that the Scriptures of the prophets might be fulfilled."

Then all the disciples left him and fled. ⁵⁷ Those who had taken Jesus led him away to Caiaphas the high priest, where the scribes and the elders were gathered together. ⁵⁸ But Peter followed from a distance, to the court of the high priest, and entered in and sat with the officers, to see the end. ⁵⁹ Now the chief priests, the elders, and the whole council sought false testimony against Jesus, that they might put him to death; ⁶⁰ and they found none. Even though many false witnesses came forward, they found none. But at last two false witnesses came forward ⁶¹ and said, "This man said, 'I am able to destroy the temple of God and to build it in three days.'"

⁶² The high priest stood up, and said to him, "Have you no answer? What is this that these testify against you?" ⁶³ But Jesus held his peace. The high priest answered him, "I adjure you by the living God, that you tell us whether you are the Christ, begotten of God."

⁶⁴ Jesus answered, "You have said it. Nevertheless, I tell you, after this you will see the Human One sitting at the right hand of Power, and coming on the clouds of the sky."

⁶⁵ Then the high priest tore his clothing, saying, "He has spoken blasphemy! Why do we need any more witnesses? Observe now, you have heard his blasphemy. ⁶⁶ What do you think?"

They answered, "He is worthy of death!" ⁶⁷ Then they spat in his face and beat him with their fists, and some slapped him, ⁶⁸ saying, "Prophesy to us, you imposter! Who hit you?"

⁶⁹ Now Peter was sitting outside in the court, and a maid came to him, saying, "You were also with Jesus, the Galilean!"

⁷⁰ But Peter denied it before them all, saying, "I don't know what you are talking about."

⁷¹ When he had gone out into the gateway, someone else saw him, and said to those who were there, "This man was also with Jesus of Nazareth."

⁷² Again he denied it with an oath: "I don't know the man."

⁷³ After a little while those who stood by came and said to Peter, "Surely you are also one of them, for we recognize you by your speech."

⁷⁴ Then he began to curse and to swear, "I don't know the man!"

Immediately the rooster crowed. ⁷⁵ Peter remembered the word which Jesus had said to him: "Before the rooster crows, you will deny me three times." Then he went out and wept bitterly.

ᵃ Zechariah 13:7

Twenty-seven

In this chapter, Matthew tells the story of Jesus' torture, death on the cross, and burial. Through the ages, Christians have considered these verses to be truly the "crux" of their faith. The crucifixion is the focal point of Christian theology.

THE MEANING OF THE CROSS

Although the crucifixion has always been essential to Christianity's meaning, the way in which Christians have defined that meaning has changed over the centuries. The Celtic saints understood it quite differently from the way in which many Christians do today.

The theory of the cross most modern Christian denominations hold is that of "substitution." This theory goes like this: all humans are sinners who deserve God's wrath, but Jesus' death satisfied the cost of human sin. Scripture cited to support this view is Isaiah 53: "He was punished for our transgressions." While common today, this theory

294 THE GOSPEL OF MATTHEW

CHAPTER TWENTY-SEVEN 295

of redemption has only been popular since Archbishop Anselm of Canterbury promoted it around the year 1100, more than a thousand years after the birth of Christianity.

The Celts understood the crucifixion quite differently; their understanding was based on the perspective of the "Christus Victor" model of atonement. The Christus Victor premise was that Jesus' death was not a legal settlement with God (where God had to punish someone for human sin, so Jesus substituted himself for humanity) but instead a victorious battle against the forces of darkness. On the cross, Christ stepped into the human arena where we all confront death and the other works of Satan. Like the bravest of knights, he fought with these terrifying enemies and was triumphant; he forced them to release humanity from their grip.

In a world where battle was common and warriors honored, this perspective must have been particularly appealing. The ancient Celts spent long evenings around the fire extolling the triumphs of their heroes. Christ's feats were as brave and thrilling as the Irish hero Cuchulain's.

The Iona monastery, one of Celtic Christianity's vital nerve centers, had an extensive library, which included the Acts of Pilate, an apocryphal Gospel that describes the "Harrowing of Hell." After Jesus dies—and before the Resurrection—he descends into hell to rescue those who have been languishing there. When Christ reaches hell's gates, he demands, "Open thy gates that the King of Glory may come in." The demons refuse him entrance, but then "suddenly Hell did quake, and the gates of death and the locks were broken small, and the bars of iron broken, and fell to the ground, and all things were laid open." Christ then frees a jubilant crowd of captives.

Afterward, according to the Acts of Pilate, "all the saints of God besought the Lord that he would leave the sign of victory—even of the holy cross—in hell, that the wicked ministers thereof might not prevail to keep back any that was accused, whom the Lord absolved.

And it was so done, and the Lord set his cross in the midst of hell, which is the sign of victory; and it shall remain there forever." For the ancient Celts, the cross was a symbol of Christ's heroic and eternal victory over hell and death. They believed if they descended to the very depths of hell, they would find the cross waiting for them, offering them hope and salvation even there.

The Celtic saints identified with Jesus' death on the cross as a way for them to offer up their own lives in the battle against evil. They joyfully chose to join their Hero as he hung from the cross. And they kept tangible signs of the cross always nearby, claiming the cross as part of their daily lives, an aspect of their most intimate identities.

This ancient Celtic prayer reflects this perspective:

Christ's cross over this face I wear, and over my ear.
Christ's cross over my eye.
Christ's cross over my nose.
Christ's cross to accompany me before.
Christ's cross to accompany me behind me.
Christ's cross to meet every difficulty both on hollow and hill
Christ's cross eastwards facing me.
Christ's cross back toward the sunset.
In the north, in the south, increasingly may Christ's cross straightway be.
Christ's cross up to broad Heaven.
Christ's cross down to Earth.
Let no evil or hurt come to my body or my soul.

Chapter Twenty-Seven

Christ's cross over me as I sit.
Christ's cross over me as I lie.
Christ's cross be all my strength until we reach the King of Heaven.
From the top of my head to the end of my toenail,
O Christ, against every danger I trust in the protection of the cross.
Till the day of my death, when my flesh goes into the clay,
And I shall once more take
Christ's cross over this face.

—Kenneth McIntosh

27

¹ Now when morning had come, all the chief priests and the elders of the people took counsel against Jesus to put him to death; ² and they bound him, and led him away, and delivered him up to Pontius Pilate, the governor. ³ Then Judas, who betrayed him, when he saw that Jesus was condemned, felt remorse, and brought back the thirty pieces of silver to the chief priests and elders, ⁴ saying, "I have done wrong in that I betrayed innocent blood."

But they said, "What is that to us? You see to it."

⁵ He threw down the pieces of silver in the sanctuary, and departed. He went away and hanged himself. ⁶ The chief priests took the pieces of silver, and said, "It's not lawful to put them into the treasury, since it is the price of blood." ⁷ They took counsel, and bought the potter's field with them, to bury strangers in. ⁸ Therefore that field was called "The

Field of Blood" to this day. ⁹ Then that which was spoken through Jeremiah the prophet was fulfilled, saying,

> "They took the thirty pieces of silver, the price of the One upon whom a price had been set by the children of Israel, ¹⁰ and they gave them for the potter's field, as the Eternal One commanded me." [a]

¹¹ Now Jesus stood before the governor: and the governor asked him, saying, "Are you the Ruler of the Jews?"

Jesus replied, "So you say."

¹² When he was accused by the chief priests and elders, he answered nothing. ¹³ Then Pilate said to him, "Don't you hear how many things they testify against you?"

¹⁴ Jesus gave no answer, not even one word, so that the governor marveled greatly. ¹⁵ Now at the feast, the governor was accustomed to release to the crowd one prisoner, whomever they desired. ¹⁶ They had then a notable prisoner, called Barabbas, ¹⁷ so when they were gathered together, Pilate said to them, "Whom do you want me to release to you? Barabbas, or Jesus, who is called the Christ?" ¹⁸ For he knew that because of envy they had delivered him up.

¹⁹ While he was sitting on the judgment seat, his wife sent to him, saying, "Have nothing to do with that righteous man, for I have suffered many things today in a dream because of him." ²⁰ Now the chief priests and the elders persuaded the crowds to ask for Barabbas and destroy Jesus. ²¹ But the governor answered them, "Which of the two do you want me to release to you?"

They said, "Barabbas!"

²² Pilate said to them, "What then shall I do to Jesus, who is called the Christ?"

They all said to him, "Let him be crucified!"

²³ But the governor said, "Why? What evil has he done?"

But they shouted, "Let him be crucified!"

²⁴ So when Pilate saw that nothing was being gained but rather that a disturbance was starting, he washed his hands in water before the crowd, saying, "I am innocent of the blood of this righteous person. You see to it."

²⁵ All the people answered, "May his blood be on us, and on our children!"

²⁶ Then he released to them Barabbas, but Jesus he flogged and delivered to be crucified. ²⁷ Then the governor's soldiers took Jesus into the governor's residence, and gathered the whole garrison together against him. ²⁸ They stripped him and put a scarlet robe on him. ²⁹ They braided a crown of thorns and put it on his head, and a reed in his right hand; and they kneeled down before him and mocked him, saying, "Hail, King of the Jews!" ³⁰ They spat on him, and took the reed and struck him on the head. ³¹ When they had mocked him, they took the robe off him and put his clothes on him, and led him away to crucify him.

³² As they came out, they found a man of Cyrene, Simon by name, and they compelled him to go with them, that he might carry his cross. ³³ When they came to a place called "Golgotha," that is to say, "the place of a skull," ³⁴ they gave him sour wine to drink mixed with a bitter herb. When he had tasted it, he would not drink. ³⁵ When they had crucified him, they divided his clothing among them, casting lots, ³⁶ and they sat and watched him there. ³⁷ They set up over his head the accusation against him written, "THIS IS JESUS, THE KING OF THE JEWS."

³⁸ Then there were two robbers crucified with him, one on his right hand and one on the left. ³⁹ Those who passed by hurled abuse at him, wagging their heads ⁴⁰ and saying, "You who destroy the temple, and

build it in three days, save yourself! If you are the Son of God, come down from the cross!"

⁴¹ Likewise the chief priests also mocking, with the scribes, the Pharisees, and the elders, said, ⁴² "He saved others, but he can't save himself. If he is the Ruler of Israel, let him come down from the cross now, and we will believe in him. ⁴³ He trusts in God. Let God deliver him now, if he wants him; for he said, 'I am the Son of God.'" ⁴⁴ The robbers also who were crucified with him cast on him the same reproach.

⁴⁵ Now there was darkness over all the land from noon until three in the afternoon, ⁴⁶ and then, at about three, Jesus cried with a loud voice, saying, "Eli, Eli, lima sabachthani?" That is, "My God, my God, why have you forsaken me?" [b]

⁴⁷ Some of them who stood there, when they heard it, said, "This man is calling Elijah."

⁴⁸ Immediately one of them ran, and took a sponge, and filled it with vinegar, and put it on a reed, and gave him a drink. ⁴⁹ The rest said, "Let him be. Let's see whether Elijah comes to save him."

⁵⁰ Jesus cried again with a loud voice, and yielded up his breath. ⁵¹ Suddenly the veil of the temple was torn in two from the top to the bottom. The earth quaked and the rocks were split. ⁵² The tombs were opened, and many bodies of the saints who had fallen asleep were raised; ⁵³ and coming out of the tombs after his resurrection, they entered into the holy city and appeared to many. ⁵⁴ Now the centurion, and the others gathered around were watching Jesus, when they saw the earthquake and

the things that were done, were very afraid and said, "Truly this was the Son of God."

⁵⁵ Many women were there watching from afar, who had followed Jesus from Galilee, serving him. ⁵⁶ Among them were Mary Magdalene, Mary the mother of James and Joses, and the mother of the sons of Zebedee. ⁵⁷ When evening had come, a rich man from Arimathaea named Joseph, who himself was also Jesus' disciple, came ⁵⁸ and went to Pilate and asked for Jesus' body. Then Pilate commanded the body to be given up. ⁵⁹ Joseph took the body and wrapped it in a clean linen cloth, ⁶⁰ and laid it in his own new tomb, which he had cut out in the rock, and he rolled a great stone against the door of the tomb and then departed. ⁶¹ Mary Magdalene was there, and the other Mary, sitting opposite the tomb.

⁶² Now on the next day, which was the day after the Preparation Day, the chief priests and the Pharisees were gathered together to Pilate, ⁶³ saying, "Sir, we remember what that deceiver said while he was still alive: 'After three days I will rise again.' ⁶⁴ Command therefore that the tomb be made secure until the third day, lest perhaps his disciples come at night and steal him away, and tell the people, 'He is risen from the dead,' and the last deception will be worse than the first."

⁶⁵ Pilate said to them, "You have a guard. Go, make it as secure as you can." ⁶⁶ So they went with the guard and made the tomb secure, sealing the stone.

ᵃ Zechariah 11:12–13; Jeremiah 19:1–13, 32:6–9
ᵇ Psalm 22:1

Chapter Twenty-Eight

In the final chapter of this Gospel, the author describes the resurrection of Jesus after his crucifixion and burial. As Mary Magdalene and another woman mourn at Jesus' tomb, an earthquake occurs and an angel appears, shocking the guards into catatonia. The angel gives the message of Jesus' resurrection to the women, and tells them to take the message to Jesus' other followers. The fact that Matthew records this detail is significant, for it elevates the role of women in a way that was not consistent with the culture of the day; women are commissioned by heavenly authority to be the first to carry the Good News.

The author does not spend much more time on the resurrected Jesus. For Matthew, this concludes his story. What is most important to him is that before Jesus' ascension, he commissions the rest of his followers—citing his own heavenly authority—to spread his teachings.

⋈ WITH YOU ALWAYS ⋈

Having written some published fiction I can tell you: the ending of a story is the hardest part to write. The author that we call Matthew did an amazing job finishing his story of Jesus' life, with Christ giving this speech: "All authority has been given to me in heaven and on earth. Go and make disciples of all nations. . . . I am with you always, even to the end of the age" (vss. 19–20). The genius of this speech is that it makes Jesus' story become our story. It expands the tale of the twelve apostles to all of us "disciples" who have followed in the centuries since, from Galilee in the Middle East to "all nations," and from 33 CE to "the end of the age."

Down through the centuries, Jesus' followers—including the Celts—have interpreted these final words of Matthew's Gospel in various ways. Saint Patrick, for instance, believed that his evangelization of Ireland was the literal fulfillment of Jesus' final statement in verse 20. In his autobiographical treatise, Patrick alluded repeatedly to the eschatological ("end-times") significance of his work. From his perspective, Ireland was perched on the very edge of the world, and was thus the last remaining nation to receive the gospel. Since he had succeeded in delivering the Good News to the final region (completing Jesus' reference to "all nations"), Patrick assumed that his life was also perched on the end of time.

Sixteen centuries later, Patrick's confidence in his end-times role seems naive. He had no idea how much more there was to the geographical globe, nor how much more history was yet to unfold. Patrick wasn't the only one to make this mistake, however: for as long as Christianity has existed, every few years someone has predicted the imminence of Jesus' physical return to earth—and it hasn't happened yet.

Patrick's sense of his role in Jesus' promise did not make him so focused on the future, however, that he lost interest in the present reality. Instead, it convinced him that the actions and choices he made now were of vital importance to the Reign of God. While the modern-day belief that we are in the "end times" has sometimes led to the assumption that we live in a disposable, throw-away world, Patrick's beliefs made him more aware of the preciousness of this world. They gave him a sense of urgency about building Heaven's realm on earth. As he built churches, formed relationships, and prepared for others to continue his work after his death, his actions indicated that he had a practical grasp on the necessity of living in this world even while preparing for the next.

Jesus' modern-day followers continue to hope for God's consummation of history. Some forms of Christianity have taken this to mean that we do not have to work hard to protect this Earth—the planet on which we live—since they believe God will destroy creation as we know it; they do not believe our world is a continuing part of the Divine plan for the Reign of God. Others, however, believing that God will someday act decisively and powerfully to make all things well, are inspired to work all the more urgently for justice and peace, even if their efforts appear futile in the short run.

Perhaps we'd be better off regarding "the end of the age" in Matthew 28 not as a fixed destination point but a promise of Jesus' presence in every era of history. This understanding may have also been part of the Celtic perspective, alongside their belief in the imminent physical return of Jesus. For the Celtic saints, the Reign of Heaven had already begun, now, in the present moment, in the ordinary world.

In a story from Ireland's oral tradition, Patrick's farewell to a friend illustrates that perspective. "From myself to yourself," Patrick says, "in the house or out of the house, in whatever place God will lay His hand on you, I give you Heaven." In another story, Patrick warns against being too preoccupied with either the past or the future: "You have your thoughts too much taken up with them. They stand between your eyes and the Heaven that is all around you."

Jesus' promise to be with us is more than mere comforting words. It is an assurance that Jesus continues to be a present-tense reality in the world where we live. Unlike King Arthur, who has been called the "once-and-future king," Jesus is *now*. That understanding should give us a sense of the importance of the time in which we live, an understanding that is similar to Patrick's, for Jesus' presence means the Reign of Heaven is here and now. We are each a valuable part of the great, ongoing tale that extends from the Jesus who walked the earth more than two thousand years ago, to Patrick's medieval mission, to the twenty-first-century and beyond. We are actors, each with a vital and urgent role to play, in Heaven's continuing story.

—Kenneth McIntosh

28

¹ Now after the Sabbath, as morning began to dawn on the first day of the week, Mary Magdalene and the other Mary came to see the tomb. ² And suddenly there was a great earthquake, for an angel of the Eternal One descended from the sky, and came and rolled away the stone from the door, and sat on it. ³ The angel's appearance was like lightning, with clothing white as snow. ⁴ The guards trembled with fear and fell senseless to the ground as though dead. ⁵ The angel said to the women, "Don't be afraid, for I know that you seek Jesus, who has been crucified. ⁶ He is not here, for he has risen, just like he said. Come, see the place where The Great One lay. ⁷ Go quickly and tell his disciples, 'He has risen from the dead, and now, look!—he goes ahead of you into Galilee; there you will see him.' Pay attention to what I have told you."

CHAPTER TWENTY-EIGHT ☘ 309

⁸ The women departed quickly from the tomb with fear and great joy, and ran to bring the news to Jesus' disciples. ⁹ As they went, look!—Jesus met them, saying, "Rejoice!"

They came and took hold of his feet, and worshiped him.

¹⁰ Then Jesus said to them, "Don't be afraid. Go tell my brothers and sisters that they should go into Galilee, and there they will see me."

¹¹ Now while they were going, look!—some of the guards came into the city and told the chief priests all the things that had happened. ¹² When they were assembled with the elders and had talked about it, they gave a large amount of silver to the soldiers, ¹³ saying, "Say that his disciples came by night, and stole him away while we slept. ¹⁴ If this comes to the governor's ears, we will see to it that you are kept out of trouble." ¹⁵ So they took the money and did as they were told. This saying was spread abroad among the Jews and continues until today.

¹⁶ But the eleven disciples went into Galilee, to the mountain where Jesus had sent them. ¹⁷ When they saw him, they bowed down to him, but some doubted. ¹⁸ Jesus came to them and spoke to them, saying, "All authority has been given to me in heaven and on earth. ¹⁹ Go therefore and make disciples of all nations, baptizing them in the name of Abba and of the Son and of the Holy Wind, ²⁰ teaching them to guard all things with which I have charged you. And now I am with you always, even to the end of the age."

A Few Notes

It is well known in the study of languages that "every translation is an interpretation." For that reason, every new Bible translation is provisional, an unending quest by modern readers to understand ideas that began thousands of years ago. Profusion of translations creates opportunities for better understanding, as each variation creates a new way to approach the text. In fact, there has never been a time when the Christian church had an un-translated Bible, for even the original Gospel books were translations of Jesus' Aramaic words into Greek.

Celtic scholars of the Early Middle Ages faithfully copied the texts they had received, and they made choices in that process. They had multiple, varying versions of the Bible in Latin, or they had more ancient varying texts in Greek or Hebrew. So they prayed, consulted with one another, and made choices as to which manuscripts they should follow in their copying, and which words to choose in their Latin translations. In the same way, those of us editing each of the volumes of the Celtic Bible Commentary have made translation choices. We hope that you will be pleased with the text of this Bible commentary, and have included this brief explanation of the methods and choices involved in its rendering.

The Celtic Bible Commentary (CBC) text is based to large degree on the *World English Bible* (WEB) but with substantial changes. The *World English Bible* is a copyright-free translation of the Scriptures, the fruit of extraordinary effort by Michael Johnson, a Navy veteran, Bible translator, and now a missionary. He has done a great work translating and offering the WEB, free of charge, to the world. However, the Celtic Bible Commentary is not the WEB translation. The WEB website requests that "if you CHANGE the actual text of the World English Bible in any way, you not call the result the World English Bible any more." We have indeed changed it substantially, and it is now the CBC text. The WEB Bible is entirely free of blame for any errors that readers might perceive in the CBC translation.

The Celtic Bible Commentary follows an honored tradition of Bible translations that built on previous works. The *World English Bible* is based upon the *American Standard Version* (1901), which was a major rewrite of the *King James Version* (1611)—and even that hallowed translation was substantially modeled on the *Geneva Bible* (1599). Since it is a revision of the WEB version, the Celtic Bible Commentary is a continuation of this stream of biblical derivations.

The first decision regarding a text for the CBC was this: should we try to emulate the Bible used in the Early Middle Ages, at the time in which the first Celtic saints were engaged in serious Bible study? That would be an early Latin translation, and an English translation of what is now known as the Vulgate could be used to approximate that. We noted, however, that Bible scholars in the "Golden Age" of Celtic Christianity were committed to finding the best texts that they could get their hands on. (An unfortunate example of this is Saint Columba's willingness to begin a war between clans in order to possess a copy of Jerome's translation of Psalms.) We decided that a good modern translation would best serve the intentions of ancient Celtic scholarship.

I examined several copyright-free texts and chose the WEB for its clarity and veracity, while at the same time deciding a substantial rewrite was in order. Again, there is good precedent for modifying earlier translation work: most of the Early Medieval Insular Gospel texts did not follow one translation. The Book of Kells, for example, is in large part copied from Jerome's Vulgate but there are significant amounts of text derived from other Latin versions; in short, it is a hybrid. Insular scholars in the Early Middle Ages considered such hybrid renditions of the biblical texts to be normative.

The most significant change we have made is that the CBC follows the Nestle-Aland *Novum Testamentum Graece* (NA) for its base text, whereas the WEB follows the Textus Receptus (TR). The *Novum Testamentum Graece* is the Latin name of a compendium source document of the New Testament in its original Greek-language. The first printed edition was early in the sixteenth century, but today the *Novum Testamentum Graece* normally refers to the Nestle-Aland editions, named after the scholars who led the critical editing work. The text is currently in its twenty-eighth edition, and is the primary source for most contemporary New Testament translations. The *Textus Receptus* (Latin for "received text") is the name given to the succession of printed Greek texts of the New Testament that were the translation base for the original German Luther Bible, the translation of the New Testament into English by William Tyndale, the King James Version, the Spanish Reina-Valera translation, the Russian Synodal Bible, and most Reformation-era New Testament translations throughout Western and Central Europe. The series originated with the first printed Greek New Testament, published in 1516, and was based on the Orthodox Church's version, which had been used since the fourth century. This was used in most Protestant denominations before the nineteenth century adoption. Today, however, the NA is preferred over TR by a majority of New Testament scholars.

A FEW NOTES ☘ 313

The second major change we made to the WEB was to opt for gender-neutral pronouns: "people" rather than "men," unless referring to specific individuals of a certain gender. The use of male-gendered pronouns in the twenty-first century signals a deliberate assertion of male privilege, a statement that was not intended by the authors of Sacred Scripture.

We also chose to avoid gendered pronouns when referring to God. There is growing theological consensus that God is neither male nor female, due in part to biblical examples of feminine God imagery. For example, a common Hebrew term for God, *El Shaddai*, translates as "the many breasted one," and Jesus in Matthew 23:37 declares, "I have longed to gather your children together, as a hen gathers her chicks under her wings." Masculine gendered pronouns when referring to God, in an age when most communication is gender-neutral, creates a deceiving impression of God's "maleness."

While modifying the text, we stayed faithful to the inspired writers' word selections by choosing English words that fit the meaning of those used in the original Greek. Scholars refer to "semantic domain" when speaking of the set of words that can convey the meaning of a single given word. So "Kingdom of God" can be properly rendered "Realm of God," or "Reign of God," depending upon context.

We chose the word "Abba" or "Abba God" in place of "Father" when Jesus refers to God-who-sent-him. "Abba" is the Aramaic word for a male parent, and this was the form of address used by Jesus and by Saint Paul when praying to God. It expresses both trust and affection. We also retain "Son," when referring to Jesus, because Jesus was a specific male individual. Exceptions to this are the four cases in John's Gospel where we correctly render the Greek word *monogeneous* as "only begotten" rather than "only begotten son."

One of the richest New Testament words, with a broad range of meaning, is κυριοσ. The word can be translated as "Sir" or "Great One," as a title; "rabbi," "teacher," "ruler," or "lord," describing function in society; or as a circumlocution used by ancient Jews for the Divine Name YHWH. We have rendered the Divine Name as the "Eternal One," and used a number of different words to translate references to Jesus, to signify the word's fullness of meanings when applied to him. In the post-resurrection portion of the Gospel of John and in the Acts of the Apostles, Jesus is constantly referred to as κυριοσ, so that word becomes the main designation for Jesus after he is raised from death and ascended into glory, a reminder that he is more than just a great human being.

We have done the best we can to carry the meanings of God's Word into today's world, believing that our relationship with the Bible mirrors our relationships with human significant others: when first we encounter our beloved, we are fascinated and intrigued, but as time goes by we may lose that glow of new romance. Passion—for a human partner or for the Sacred Book—depends on falling in love over and over as we perceive the beloved in fresh ways.

This is an especially important time in history for a fresh understanding of the Bible. On one hand, some Christians have hardened their interpretations to such a degree that the Scriptures can serve as a cudgel against those with opposing views. At the same time, others have focused on aspects of the Scriptures they find troubling, leading them to disparage the Bible's worth and lose their passion for reading it. The ancient Celts, however, were able to read Scripture in ways that avoided both horns of our contemporary dilemma. Their insights can rekindle our passion for the Bible today.

—Kenneth McIntosh

GLOSSARY OF CELTIC NAMES & TERMINOLOGY

Abban (died 520?): Irish saint, the son of Cormac, who was King of Leinster, and the nephew of Saint Ibar. He is said to have preached in Ireland *before* the arrival of Patrick.

Adomnán (627–704): Ninth abbot of the monastery at Iona, he was also Columba's biographer.

Aelred (1110–1167): Born in Northumbria, he became the abbot of Rievaulx in North Yorkshire. He was the author of several books.

Aidan (died 651): An Irishman who became known as the Apostle to the English, he is the founder and first bishop of the Monastery of Lindisfarne in Northumbria.

Bede (673–735): Born in Northumbria, he is known as "the first English historian."

Boisol (died 661): Also known as Boswell, he was the Bishop of Melrose Monastery. He was a pupil of Saint Aidan, and he was Saint Cuthbert's teacher.

Book of Kells: The most famous early-medieval illuminated copy of the Gospels, now on display at Trinity College, Dublin. It was produced around 800 in one of the monasteries associated with Saint Columba.

Brendan the Navigator (484–577): Established monasteries in Western Ireland, but is most famous for his nautical travels related in the *Voyage of Saint Brendan*.

Brigid (also Brighid, Brigit, 451–525): The most influential Celtic saint (after Patrick), who was the founder and abbess of the great monastery in Kildare, Ireland. Legends of Saint Brigid have taken on many aspects of the older goddess of the same name. She is intimately connected—as is the Goddess Brigid—with the feast of Imbolc, the Celtic beginning of spring.

Cadog (born 497): Also known as Cadoc, he was abbot of Llancarfan, Wales, and founded churches in Wales, Brittany, and Scotland.

Caedmon: The earliest known English poet, who is mentioned in Bede's *Ecclesiastical History* as being given miraculous gifts of composing poetry in song, an event that took place sometime during the abbacy of Saint Hilda at Whitby (657–680).

Carmina Gadelica: A published collection of Gaelic language poems, songs, chants, hymns and spells collected between 1860 and 1900 in Scotland by folklorist Alexander Carmichael.

Cellach: Sixth-century bishop of Killala Ireland

GLOSSARY 317

Columba (521–597) Also known as Columcille, he established monasteries in Ireland before (according to legend) being exiled from Ireland and subsequently founding the monastery on Holy Island Iona off the Pictish coast (modern-day Scotland).

Comgall (died either 597 or 602): Founder and abbot of the Monastery in Bangor, Ulster.

Cuchulain (also spelled CuChullain, pronounced "koo-hoo-len"): Mythic Irish warrior hero who singlehandedly fended off the armies of Queen Maeve. Known as the "Hound of Ulster," he is thought to be both the son on the god Lugh and his incarnation.

Cummian (591–661 or 662): Bishop of Clonfert Ireland and foster-son of Ita, who was famous for his theological writing.

Cuthbert (634–687): Patron saint of northern England, he was an Anglo-Saxon monk trained at the Scottish monastery of Melrose and later bishop of Lindisfarne. His remains today are in Durham Cathedral.

Finian (c.495–589): Studied in Rome, and returned to Ireland in 540 with a copy of St. Jerome's Vulgate. He founded a school of his own at Movilla (Maigh Bhile) in County Down in Ireland. At a time when books were rare, this text brought honor and prestige to his school, where he taught Columba (who would later try to copy his teacher's manuscript).

Gildas (500?–570): A sixth-century British monk who is best known for his history of the Britons before and during the coming of the Saxons.

Hilda (614–680): Born into Anglian royalty, she became the founder of monastic centers in Hartlepool and Whitby and was important in the conversion of the Anglo-Saxons. She presided over the Synod of Whitby, at which it was decreed that Celtic churches would begin following Roman traditions.

Ibar (died about 500): An early Irish saint, who is said to have been one of the "four most sacred bishops" who preceded Patrick in Ireland.

Iona: A small island in the Inner Hebrides off the Ross of Mull on the western coast of Scotland. Columba founded a monastery there in 563, and it remained a center of Celtic monasticism for four centuries

Irish Augustine: An anonymous Irish scholar who wrote "On the Miracles of Holy Scripture" in 655, a work that explains Bible miracles as natural phenomenon. His work was misattributed to Saint Augustine, hence the name.

Kevin (died 618): Founder and abbot of the monastery in Glendalough, Ireland, he is known as the "Irish Saint Francis" due to his love of nature.

Lindisfarne Gospel: An illuminated manuscript produced around the year 700 in a monastery off the coast of Northumberland at Lindisfarne, which is now on display in the British Library in London.

Loegaire: High King of Ireland in the time of Saint Patrick.

Missal: A book containing the instructions and texts used in church services throughout the Christian liturgical year.

GLOSSARY

Muirchu: Seventh-century monk at Leinster, Ireland who wrote the first life of Saint Patrick.

O'Neill: A proud and important Irish clan descended from the High Kings of Ireland.

Patrick: A fifth-century British Christian missionary and bishop in Ireland, he is known as the "Apostle of Ireland" and is the primary patron saint of Ireland, along with Saint Brigid of Kildare.

Pelagius (354–420): Also known as Saint Morgan of Wales, he was the first Celtic theologian. He emphasized humanity's free will, based on the Divine Image. Saint Augustine of Hippo fiercely contested Pelagius and eventually succeeded in condemning him as a heretic. However, his teachings continued to have great influence over Celtic Christians.

Penitentials: Irish manuals produced in the Early Middle Ages, prescribing 'cures' for various "illnesses" of sin.

Tirechan: A seventh-century Irish bishop and biographer of Saint Patrick.

SUGGESTED READINGS

ON THE BIBLE

Raymond E. Brown: *An Introduction to the New Testament* (Doubleday). Despite being somewhat dated, this may be the best overall New Testament introduction. The late Raymond Brown was a foremost expert in New Testament studies, combining his vital Christian faith with outstanding scholarship, resulting in this finely balanced work. Brown has the rare honesty and wisdom to distinguish between what is known and what can only be conjecture, enabling him to make statements or pose questions as appropriate.

Common English Bible (CEB, Common English Bible Publisher). A recent translation that combines simple language with careful translation choices. Unlike most translations, the CEB retains ambiguity where the texts in the original languages defy easy understanding. The translation team consists of members from a broad variety of Christian denominations, ensuring that the translation is free from theological bias.

SUGGESTED READINGS

Michael D. Coogan, Editor: *The New Oxford Annotated Bible* (Oxford University Press). The go-to general-purpose study Bible, from a mainline Christian perspective, with commentary by top-notch scholars.

Sandy Eisenberg Sasso: *Midrash: Reading the Bible with Question Marks* (Paraclete Press). A rabbi presents this fun, easy-to-read introduction to Jewish Bible interpretation, including "how-to" sections. This is an excellent brief book to read alongside the Celtic Bible Commentary's volumes.

Peter Enns: *The Bible Tells Me So...Why Defending Scripture Has Made Us Unable to Read It* (Harper One). A professor of biblical studies explains how he re-learned the value of the Bible after struggling with it. If the Bible has never seemed like a stumbling block to you, you don't need this book; but if you are struggling with doubts about the Scriptures, this could be valuable.

Harry Y. Gamble: *The New Testament Canon: Its Making and Meaning* (Wipf and Stock). A brief but scholarly guide to this very complex topic.

Gregory Mobley: *The Return of the Chaos Monsters—and Other Backstories of the Bible* (William B. Eerdmans). Mobley, Bible professor at Andover-Newton Seminary, presents an absolute treasure. He shows how the entire Bible is better understood when heard as storytelling. The medium suits the message, as Mobley's exquisite prose seems more like poetry. This book may revolutionize the way you read Scripture and makes a fine companion to the Celtic Bible Commentary's volumes.

ON CELTIC CHRISTIANITY

Adomnán of Iona: *Life of St Columba* (Penguin Books). This life of the saint, grouped by categories of miracles, written by the ninth abbot of Iona, is a good entryway into the thinking of a Celtic Christian in the heyday of the Iona Monastery.

Bede: *The Ecclesiastical History of the English People* (Penguin Books). In this first English history book, Bede displays grudging admiration for his Celtic neighbors and records numerous events of the Early Middle Ages that would otherwise be unknown.

Robert Boenig: *Anglo-Saxon Spirituality: Selected Writings* (Paulist Press). The similarities between Celtic and Anglo-Saxon Christians in the Early Middle Ages far outweigh the differences; they reflect a common Insular outlook. This is the best single volume of translated Anglo-Saxon documents.

Thomas Cahill: *How the Irish Saved Civilization: The Untold Story of Ireland's Heroic Role from the Fall of Rome to the Rise of Medieval Europe* (Doubleday). This popular history, written like a novel, is a good first introduction to Celtic Christianity for many readers.

John Carey: *King of Mysteries: Early Irish Religious Writings* (Four Courts Press). Along with Davies' *Celtic Spirituality* (below), this is the best source of translated Celtic Christian documents.

SUGGESTED READINGS

Paul Cavill: ***Anglo-Saxon Christianity: Exploring the Earliest Roots of Christian Spirituality in England*** (Fount). A professor of Old English mixes translated documents with his own Christian insights. If you enjoyed *Water from an Ancient Well* (McIntosh) or *Celtic Christianity* (Simpson), you will also benefit from this book.

Oliver Davies: ***Celtic Spirituality: Classics of Western Spirituality*** (Paulist Press). A treasure trove of translated primary documents, nicely explained and arranged.

Leslie Hardinge: ***The Celtic Church in Britain*** (Teach Services). Hardinge did a formidable amount of research for this book, which is unfortunately marred by being dated and by his denominational biases. Nonetheless, this book contains valuable information not found elsewhere.

Michael W. Herren and Shirley Ann Brown: ***Christ in Celtic Christianity: Britain and Ireland from the Fifth to the Tenth Century*** (Boydell Press). Writing on a scholarly level, combining analysis of written and artistic expressions, the authors argue that there was a distinctly Celtic Christology in the Early Middle Ages, largely due to the continuing influence of Pelagius.

Meg Llewellyn: ***Celtic Miracles and Wonders: Tales of the Ancient Saints*** (Anamchara Books). You can almost hear the voice of a bard relating these folktales of the saints. An easy-to-read and fun introduction to the ethos of Celtic Christianity, with brilliant short introductions.

Kenneth McIntosh: *Water from an Ancient Well: Celtic Spirituality for Modern Life* (Anamchara Books). Father Richard Rohr says that this book "allows us to rediscover the depth and wisdom of Celtic Christianity."

Thomas O' Loughlin: *Celtic Theology: Humanity, World and God in Early Irish Writings* (Continuum). Written on a scholarly level, this is a deeper, richer treatment of the themes in *Journeys on the Edges* (below). It will be valuable if you have already read the more basic books in this list.

Thomas O'Loughlin: *Journeys on the Edges: The Celtic Tradition* (Orbis Books). A neglected gem and "must" reading for anyone interested in Celtic Christianity. O'Loughlin is unusual insofar as he is a professor at the Centre for the Study of Religion in Celtic Societies, University of Wales (so he works vocationally with primary materials) *and* he writes this book in simple language for laypeople, with the aim of spiritual guidance. This book is unique in its combination of sober scholarship and spiritual discernment.

Edward C. Sellner: *Wisdom of the Celtic Saints* (Ave Maria Press). An excellent, popular-level overview of the chief Celtic saints (and a few lesser-known ones) with a fine set of introductions to Celtic Christianity.

Ray Simpson: *Celtic Christianity: Deep Roots for a Modern Faith* (Anamchara Books). Ray Simpson is one of the founders of the Community of Aidan and Hilda. This is one of the finest overviews on Celtic Christianity, aimed to spiritually enrich the reader.

Ray Simpson: *The Celtic Book of Days: Ancient Wisdom for Each Day of the Year from the Celtic Followers of Christ* (Anamchara Books).

This is a daily devotional with insights from Scripture and the lives of the Celtic saints for each day of the year.

Lilly Weichberger & Kenneth McIntosh: *Brigid's Mantle: A Celtic Dialogue Between Pagan & Christian* (Anamchara Books). Using the saint and goddess who share the same name as a common point for Pagans and Christians, this book has much to offer in terms of both history and modern inspiration from Celtic spirituality, from two separate—yet overlapping—perspectives.

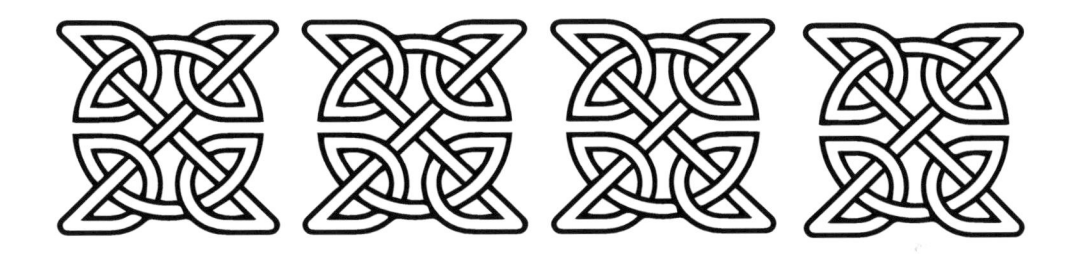

CONTRIBUTORS

DAVID COLE is an international Christian speaker and retreat leader; an award-winning author; "Explorer Guide" for the Community of Aidan and Hilda, a globally dispersed Celtic New Monastic Community; and founder of Waymark Ministries. David has been studying and teaching Celtic Christianity for twenty years, giving talks and running regular Celtic retreats and workshop days. David lives in the beautiful New Forest National Park on the southern coast of England with his wife and children. For more information visit www.waymark-ministries.com.

TERESA MONICA CROSS is a Celtic historian and theologian, who has been a scholar of Celtic history and religions since the mid-1980s. She has taught Bunrang Gaeilge for the Conradh na Gaeilge and Celtic Mythology for Richland College, and been a priest in the Celtic Christian Communion, a member of the Ceili De (Culdees), and a deacon in both the Celtic Orthodox Christian Church and Celtic Episcopal Church. She is descended from the Mac an Chrosains, O'Connors, and the Ballards of Ireland (to name a few); the Stewarts, MacGregors,

CONTRIBUTORS 327

and Clan Fraser of Scotland; and the Jones of Wales. A former resident of Texas, she has lived in Arizona since her retirement.

JACK GILLESPIE has been a follower of Jesus since childhood. He's a professed member and ordained Celtic priest in the Lindisfarne Community, an independent, ecumenical religious community in the Anglo-Celtic tradition with apostolic succession. He has studied the Bible, church history, and theology for more than thirty years. Jack lives in Oklahoma with his wife, daughter, and their two dogs.

PAUL JOHN MARTIN is a former Episcopal priest and retired business-owner. He holds a master's degree in Greek from Oxford University, and a seminary diploma from Durham University. He serves as U.S. Guardian of the Community of Aidan and Hilda, a dispersed, ecumenical fellowship drawing inspiration from the lives of the Celtic saints. Brought up in England, he has lived in the United States for thirty years. He now lives in St. Louis Park, Minnesota, and is a member of Union Congregational Church (United Church of Christ), where his wife Barb is the pastor. He follows English soccer and American college football, enjoys travel, and loves choral singing.

KENNETH McINTOSH serves as pastor of the United Church of Christ church in Flagstaff, Arizona, and also works as Lutheran Campus Minister at Northern Arizona University. He is the author of many nonfiction books for young adults, as well as the young adult fantasy fiction *Magic Reversed* and the best-selling *Water from an Ancient Well: Celtic Spirituality for Modern Life*. Ken has traveled throughout the UK, and he is constantly seeking out new insights into Celtic sprituality. He co-authored *Brigid's Mantle: A Celtic Dialogue Between Pagan and Christian Perspectives* with Lilly Weichberger, and he and Lucie Stone (Ellyn Sanna) created a collection of Celtic prayers titled *Prayers from an Ancient Well: Celtic Nature Prayers*.

STEVE ROBINSON, whose ancestry is Welsh, has been learning about Celtic history, culture, and mythology for more than forty years. As a committed believer in Jesus during that same period, he never felt completely comfortable in much of current Christian culture. When he was introduced to Celtic Christian spirituality about twelve years ago, he felt as though he had finally "come home." Today he is a member of the Community of Aidan and Hilda (CA&H), an international community seeking inspiration from the early Christian believers in the Celtic lands. He is the author of *The Oenologic Holmes: The Role of Wine in the Life and Times of Sherlock Holmes*, as well as a Celtic books column for the quarterly CA&H newsletter, *The Wild Goose*.

ELLYN SANNA is the executive editor of Anamchara Books, and the author of many books, both fiction and nonfiction. Most recently, she wrote *All Shall Be Well: A Modern-Language Version of the Revelation of Julian of Norwich* and the spiritual fantasy *The Thread*, written under the name Lucie Stone. The daughter of a Wesleyan minister, she grew up immersed in the Bible and its stories. Ellyn has been studying Celtic theology and mythology for more than twenty years. A resident of upstate New York, she spends as much time as she can each year in Devon, the Celtic south of England.

CELTIC BIBLE COMMENTARY

⋈ Sometimes, illumination from the ancient past can reveal the road ahead. ⋈

Each volume of the Celtic Bible Commentary contains a new translation of that book of the Bible, with commentaries, written by Celtic and Bible scholars, for all chapters. These commentaries include insights from the ancient Celts—and apply them to our own lives in the twenty-first century, challenging us to weave the Bible's stories into our own. Each commentary encourages us to read scripture "the Celtic way," encountering it as fresh, living, and radical.

For the Celts, the Bible was something amazing and wondrous. It was to be read attentively, with the commitment and fascination the lover feels for the beloved. Their approach to reading scripture need not be lost to us. We too can learn to open our hearts and minds to the gift of the Divine Word, allowing the Breath of God to inspire us and transform us in unpredictable ways—and then sweep through us like a flame that kindles new life and healing in the world around us.

THE WINGED LION:
The Good News According to Mark
CELTIC BIBLE COMMENTARY: VOLUME TWO

Paperback Price: $24.99
E-book Price: $9.99
ISBN: 978-1-62524-459-8

In the fifth century, Saint Jerome assigned to each of the four Gospel authors a winged creature that is still associated with that particular account of the life of Jesus. Mark's symbol is a winged lion, an image of courage and triumph, representing Christ's authority over life and death. With the Celtic saints, we find in this Gospel a vision of Jesus that is always larger than anything we have experienced in ordinary life—a vision that challenges us to live life in a new and deeper way. ⊕

THE WINGED CALF:

The Good News According to Luke

CELTIC BIBLE COMMENTARY: VOLUME THREE

Paperback Price: $24.99
E-book Price: $9.99
ISBN: 978-1-62524-469-7

The Gospel author we know as Luke is traditionally represented by a winged calf, a figure of otherworldly sacrifice, service, and strength. This account of Jesus' life begins with the sacrificial duties of Zacharias in the temple, and it focuses on Christ's self-giving on the Cross. The Gospel of the Calf struck a chord that resonated in the heart of Celtic faith. For the Celts, this was a metaphor that embraced the deepest meaning of Christian life—giving ourselves away on behalf of others. As one ancient Celtic author put it, "A person who has compassion for the needs of neighbors truly carries the cross." Luke's Gospel points us toward the Way of Jesus, the way of the calf.

THE FAR-SEEING EAGLE:

The Good News According to John

CELTIC BIBLE COMMENTARY: VOLUME FOUR

Paperback Price: $24.99
E-book Price: $9.99
ISBN: 978-1-62524-470-3

John's symbolic animal is an eagle, a far-seeing creature of the sky that was believed to be able to look straight into the sun. The author of this Gospel differed from the others in that he describes Jesus as the eternal Word, focusing throughout his account on Jesus' Divine nature. The same man who walked the streets of Nazareth, writes John, is also the universe-filling Wisdom of God who existed from the beginning of Creation. For the Celts, who loved seeing more-than-literal meaning throughout the Bible, this Gospel is a treasure trove of symbolism. As we read it, we too are challenged to live differently but also to see differently, to perceive the deep spiritual Mystery that is hidden everywhere we look.

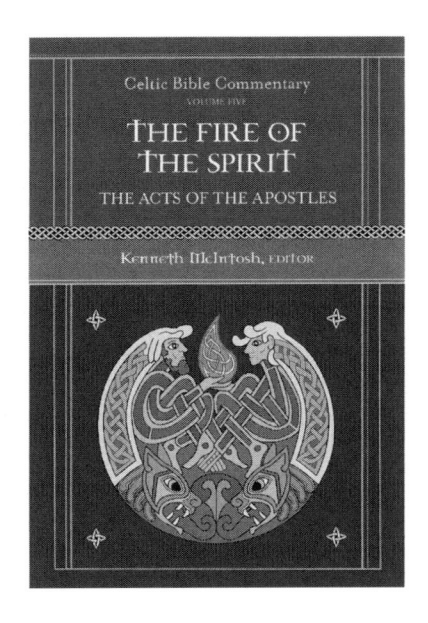

THE FIRE OF THE SPIRIT:
The Acts of the Apostles
CELTIC BIBLE COMMENTARY: VOLUME FIVE

Paperback Price: $24.99
E-book Price: $9.99
ISBN: 978-1-62524-471-0

Although this book is traditionally titled "The Acts of the Apostles," a better title might be "The Acts of the Holy Spirit." In Acts, God's Breath (or Spirit) does not descend as the traditional dove but instead falls as fire. The Spirit's flaming presence is the motif for Pentecost, and afterward Spirit spreads like wildfire from Jerusalem outward, transforming lives as it advances. Acts is an account of how people came to believe in the Way of Jesus, but it is even more the story of how Spirit brought people to venture beyond their traditional religious boundaries. Throughout Acts, the inclusive Breath of God works continually to break down barriers erected by prejudice, ego, or insecurity. The ancient Christian Celts opened their hearts to this message, and they challenge us to join the Spirit in extending God's welcome to everyone, without exception.

Anamchara Books
Books to Inspire Your Spiritual Journey

In Celtic Christianity, an *anamchara* is a soul friend, a companion and mentor (often across the miles and the years) on the spiritual journey. Soul friendship entails a commitment to both accept and challenge, to reach across all divisions in a search for the wisdom and truth at the heart of our lives.

At Anamchara Books, we are committed to creating a community of soul friends by publishing books that lead us into deeper relationships with God, the Earth, and each other. These books connect us with the great mystics of the past, as well as with more modern spiritual thinkers. They are designed to build bridges, shaping an inclusive spirituality where we all can grow.

To find out more about Anamchara Books and order our books, visit www.AnamcharaBooks.com today.

Anamchara Books
Vestal, New York 13850
www.AnamcharaBooks.com

Printed in Great Britain
by Amazon